In *Ideologies of Experience*, Matthew H. Bowker is onto an idea of profound significance. His concept of an ideology of experience may very well hold a key insight into the contemporary psychological processes behind our politics of fantasy over reality, and false attributions and assertions over valid information. Once we as individual selves are taught to mistrust our own capacity for reality testing and knowing good from bad, stripped of critical thinking we forfeit the essence of citizenship in a democratic society.

Michael A. Diamond, Professor and Director, Center of the Study of Organizational Change, Harry S. Truman School of Public Affairs, University of Missouri

A critical and provocative interdisciplinary inquiry into experience, and the ways it might be manipulated, Matthew H. Bowker challenges us to question basic assumptions we make about our society and our lives. *Ideologies of Experience* is a work from which all of us can profit.

Stephen Eric Bronner, Board of Governors Professor of Political Science, Rutgers University, USA

Bowker explores a fascinating array of ideas dealing with the self and the impact of what he calls 'ideologies of experience' on the self. This is a fascinating and stimulating excursion through philosophy and psychoanalytic theory that enriches our understanding of how the self relates to itself, to others, to the community and to the often difficult and traumatic ways experience attacks and engages the very foundations of our being.

James M. Glass, Distinguished Scholar/Teacher and Professor, University of Maryland, College Park, USA

In the aftermath of radical changes to traditional assumptions about subjectivity, and selfhood, this book offers a useful and original re-interpretation of key contested concepts—experience, ideology, trauma, solitude

Marshall Alcorn, George Washington University, USA, author of Changing the Subject in English Class

IDEOLOGIES OF EXPERIENCE

Matthew H. Bowker offers a novel analysis of 'experience': the vast and influential concept that has shaped Western social theory and political practice for the past half-millennium.

While it is difficult to find a branch of modern thought, science, industry, or art that has not relied in some way on the notion of 'experience' in defining its assumptions or aims, no study has yet applied a politically-conscious and psychologically sensitive critique to the construct of experience. Doing so reveals that most of the qualities that have been attributed to experience over the centuries – particularly its unthinkability, its correspondence with suffering, and its occlusion of the self – are part of unlikely fantasies or ideologies. By analyzing a series of related cases, including the experiential education movement, the ascendency of trauma theory, the philosophy of the social contract, and the psychological study of social isolation, the book builds a convincing case that ideologies of experience are invoked not to keep us close to lived realities and 'things-in-themselves,' but, rather, to distort and destroy true knowledge of ourselves and others.

In spite of enduring admiration for those who may be called champions of experience, such as Michel de Montaigne, Ralph Waldo Emerson, and others treated throughout the work, ideologies of experience ultimately discourage individuals and groups from creating, resisting, and changing our experience, urging us instead to embrace trauma, failure, deprivation, and self-abandonment.

Matthew H. Bowker is Visiting Assistant Professor of Liberal Arts at Medaille College in Buffalo, NY. His work applies psychoanalytic and literary-critical approaches to topics in political philosophy.

IDEOLOGIES OF EXPERIENCE

Trauma, Failure, Deprivation, and the Abandonment of the Self

Matthew H. Bowker

Routledge
Taylor & Francis Group

NEW YORK AND LONDON

First published 2016
by Routledge
711 Third Avenue, New York, NY 10017

and by Routledge
2 Park Square, Milton Park, Abingdon, Oxon OX14 4RN

Routledge is an imprint of the Taylor & Francis Group, an informa business

Library of Congress Cataloging in Publication Data
A catalog record for this book has been requested

ISBN: 978-1-138-18267-7 (hbk)
ISBN: 978-1-138-18268-4 (pbk)
ISBN: 978-1-315-64626-8 (ebk)

Typeset in Bembo
by Taylor & Francis Books

For Julie and Zoe, my beloveds

CONTENTS

ACKNOWLEDGMENTS

David Levine, once my teacher, still my teacher, read substantial portions of this manuscript and offered deeply thoughtful critiques. Our correspondence and collaborations, even on subjects having little to do with 'experience,' have been extraordinarily helpful and have surely influenced the shape of this book. I regularly find myself turning to David's published work for the depth of his understanding and the seemingly effortless clarity he brings to each of his topics.

I am truly fortunate that Fred Alford, my former doctoral advisor and mentor at the University of Maryland, College Park, continues to teach me through our conversations, correspondence, and occasional conference panels, as well as through his published work, to whose riches I feel, quite irrationally, I retain some sort of privileged access. Fred read early portions of this manuscript, asked provocative questions, and offered sage advice.

Marshall Alcorn, Julie Bowker, Jim Butters, Patrick Fazioli, and Lynne Layton read portions of this manuscript at various stages of its development. I am grateful for their helpful comments and appraisals.

An early version of Chapter 3 was presented at the 2014 Annual Conference of the Association for the Psychoanalysis of Culture and Society (APCS) at Rutgers University in New Brunswick, NJ. An early version of Chapter 8 was presented at the 2015 Annual Conference of the Midwest Political Science Association (MPSA) in Chicago, IL. An early version of Chapter 7 was published in the *Journal of Psycho-Social Studies* 9(1). This portion of the present work benefited enormously from the wisdom of Helen Lucey and the anonymous reviewers.

For the second time, I have been blessed by the expertise, insight, and confidence of Taylor and Francis' Senior Editor of Political Science Research, Natalja Mortensen. Lillian Rand's thoughtful guidance through all stages of this book's development and Justin Dyer's astute editorial assistance have likewise been essential to the completion of this work.

1

INTRODUCTION

In this book, I try to make sense of discourses and attitudes that emphasize the importance of trauma, failure, and deprivation. I believe it is fair to call these discourses and attitudes, if not a single ideology, at least a family of ideologies. Because what unites these ideologies is an identifiable set of presumptions concerning the value of certain kinds of experiences and our relation to them, I refer to them collectively as 'ideologies of experience.'

The ideologies of experience discussed here share an intellectual history that begins in the modern era and is remarkable throughout the Protestant Reformation, the European Renaissance, the Scientific Revolution, and the early Romantic movement, for instance, in the work of Martin Luther, Michel de Montaigne, Francis Bacon, and the young J.W. Goethe, among many others. Some have argued that the ancient Greeks and early Christians, too, upheld ideals of experience (see Jay 2005, 13–19; Lloyd 1979), citing Aristotle, the Hellenistic Skeptics and Cynics, and Augustine. Yet, while it is inadvisable to generalize about intellectual history, and while there are certainly exceptions to the rule, it is not the classical but the modern era that truly enshrines *empeiria, scientia*, and individualism, from whose influences arise the need to locate moral and epistemic authority in experience. In the modern era, Francis Bacon would recommend *experientia literata* (learned experiences) as a first "step to essential knowledge" (Jay 2005, 31), and Michel de Montaigne would claim that "in the experience I have of myself, I find enough to make me wise" (1993, 354). In the classical era, by contrast, Plato's cave-dwellers would be condemned to their shadowy existence not primarily by the bonds restraining their legs and necks (1987, 317–318), but by the shackles of experience, custom, and conventional wisdom, tightened daily.

Regardless of their point of origin, ideologies of experience exert tremendous influence over contemporary intellectual, social, and political life: They shape and guide popular epistemologies, approaches to both personal and collective traumas, definitions of the purpose of higher learning, orientations toward citizens and civil institutions, and much more. The basic premise uniting ideologies of experience is that experience is a privileged means of accessing reality. Of course, from this premise a variety of secondary postulates have been advanced, many of which carry normative force, and most of which are surprisingly antithetical to the self-liberatory aims of experience's early champions.

I strive to show that ideologies of experience endorse immediate identification with and incorporation of experience's objects, the splitting of experience from thinking, the repetition and transmission of experience in unthought forms, and the over-reliance upon the psychic mechanisms of projection and introjection. An important consequence of the ascendency of experience in its ideological form has been the putative demonstration of the artificiality, undesirability, and even impossibility of mature selves and groups. Instead, ideologies of experience recommend that we regenerate and preserve what are thought to be 'natural' experiences of psychic devastation in our private and civil lives.

To ideologies of experience, I oppose an ideal of selfhood, which values the mediation of experience via thinking and knowing, the potential for creative action, and the capacity to be alone, which entails the possibility of ethical relatedness with others. A critic of ideals of selfhood might object that I am merely opposing ideologies of experience with an ideology of the self. There is no way to defeat this objection. There are, however, reasons to suspect it. The best reason is that such objections deny the value of preserving a distinction between ideal and ideology. If all ideals – and perhaps, by extension, all ideas – are, at bottom, ideologies, then we find ourselves already entangled with a woeful ideology in which no idea, proposition, or claim of value can express more than coercive force. Such a condition would be, of course, quite inimical to the development of thinking, willing, acting selves. Although not treated in this book as thoroughly as in my earlier work (see, e.g., Bowker 2014), the refusal to distinguish ideal from ideology, reasoning from rationalization, and self from selfishness may be among the most dangerous of contemporary intellectual pathologies. Undertaken in the name of defending the victimized and the oppressed, such a view lamentably undermines investment in the very capacities by which mature, secure selves and ethical, non-oppressive groups are formed.

I hope the reader will not be disappointed that in this book I leave aside not only the rich intellectual history of the concept of experience, but what I consider to be the unanswerable question, 'What is experience, itself?,' not to mention the equally unanswerable question Richard Kuhns calls "*the* philosophical question" (1970, 53–55): 'How is experience possible?' These questions, which concern the foundations of empiricism, idealism, skepticism, phenomenology, pragmatism, and existentialism, have been treated exhaustively in the works of Baruch Spinoza,

John Locke, Immanuel Kant, David Hume, G.W.F. Hegel, Edmund Husserl, William James, Walter Benjamin, Jean-Paul Sartre, and others, and in the secondary and tertiary literatures surrounding them.

Several comprehensive volumes have already been dedicated either to parsing the idea of experience, such as Michael Oakeshott's seminal *Experience and Its Modes* (1933), or to retracing the intellectual history of the concept of experience, itself, such as Martin Jay's truly exceptional *Songs of Experience* (2005). These works permit us to dispense with laborious enumerations of past and present ideas of experience and, instead, to explicate some subtler dynamics that unite conceptions of experience across a wide range of intellectual, political, and popular discourses.

This work, then, explores a rather limited set of questions regarding experience, conceived as a psycho-social construct with normative force: 'How have our approaches to certain types of experience shaped contemporary thinking about the self?,' 'What conscious and unconscious aims are served by valorizing experience, especially experiences of disaster?,' and 'Against what, if anything, does the construct of experience, so construed, defend?' Since 'experience' has been invoked in hundreds of different ways by philosophers, theologians, psychologists, scientists, poets, teachers, advertisers, and many others, it should be clarified at the outset that this book is concerned with but one strain – although it will be recognized by the reader as a *dominant* strain – of both scholarly and popular orientations to experience.

The term 'experience' has no suitable synonym in any language of which I am aware, and retains the quality of a 'slippery signifier,' capable of referring to almost anything. An adequate illustration of both the slipperiness of the concept and the necessity of my approach comes from an excerpt of Alfred North Whitehead's defense of his event- and process-oriented philosophy. Whitehead argues:

> In order to discover some of the major categories under which we can classify the infinitely various components of experience, we must appeal to evidence relating to every variety of occasion ... experience drunk and experience sober, experience sleeping and experience waking, experience drowsy and experience wide-awake, experience self-conscious and experience self-forgetful, experience intellectual and experience physical, experience religious and experience sceptical, experience anxious and experience care-free, experience anticipatory and experience retrospective, experience happy and experience grieving, experience dominated by emotion and experience under self-restraint, experience in the light and experience in the dark, experience normal and experience abnormal.
>
> *(1933, 226)*

Of course, the irony of Whitehead's attempt to display the myriad components of experience is that with each new mode, with each item on his list, we find ourselves increasingly perplexed about what "experience" could possibly denote. In the end, it seems an unnecessary word, or, alternatively, a super-word, capable of signifying a temporary condition ("drunk"), a mode of being ("physical"), an attitude ("skeptical"), a psychological state ("grieving"), a circumstantial environmental condition ("in the dark"), a moral or ethical self-relation ("under self-restraint"), and a relation to a group ("abnormal").

Perhaps the only way to make sense of Whitehead's usage is to imagine that experienc*ers* hold these varieties of experience together, making them into something more than chaos. But that is not Whitehead's point. It is, in part, *my* point, as I hope to show that modern and contemporary ideologies of experience routinely eclipse an ideal type of *experiencer* – a self – in favor of less capable, less integrated experiencers, wedded in less mature ways to their experiences and their experiences' objects. In so doing, ideologies of experience misconstrue what a self does, what it needs, what it offers, and how its relation to experience can become either fortifying or oppressive.

Although one might imagine that an exhaustive study of the great phenomenologists, such as Edmund Husserl, Martin Heidegger, and Maurice Merleau-Ponty, would permit us to pin down the meaning of experience, we find that, despite their 'bracketing' (*Einklammerung*) of assumptions about the noumenal world, and despite their attention to the properties of human experience – its directedness, its embeddedness, its 'qualia' – phenomenologists rarely inspect the concept of experience in its own right. Indeed, for many phenomenologists, as for Whitehead, 'experience' may refer to almost anything, from actions to thoughts to sensations to dreams, just as 'experience' may occur in active or passive modes and upon conscious or unconscious registers.

It may be unfair to ask phenomenologists, dedicated to a 'first-person' orientation to phenomena, to impose a definition of experience upon experience. Nevertheless, it is difficult to find a cogent defense, from within the schools of phenomenology, of the assumption that individuals 'experience' anything at all, or that 'experience' is more than a catch-all term for anything human beings may see, feel, sense, think, encounter, or do.

Perhaps the best-known philosophical debate concerning experience involved David Hume and Immanuel Kant. To vastly simplify their argument, Hume argued that experience – as in the impressions given to the human senses – was both the only ground, and yet also a limited ground, upon which knowledge could rest (1993, 2001). Kant claimed that experience (*Erfahrung*) included both the sensory perceptions that give rise to cognitions and the *a priori* concepts and categories, including the faculties of intuition, understanding, and reason, that made experience meaningful (1998). At least half of Kant's vision – his defense of the *a priori* claim or concept – has been questioned by some of today's empirically oriented philosophers. At the same time, Kant's argument that we cannot directly know things-in-themselves, like his related reflections on what might be called the aesthetic 'limit-experience' of the sublime, has given rise to a good deal of postmodern theorizing about experience (2001).

Indeed, the question of the 'sublimity' we afford to experience is not entirely beyond the scope of this inquiry. If Martin Luther was able to challenge a millennium of Church authority by claiming that "experience alone makes a theologian" (quoted in Gerrish 1993, 186), it is curious that the experience he defended would so quickly come to resemble the mysterious and overpowering Church he opposed. Consider, for instance, how individual experiences of the sacred often take on the qualities of precarity and *supplice* – 'precarity' comes from the Latin *prex*, meaning begging or prayer, while *supplice*, the French word for torture derived from the Latin *supplicare*, was famously praised by Georges Bataille as a paradoxically liberating and self-destructive vulnerability (1988, 33–61; see also Bowker 2014, 60–63).

American mystic Andrew Jackson Davis offers an illustrative example. Davis contends that abstract thought :

> bears the same relation to the Real Truth … that a dream sustains to the substantial events of wakeful experience," for when the "hour of real prayer comes over the throbbing soul … inexorable experience steps in, prescribes its own remedies, its own penalties; and becomes, at last, the only 'divinity school' from which the mind can derive its imperishable education.
>
> *(1869, 33)*

For Davis, "inexorable" experience is the only "school" capable of saving our "throbbing soul[s]" by prescribing "*its own* remedies … [and] penalties" upon us; if, that is, we are desperate enough to offer ourselves up in "*real* prayer." The "imperishable education" tendered by experience is quite often, as we shall see in the following chapters, a lesson in the necessity of submitting to experiences of suffering, deemed necessary and good.

Without being overly naïve about it, we might imagine that our experience, even our experience of the sacred, ought to make us feel at home, alive, and whole, but these feelings are quite at odds with the "numinous dread," "awefulness," and quality of *mysterium tremendum et fascinans* (overwhelming and fascinating mystery before which we tremble) that have continued to mark off sacred experience from the banal and the ordinary (Otto 1992, 78–85). Thus, in his book on *The Throe of Wonder*, Jerome Miller writes of the foolishness of removing ourselves from crisis, horror, and death. Miller recommends, instead, "allow[ing] the experience of horror, and specifically horror in the face of death, to shatter the accepted understanding of ourselves both as selves and as philosophers" (1992, 124).

Emmanuel Levinas, the famous Lithuanian-French philosopher and Talmudic scholar, has advanced an extremely influential spiritually sponsored philosophy in which our experience of others must be non-relational in order to be ethical (see Levinas 1996, 1998). The other must beset us like a god, must invade us, and must put "into question" the self's very existence (Levinas 1969, 43). What this means, for Levinasians and even for more judicious social theorists like Judith

Butler, is that our selves must be "gripped and undone" by our experiences with others, in order that we be instructed, or at least reminded, of our essential precariousness, of "the thrall in which our relations with others hold us ... in ways that often interrupt the self-conscious account of ourselves as autonomous and in control" (Butler 2004, 23).

Our experience with others must shatter our autonomy, must "clutter [our] speech with signs of its undoing," must leave us "throbbing," "disrupted," and perhaps "awefully" attuned to those experiences that make attempts at self-awareness and self-narration absurd (see Bowker 2014, 64–65). "My narrative falters, as it must," writes Butler. "Let's face it. We're undone by each other. And if we're not, we're missing something" (2004, 23). If we are *not* undone, what we are missing is not our selves but their opposites: experiences of self-destruction, experiences taken to be natural, inevitable, and ethically and politically necessary. We must undo our selves in order to become not more human but "posthuman," as Lauro and Embry propose in their "Zombie Manifesto":

> Posthumanity can only really be attained when we pull the trigger on the ego. To kill the zombie, you must destroy the brain, and to move posthuman, to lay humanism and its legacy of power and oppression in the grave, we have to undo our primary systems of differentiation: subject/object, me/you.
> *(2008, 107)*

Thus, "the only way to truly get posthuman is to become antisubject" (87).

Such orientations to subject and self are not distinct from less apocalyptic efforts to "discern our suffering's productive worth" (Davies 2012, 49). Recent works such as Norman Rosenthal's *The Gift of Adversity* (2013) and James Davies' *The Importance of Suffering* (2012) carry on the tradition of scholarly approbation for the experience of suffering, where the object supplicated in our *supplice* is not a god but an other. Deonna, Rodogno, and Teroni, in their *In Defense of Shame* (2012), and Christina Tarnopolsky, in *Prudes, Perverts, and Tyrants: Plato's Gorgias and the Politics of Shame* (2010), have also recently espoused the value of self-effacement, arguing that socio-cultural degeneration can be corrected by shame, conceived as a sort of psychic civil service, undertaken for the good of others.

Experience as ideology

We are tempted, in a neo-liberal era, to imagine that any extreme, radical, or even stringent idea is, by definition, 'ideological.' But extremity, radicalism, and stringency do not an ideology make. Rather, while ideas and ideologies are theoretically inseparable, to use the term 'ideology' is to draw attention to the fantastical and coercive aspects of ideas. The primary function of any ideology is to defend against knowledge of reality by replacing it with a mythical or fantastical (i.e., wished-for) reality that better supports the ideologists' objectives.

A Marxist, for instance, might argue that the ideology of individual freedom functions to legitimize certain institutions and practices of contemporary capitalism, institutions and practices that often undermine the genuine freedom of human beings around the world. To the extent that this ideology of freedom functions as intended, the positive value attached to 'freedom' is applied to the practices of capitalism, say, in the discourse of the 'free market,' just as criticism of or resistance to the practices and impacts of capitalism is coercively suppressed as if it were an attack on 'freedom.'

In approaching experience, trauma, failure, and deprivation as ideologies, my aim is not, of course, to connect these constructs to a Marxist critique of capitalism, but to reference the coercive force of our attitudes toward them. It is also my intention to show that ideologies of experience play a considerable role in shaping power-relations between citizens, groups, and institutions by framing the terms by which civil relationships are formed and by defining influential cultural, moral, and political ideals.

As Charles Taylor claims, and as his well-known debates with Michael Sandel imply, "if we are to do political philosophy intelligently," not only must we consider governments, institutions, laws, and groups, but we "must write about the self" (Alford 1991, 9). Why? Because the self's development, its relationships with others, and its status vis-à-vis civil institutions is one way – but not the *only* way – of defining and assessing psychological, political, and ethical achievement, a way that is particularly persuasive if we take seriously the values of individual freedom, human flourishing, and both privacy and publicity. If we do, then it is worthwhile to clarify how ideologies of experience may undermine the self and to examine what is lost, what is gained, and whether this exchange is in keeping with the values we espouse.

The fact that ideologies of experience are hardly recognized and rarely discussed in standard political-theoretical debates, such as those between liberals and communitarians, moderns and postmoderns (and post-postmoderns), or the Left and the Right, demonstrates not their apolitical nature but that, like all truly potent ideologies, ideologies of experience transcend such divisions. In keeping with current trends, it might be tempting to write of micro-ideologies, just as we now write of 'micro-democracy,' 'micro-socialism,' and even 'micro-revolution.' But ideologies, like genuine instantiations of democracy, socialism, and revolution, are always both micro- and macro-. Both intimate and ubiquitous, ideologies of experience are transmitted not just between leaders and citizens, but between parents and children, teachers and students, employers and employees, writers and readers. We find traces of their influence not only in political philosophies but in popular films, television shows, and common jokes. Ideologies of experience may be held to dearly and propagated enthusiastically by those who have never heard of the term 'ideology' nor involved themselves with politics in any substantial way. In my view, this makes ideologies of experience pressingly 'political.'

Given how profoundly our experiences are held to impact our lives, it might be equally tempting to imagine that, since ideologies of experience seem to transcend political divisions, experience must transcend ideology. In other words, we might speculate that no ideology is needed to impart experience's lessons or to instill respect for its importance. David Smail is right, and perhaps understates the case, when he notes that "there is something about the lessons they draw from their experience of life which human beings are reluctant – indeed, often almost unable – to abandon" (1984, 93).

But asserting that the lessons of experience mysteriously adhere to or inscribe themselves upon us is already to have ceded ground to ideology, already to have invested experience with that indefinable quality that differentiates 'things-in-themselves' from 'mere ideas' about them. In what follows, I do not attempt to untangle the philosophical question of whether experiences or their objects may be considered 'things-in-themselves.' More important is to reflect upon what we intend, what we gain, and what we lose when we conceive of experiences and their objects in this way. That is, while the notion of 'things-in-themselves' is philosophically troubling, more troubling is the manner of relating to experiences and objects *as if* they were 'things-in-themselves.'

Celebrants of experience often argue that experience is our last remaining *antidote* to ideology, making the matter of critiquing ideologies of experience rather complicated. Their argument proceeds by equating ideas with ideologies, then, by equating thinking with the cognitive distortions that result from ideological pressure. The ideologists of experience I discuss in this book generally insist that the reality accessible by experience is valuable precisely because it *cannot* be thought, cannot be transformed into an idea, cannot be interfered with by the self, because experience is incommensurate with and superior to the self. Of course, the notion of idea-proof, thought-proof, self-proof experience is, itself, mythical and ideological: It is the mythology and ideology of the *in-itself-ness* of experience.

In conversing with colleagues and students about this book, I have been asked, more than once: "Do we *really* need to think this much about experience?" It is a telling objection, and an ideological one. If we do not need to think about experience, it must be because we already know enough, or because no good can come from trying to know more. In either case, we confront more than a worry that we will waste time. We confront a fear that in thinking about experience, we will lose touch with experience, that our experiences may lose their special-ness and value. This attitude implies that experience must be kept away from thought and its concomitants: analysis, questioning, and doubt. If thought, analysis, questioning, or doubt is brought into contact with our experience, then it may threaten our relationships to our experiences, relationships to which we may be more committed than we know.

To be clear, if ideologies of experience held merely that experiences were special and valuable, or that we should not like to lose touch with them, there would be no need to undertake the sort of ideology-critique pursued in this book. Experience *is* special: If one wishes to *experience* a roller-coaster, no amount of talking or thinking about a roller-coaster will do. And experience *is* valuable: Without experience, human beings could not experiment – 'experiment' is rooted in the Latin *experiri* and cognate with 'experience' – develop, learn, change, or sustain the vitality of selves and groups.

In this book, I do not argue that experience is bad, nor that an alternative to experience – if there could be such a thing – is superior to it. On the contrary, the value we place on experience is likely born of healthy desires, such as the desire to feel real, to express curiosity, and to be creative. We may seek experience to expand our horizons, to test our limits, or to reach out and find others and the world in new ways. And experience frequently serves these aims. But ideologies of experience go further, insisting not only that experiencing is the ultimate mode of human being, but that the most valuable types of experiences are those in which the self and its distinctive capacities are eclipsed or destroyed by experience's objects, as they are in trauma, failure, and deprivation.

Therein lies the problem. While experiences do form special and valuable parts of human lives, the most venerated experiences too often become those in which the qualities of selfhood are negated or lost, in which the experiencer finds, instead, an ambivalently attractive and agonizing – *tremendum et fascinans* – connection with an overwhelming object. If ideologies of experience exhort us to cherish such connections and to repeat such self-occlusive experiences, then, contrary to their stated aims, they may substantially limit the range and depth of experience available to human beings.

The ideal of selfhood

There are likely as many definitions of 'self' as there are of 'experience.' And selfhood, unfortunately, cannot be distilled to a single criterion. Rather, selfhood is a constellation of capacities and qualities, all inter-related. Since 'self,' like 'experience,' is a term thrown around hastily, it is desirable to explore very briefly some of the meanings and aspects of selfhood, not to pronounce with any finality upon what a self is or may be, but merely to clarify my intended usage of the concept in this work.

My approach to the self is derived largely from the – sometimes contrasting – premises of select schools of psychoanalytic object-relations theory and self psychology (see, e.g., Bion 1962, 1967, 1988; Klein 1975a, 1975b; Kohut 1971, 1977; Winnicott 1965, 1971, 1984, 1986, 1989). While others working within and around these traditions disagree, I believe it is clear that to write of the self is to invoke a value, not a substance. The ideal of selfhood pays homage to a set of psychological, political, and ethical norms that may not – and that need not – be convincing to all and that likely would not have arisen in different times and places than those in which they did. Although several advances in psychoanalytic psychology have resulted from direct observation and other forms of empirical inquiry, the theories of self that have arisen alongside them do not necessarily make the self a 'real thing' (whatever that may mean), nor do they contain 'facts' about human existence.

There is a respectable case to be made that the self does not 'exist,' but not precisely for the reasons that others offer (see, e.g., Derrida 1991, 1998; Lyotard 1984; Rorty 1987). More of those who write about the self might admit the self's non-existence if some agreement could be reached about what it means for something to 'exist,' for, even if the self does not 'exist,' its ideals may nevertheless inform the thoughts, feelings, activities, and experiences of real human beings. I agree with Christopher Bollas in this respect, when he writes that:

> there is no one unified mental phenomenon that we can term self, although … it is true to say that all of us live within the realm of illusion and within this realm the concept of self has a particularly relevant meaning.
>
> *(1987, 9)*

Put another way, even if the self is an illusion, it is a *usable* illusion; usable, that is, unless it is felt to be intolerably threatening to one's cherished objects, or to experience, or to others, or to groups. When the illusion of the self is threatening, it becomes necessary to evacuate the illusion and incapacitate those who would use it (Bowker 2014, 59).

Although the self may not 'exist,' there are real differences between human beings who feel, act, and think like selves and those who do not. A good many conversations between psychotherapists and clients – and teachers and students, and parents and children, and legislators and constituents – carry in their subtext a struggle over who is feeling, acting, or thinking like a self and who is not, over who can be a self and who cannot. While the presence of self in any encounter, even a solitary one, may be perceptible, it is hardly objectifiable or quantifiable. Indeed, that selfhood is *not* empirically verifiable, quantifiable, nor objectively resolvable in any ultimate sense, turns out to be a pivotal insight for those who seek to enliven and integrate their selves, particularly for those who pursue such aims via psychoanalytic psychotherapy.

Most ideas of self rely upon the imagination of a boundary, a porous psychic "membrane" (see, e.g., Grey 2008, 85), that permits the self both to separate itself from and to make contact with others and the environment. The metaphorical boundary of the self, then, delineates the 'inner' and 'outer' worlds. This metaphor is as useful as it is dangerous, for it tempts us to reify the self's boundaries, to think of them as material substances or psychic infrastructures. This is particularly the case in contemporary trauma theorizing, where the medical definition of trauma – the piercing of the body's boundary by a foreign object – has subtly informed contemporary conceptions of self. That psychic trauma could be thought to violate or puncture the self's boundary and shatter its integrity reveals an error in overly objectifying and concretizing the psyche. This error, among others, has made it difficult for those participating in these discourses to distinguish the agony of an intrusive trauma from the ideal of an indelible truth.

It is more helpful to imagine the self and its boundaries as capacities, dynamics, and tendencies that come and go. Our selfhood is never settled, such that, in Melanie Klein's language, the individual in the "depressive position" lives with or alongside – and not above or free from – a "paranoid-schizoid" orientation to self and others, which may exert its influence at any time (see Klein 1975b, 64; Minsky 1998, 33–34; Segal 1964, xii–xiii). If we can remember that the "paranoid-schizoid" and "depressive" positions are not mileposts achieved along a developmental trajectory but, rather, are paradigms or perspectives that co-exist throughout life, then we may see what is so inspired about Klein's understanding of human psychic experience: the primacy she affords to the struggle between (a) projecting hate, destructiveness, and threats of annihilation outward while internalizing and identifying with split-off aspects of nurturing forces (the paranoid-schizoid position) and (b) recognizing and taking in whole objects, combinations of good and bad, and, in doing so, confronting the ego's own capacity for sadism and violence (the depressive position) (see Klein 1975a, 272–273, 286–289; Segal 1964, 55–57).

In the paranoid-schizoid position, there can be no self, only forces of good and bad, shuttled inside and out in an attempt to safeguard the good and neutralize the bad. In the depressive position, there is a possibility of selfhood because there is a possibility of thinking and knowing another as a whole self and, therefore, of knowing and of being known as a whole self. Needless to say, selfhood is never a *fait accompli* but a life's work, as we strive, sometimes successfully, sometimes not, to tolerate, understand, and integrate aspects of ourselves and others.

While I do not always use Kleinian language, borrowing equally from Bion, Freud, Kohut, Winnicott, and others, it would not be wrong to characterize my view as one in which our orientation toward experience drives our tendency to favor either a paranoid-schizoid or depressive posture, not, again, as a stepping-stone by which we advance from one position to another, but as a compass that positions us in relation to the objects in our inner and outer worlds. Ideologies of experience, I will argue, turn and return us to something not unlike a paranoid-schizoid orientation in which the project of developing the self is abandoned. There need be no self, ideologies of experience teach us, so long as we have 'good' experience. Indeed, the self that we are 'given' – what is typically construed as a 'bad' self – is presupposed, even hypostatized, primarily to be overcome, gotten rid of. If it is not gotten rid of, it gets in the way.

I hope to differentiate the self described in this book from the self imagined in so much contemporary theorizing, from the much-maligned Kantian "disembodied subject" (see, e.g. Sandel 1998), to the absolutist of Reason (see, e.g., Horkheimer 2002), to the "*I think* as substantial as a stone" (Levinas 1998, 71), to the "rational murderer" (Camus 1991, 253) who combines destructive impulse with Hegelian logic to negate the other. The vision of selfhood advanced here is meant to be distinguishable from the creature driven by biological impulse as well as from the rational egoist whose "supercelestial thoughts" lead only to "sub-terrestrial conduct" (Montaigne 1993, 405). The self I and others have imagined need not act out every impulse, need not react with excessive fear or violence to the demands of others, need not compulsively defend against perceived threats of annihilation, and need not deny the realities of dependence to escape narcissistic injury.

There remain important distinctions between various criteria of selfhood that should not be glossed over, especially for the reader who wishes to consider more deeply the meaning of the self. I have found it helpful to consider the idea of selfhood along three main axes: feeling, acting, and thinking. Because selfhood is a constellation and not a singular achievement, these axes inter-relate and overlap.

Winnicott famously writes of the "feeling of real" (1971, 80), a feeling that belongs presumably to the "vital moment[s] of being" in which we express our selves – or even express our "protoselves" – spontaneously (Levine 2011, 16–20). What Winnicott refers to as a "feeling of existing … as a basic place to operate from" (1986, 39) and as "feeling real" (1971, 117) may be considered a relatively primitive "sense of self" (Stern 1985, 7), one that is nonetheless crucial to sustaining more complex feelings, such as the feeling of "ontological security" (Laing 1969, 39), as well as the more complex activities and thoughts appropriate to selves.

For R.D. Laing, "ontological security" is a feeling of the self's reality, an experience of the self as "real, alive, whole, and, in a temporal sense, a continuous person" (1969, 39). "Ontological security" implies, we might say, a personal history of "feeling real," a history of connection with one's body, one's sensations, and one's emotions, and, most importantly, a capacity to hold that history in a sort of psychic trust upon which the self can rely. From this secure self-feeling, one may "live out into the world and meet others … encounter[ing] all the hazards of life, social, ethical, spiritual, biological, from a centrally firm sense of [one's] own and other people's reality and identity" (39). Although Laing here makes an unfortunate leap from the feeling of existing to the formation of an identity that is unique and self-conscious as such, his point is not entirely distinct from Winnicott's well-known assertion that the activities (the "doing") appropriate to selves must arise from their sense of themselves (from their "being") (1986, 39).

From the feeling of reality there may arise at least two sorts of *activities* appropriate to selves: spontaneous gestures and willful, purposive acts. Clearly, the latter involve a higher degree of cognitive complexity than the former. That is, willful, purposive action requires thought, and is therefore related to the third axis of thinking, to be discussed momentarily. Nevertheless, if the self may be said to act in a meaningful sense, it must do so as "a unit, cohesive in space and enduring in time" (Kohut 1977, 99), as a being that has, even momentarily, achieved "unit status" (Winnicott 1971, 70). "Unit status" implies not only a measure of integration and cohesiveness but, perhaps more importantly, differentiation from, negation of, and tolerance of tension with others and the environment. The ability to act as a self requires a degree of freedom from both biological impulse and external determination such that the active self can function as the "organizing center of the ego's activities" (Kohut 1971, 120), making the self a creative force (Winnicott 1986, 39–70), or "a center of initiative" (Kohut 1977, 99), in the world.

The *thinking* appropriate to the self is not primarily a Cartesian "*cogito ergo sum*" (Descartes 1985), but is, rather, a thinking that entails the refusal of experience as a given and the willingness to engage experience creatively and interactively. The thinking of the self is perhaps the most difficult aspect of selfhood to tackle, not least because of the considerable recent emphasis on the relationship between subjectivity, the unconscious, and language made possible by the work of Jacques Lacan (1977). It is fair to say that Lacanian psychoanalysis and philosophy afford no place for the self. Indeed, to the extent that there is a self or subject for Lacan, the ego is its symptom. This is what Lacan means when he writes, famously, that the ego lies "at the heart of the subject … a privileged symptom, the human symptom par excellence, the mental malady of man" (1988, 16).

Lacan's critique is far-reaching. For Lacan, all "desire is desire of the Other" (1998, 235), and this desire is essentially enigmatic and impossible to fulfill, leaving us with an inescapable lack (*manque*) instead of a self. Even if this desire, this lack, were fulfillable, it would have nothing to do with the creation of a self but would more closely resemble its opposite: perfect union or fusion with the other, making the self into the 'thing' of the other, a pure object of desire. What is worse, this drama of desire has been structured in fantasy according to the pressure of the "traumatic impossibility" of its symbolization (Žižek 1989, 123), meaning that the unconscious, which lies closest to what is unique or special about any human being, *chez* Lacan, holds mainly "a traumatic truth" (Žižek 2007, 3).

The symbolic order to which we turn in hope and despair does not permit of genuine expression but of what Žižek memorably compares to a Mexican soap opera in which the actors "wear tiny receivers in their ears that tell them what to do … 'Now slap him and tell him you hate him! Then embrace him!'." Our participation, that is, in thinking and symbolizing, our life in the realm of ideas, symbols, and language, which is "the second nature of every speaking being … is here, directing and controlling my acts; it is the sea I swim in, yet it remains ultimately impenetrable" (2007, 8). Thus, for Lacan, the process by which the subject is inevitably alienated from himself – by the enigmatic and impossible desire of the Other – occurs in language, so that Lacanians would say that language is both what destroys the self and what constitutes modern subjects, since language is impossible to refuse, or is refused only in madness.

Like all psychoanalytic theories, one might subject Lacan's to analytic critique and wonder why it is impossible, why it *must be* impossible, for human beings to achieve the degree of authenticity, separateness, and creativity appropriate to selfhood. For, while is it certainly possible to over-estimate the self's capacity to free itself from embeddedness, language, and unthought influences, it is also possible to over-estimate the "automatic, deterministic effects of language," making it seem as if "language lived itself in man and the reverse were not at all true" (Sass 1988, 604).

If the self, to Lacan, is an illusion, it is the same for the purposes of this book, although I see no reason to regard the capacities to feel, act, and think like a self as symptoms, defenses, or denials of reality. On the contrary, the type of activity, referred to above, that permits the self to function as the "organizing center of the ego's activities" has a correlate along the axis of thinking, whereby the self operates as a pattern- and meaning-maker of its experience. If the self includes the sum of "positions or points of view from which and through which we sense, feel, observe, and reflect on distinct and separate experiences in our being" (Bollas 1987, 9–10), then the ability to 'think,' described in more detail in the following chapter, involves the self's ability to *remove* itself from "the sea [we] swim in," to gather up and look upon its experience, upon others, and even upon itself. It is typically this ability to remove the self from its experience that is most objectionable to those who doubt or disdain the ideal of selfhood or subjectivity.

Put more plainly, to advance an ideal of self, it is necessary to proceed by defining the thinking appropriate to the self as the thinking that resists or negates given desires, given experiences, and given orders of things in favor of ideas that begin as possibilities and that may be realized through creative action. This sort of thinking means that the self is capable of relating to itself, to others, to objects in the environment, and to its own projects not as inevitabilities but as potentialities (see Levine 2011, 21–24), not as 'things-in-themselves,' but as things-that-may-or-may-not-be. Of course, a Lacanian might reply that this argument is only so much fantasy. At that point, it may only be sensible to admit to paradigmatic differences and move on.

In this book, I focus primarily on three related aspects of selfhood, which are not identical to – but, rather, cut across – the three axes of selfhood sketched out above. I argue, first, that ideologies of experience contravene the project of self-hood with respect to the self's capacity to think and know itself and its own experience in a special sense informed by Bion's theory of thinking, which also entails the internalization of feelings of reality and security within the self. This process is elaborated primarily in Chapters 2 and 3, but taken up again in Chapters 5 and 8. I strive to show that ideologies of experience discourage creative and purposeful action and recommend, instead, the kinds of compulsive and repetitive behaviors depicted in Chapter 4, Chapter 5, and, to some degree, Chapter 7. Finally, I contend that ideologies of experience interfere with the self's capacity to be alone, a complex capacity that involves feeling, acting, and thinking like a self. The problem of aloneness and its opposites is explored throughout Chapters 5, 6, 7, and 8.

Outline of this work

What follows is an evocative depiction and analysis of several ideologies of experience across what may rightly seem to be quite diverse settings. The chapters are arranged so as to gradually bring into relief the meaning and purpose of ideologies that valorize experiences of psychic devastation and the abandonment of the project of self-development. And while the examples most amenable to this theme range from the work of Michel de Montaigne to that of contemporary trauma theorists, from Enlightenment visions of the state of nature to Albert Camus' play about mistaken identity and murder, from the work of American pragmatist and pedagogue John Dewey to the experience of Japanese shut-ins, this somewhat unusual grouping of topics highlights the complex patterns concerning experience and its relationship to the self.

For instance, we will find that the individuals in *hikikomori* and those who study and treat them, described in Chapter 7, share a misguided aspiration with those who indulge in the fantasy of the state of nature, considered in Chapter 8. We will see how the protagonist of Albert Camus' well-known play *Le Mal-entendu*, analyzed in Chapter 4, mistakes the repetition of traumatic loss for the discovery of a home and an identity, an error explained in some detail in Chapters 2 and 3. And we will note how contemporary experience-based pedagogies investigated in Chapter 5 thwart the achievement of *being alone* set out in Chapter 6.

When possible, I strive to undertake *immanent* critique: to expose the flaws, contradictions, and self-defeating consequences inherent in the logic of ideologies of experience. This turns out to be a tricky endeavor, not only because advocates of experience claim that experience cannot be thought about or analyzed without doing injustice to it, but because – what amounts to nearly the same thing – ideologies of experience ask us to believe that the failures of thought generated by experience are, themselves, of great value, and so only affirm experience's worth.

In the following chapter, I set out a basic paradigm for understanding experience, one related to a witticism offered in Freud's book on *Jokes and Their Relation to the Unconscious* (1960). If experience, as we shall see, requires the conversion of the bad into the good, then it is not through the faculty of thought that this transformation is accomplished. I define what is meant by 'thinking' and 'knowing' in a psychoanalytic sense, and argue that the protection or 'fortification' of experience against intrusion is actually a defense against the internal threat of thinking.

In Chapter 3, I demonstrate that the relation imagined between trauma victim and traumatizing object is reminiscent of a relationship idealized in modern European and American literary traditions celebrating experience, traditions represented in the work of Michel de Montaigne, Ralph Waldo Emerson, Georges Bataille, and others. In the relationship between self and object depicted in accounts of both trauma and experience, we find fantasies of failure, deprivation, and self-abandonment, in which confirmations of the putative impossibility of realizing a self in the world is imagined to liberate human beings from thought and guilt. This attitude toward experience endorses not only the incorporation of trauma as an organizing principle of the psyche but the transmission of trauma to others.

Chapter 4 analyzes one of Albert Camus' best known-plays, *Le Malentendu* (*The Misunderstanding*) (1958), to display in detail the fantasy that repeated experiences of trauma will reunite the individual with experience's object. This chapter engages in an extended literary analysis of a well-known, although poorly understood, play and, with it, an even more popular moral narrative. It specifically concerns itself with the contest between, on one hand, thinking about experience in ways that can be managed and integrated by the self and by others, and, on the other hand, transmitting experience in unmitigated and unthought forms.

Chapter 5 focuses on John Dewey's famous work *Experience and Education* (1997), and its powerful legacy in pedagogical theory and practice in the United States and, now, around the world. As it has been conceived, the ideal of experience in education leads not to the development of creativity and intellectual autonomy in students but to attitudes of compliance with social organizations, norms, and ideals that are taken to be unchanging and inevitable. While ostensibly training students to serve socially redeeming ends by mastering the objects of their experience, pedagogies of experience actually coerce students to serve the narcissistic needs of educators and community members.

Most ideologies of experience link aloneness and solitude with anxieties about the self's destructive capacities, as if the separateness of the self risked the survival of the human being and the human group. Since selfhood *does* entail separation from the group – and, in some sense, from the 'human being' – the question taken up in Chapter 6 is how we conceive of this separation in the context of experience: Is solitary self-experience healthy or unhealthy, ethically necessary or morally and politically threatening? Advocates of experience sometimes appear to defend solitary experience, but are really defending a false form of aloneness that preserves self-effacing connections to experience's objects and to the groups and communal bodies that represent and house them.

In Chapter 7, I examine *hikikomori*, the experience of severe self-incarceration, often lasting several years, most commonly studied in Japan. According to some estimates, well over one million Japanese citizens, approximately twenty-five percent of Japanese young people, will experience *hikikomori* in their lifetimes. In spite of the surge in clinical and scholarly interest in the phenomenon, there remains a great degree of confusion regarding the phenomenon. I argue that difficulties in understanding *hikikomori* derive from resistances and defensive mystifications in which both individuals in *hikikomori* and those who study and treat these individuals participate, and that these defenses disguise the desire at the heart of the experience: a desire to return to a more indulgent self-experience that has been lost, leaving the individual incapable of psychically surviving contact with the self or others.

The state-of-nature theories analyzed in Chapter 8 are among the most influential ideologies of experience to date, having informed contract- and consent-oriented philosophies of modern government. To preserve the fantasy to which the state of nature refers, which is akin to the infantile illusion of omnipotence, the self must not only deny or misrecognize its dependence upon others, but must seek out experiences of 'natural' psychic devastation in private and civil life. Accomplishing this means celebrating the defeat of the 'bad' self as a means of turning 'bad' experience into 'good.' Repressed guilt and ideologically influenced fantasies of 'the real' resurface in the form of paranoid-schizoid orientations toward the self and its place in civil institutions and groups.

A note on terminology

Finally, it is worth a moment to clarify a terminological matter with epistemological and metapsychological implications. Words like 'self,' 'person,' 'ego,' 'subject,' and 'individual' are notoriously imprecise. They are often used haphazardly, and sometimes interchangeably, even by the best of thinkers. Typically, unless one wishes to devote oneself entirely to the clarification of these terms, one must make concessions to a degree of imprecision for the sake of analyzing something else one takes to be important. Because of the precise meaning I associate with the terms 'self' and 'selves,' I seek wherever possible to restrict their use to an, admittedly ideal, psychological and social achievement. One could, of course, substitute the terms 'person' and 'personhood,' or even 'subject' and 'subjectivity' for 'self,' without being in any way incorrect. To avoid confusion, I do not.

I employ the term 'individual' in discussions of the social contract, of the years-long self-incarceration that defines *hikikomori*, and of citizens of modern democratic societies such as the American society Tocqueville described. For the purposes of this book, an 'individual' is a legal individual who lacks some or all of the capacities that make up a self, or, at least, whose possession of said capacities is in doubt.

I use the terms 'family member,' 'group member,' and 'community member' to distinguish the ideal of self from the human being whose psychic existence depends largely or entirely upon shared experiences, compliance with group norms, and acquiescence to the demands of belonging.

I use the term 'human being' as a sort of baseline, or when no other term will do, as in discussions of the state of nature, where the creatures imagined by most social contract theorists are neither legal individuals, nor community members, nor family members, nor selves.

Of course, it is not only in imaginary states of nature, the locked bedrooms of *hikikomori*, or rigidly conformist groups that one encounters human beings, individuals, or group members who are not selves. The world is full of not-selves. Ideologies of experience are an important part of the reason why.

References

Alford, C.F. 1991. *The Self in Social Theory: A Psychoanalytic Account of Its Construction in Plato, Hobbes, Locke, Rawls, and Rousseau*. New Haven, CT: Yale University Press.

Bataille, G. 1988. *Inner Experience*. Translated by L.A. Boldt. Albany, NY: State University of New York Press.

Bion, W.R. 1962. *Learning from Experience*. London: Heinemann.

Bion, W.R. 1967. *Second Thoughts*. London: Heinemann.

Bion, W.R. 1988. "A Theory of Thinking." In *Melanie Klein Today: Developments in Theory and Practice. Volume I: Mainly Theory*, edited by E. Spillius, 178–186. London: Routledge.

Bollas, C. 1987. *The Shadow of the Object: Psychoanalysis of the Unthought Known*. New York: Columbia University Press.

Bowker, M.H. 2014. *Rethinking the Politics of Absurdity: Albert Camus, Postmodernity, and the Survival of Innocence*. Series: Routledge Innovations in Political Theory. New York: Routledge.

Butler, J. 2004. *Precarious Life: The Powers of Mourning and Violence*. London: Verso.

Camus, A. 1958. "The Misunderstanding." In *Caligula and Three Other Plays*. Translated by S. Gilbert, 75–134. New York: Vintage.

Camus, A. 1991. *The Plague*. First Vintage International Edition. Translated by S. Gilbert. New York: Vintage.

Davies, J. 2012. *The Importance of Suffering: The Value and Meaning of Emotional Discontent*. London: Routledge.

Davis, A.J. 1869. *The Present Age and Inner Life: Ancient and Modern Spirit Mysteries Classified and Explained*. Boston, MA: William White and Co.

Deonna, J., R. Rodogno, and F. Teroni 2012. *In Defense of Shame: The Faces of an Emotion*. Oxford: Oxford University Press.

Derrida, J. 1991. "*Différance*." In *A Derrida Reader: Between the Blinds*, edited by P. Kamuf, 59–79. New York: Columbia University Press.

Derrida, J. 1998. *Of Grammatology*. Translated by G.C. Spivak. Baltimore, MD: Johns Hopkins University Press.

Descartes, R. 1985. "Principles of Philosophy." In *The Philosophical Writings of Descartes, Volume I*, edited and translated by J. Cottingham, R. Stoothoff, and D. Murdoch, 177–292. Cambridge: Cambridge University Press.

Dewey, J. 1997. *Experience and Education*. New York: Touchstone.

Freud, S. 1960. *Jokes and Their Relation to the Unconscious*. Translated by J. Strachey. New York: W.W. Norton.

Gerrish, B. 1993. *Continuing the Reformation: Essays on Modern Religious Thought*. Chicago, IL: University of Chicago Press.

Grey, F. 2008. *Jung, Irigary, Individuation: Philosophy, Analytical Psychology, and the Question of the Feminine*. New York: Routledge.

Horkheimer, M. 2002. "The End of Reason." In *The Essential Frankfurt School Reader*, edited by A. Arato and E. Gebhardt, 26–48. New York: Continuum.

Hume, D. 1993. *An Enquiry Concerning Human Understanding*, edited by E. Steinberg. Second Edition. Indianapolis, IN: Hackett.

Hume, D. 2001. *A Treatise of Human Nature*, edited by D. Norton and M. Norton. Oxford: Oxford University Press.

Jay, M. 2005. *Songs of Experience: Modern American and European Variations on a Universal Theme*. Berkeley, CA: University of California Press.

Kant, I. 1998. *Critique of Pure Reason*, edited and translated by P. Guyer and A. Wood. New York: Cambridge University Press.

Kant, I. 2001. *Critique of the Power of Judgment*. Translated by P. Guyer and E. Matthews. New York: Cambridge University Press.

Klein, M. 1975a. *The Writings of Melanie Klein, Volume I: Love, Guilt, Reparation and Other Works, 1921–1945*. New York: Free Press.

Klein, M. 1975b. *The Writings of Melanie Klein, Volume III: Envy and Gratitude and Other Works, 1946–1963*. New York: Delacorte/Seymour Lawrence.

Kohut, H. 1971. *The Analysis of the Self: A Systematic Approach to the Psychoanalytic Treatment of Narcissistic Personality Disorders*. Chicago, IL: University of Chicago Press.

Kohut, H. 1977. *The Restoration of the Self*. Chicago, IL: University of Chicago Press.

Kuhns, R. 1970. *Structures of Experience*. New York: Basic Books.

Lacan, J. 1977. *Écrits: A Selection*. Translated by A. Sheridan. London: Tavistock.

Lacan, J. 1988. *The Seminar of Jacques Lacan: Book I, Freud's Papers on Technique, 1953–54*, edited by J. Miller. Translated by J. Forrester. Cambridge: Cambridge University Press.

Lacan, J. 1998. *The Seminar of Jacques Lacan: Book XI, The Four Fundamental Concepts of Psychoanalysis*, edited by J. Miller. Translated by A. Sheridan. New York: W.W. Norton.

Laing, R.D. 1969. *The Divided Self: An Existential Study in Sanity and Madness*. London: Penguin Books.

Lauro, S., and K. Embry 2008. "A Zombie Manifesto: The Nonhuman Condition in the Era of Advanced Capitalism." *Boundary 2* 35(1): 86–108.

Levinas, E. 1969. *Totality and Infinity: An Essay on Exteriority*. Translated by A. Lingis. Pittsburg, PA: Duquesne University Press.

Levinas, E. 1996. "Substitution." In *Basic Philosophical Writings*, edited by A. Peprzak, S. Critchley, and R. Bernasconi, 79–96. Bloomington, IN: Indiana University Press.

Levinas, E. 1998. *Of God Who Comes to Mind*. Translated by B. Bergo. Stanford, CA: Stanford University Press.

Levine, D.P. 2011. *The Capacity for Civic Engagement: Public and Private Worlds of the Self*. New York: Palgrave Macmillan.

Lloyd, G. 1979. *Magic, Reason and Experience: Studies in the Origin and Development of Greek Science*. Cambridge: Cambridge University Press.

Lyotard, J.-F. 1984. *The Postmodern Condition: A Report on Knowledge*. Translated by G. Bennington and B. Massumi. Minneapolis, MN: University of Minnesota Press.

Miller, J. 1992. *In the Throe of Wonder: Intimations of the Sacred in a Post-Modern World*. Albany, NY: State University of New York Press.

Minsky, R. 1998. *Psychoanalysis and Culture: Contemporary States of Mind*. New Brunswick, NJ: Rutgers University Press.

Montaigne, M. de 1993. *Essays*, edited and translated by J. Cohen. London: Penguin.

Oakeshott, M. 1933. *Experience and Its Modes*. Cambridge: Cambridge University Press.

Otto, R. 1992. "On Numinous Experience as Mysterium Tremendum et Fascinans." In *Experience of the Sacred: Readings in the Phenomenology of Religion*, edited by S. Twiss and W. Conser, Jr., 77–85. Hanover, NH: Brown University Press.

Plato 1987. *The Republic*. Second Revised Edition. Translated by D. Lee. London: Penguin Books.

Rorty, A. 1987. "Persons as Rhetorical Categories." *Social Research* 54: 55–72.

Rosenthal, N. 2013. *The Gift of the Adversity: The Unexpected Benefits of Life's Difficulties, Setbacks and Imperfections*. New York: Tarcher.

Sandel, M. 1998. *Liberalism and the Limits of Justice*. Second Edition. Cambridge: Cambridge University Press.

Sass, L. 1988. "The Self and Its Vicissitudes: An 'Archaeological' Study of the Psychoanalytic Avant-Garde." *Social Research* 55: 551–608.

Segal, H. 1964. *Introduction to the Work of Melanie Klein*. New York: Basic Books.

Smail, D. 1984. *Illusion and Reality: The Meaning of Anxiety*. London: J.M. Dent and Sons Ltd.

Stern, D.N. 1985. *The Interpersonal World of the Infant: A View from Psychoanalysis and Developmental Psychology*. New York: Basic Books.

Tarnopolsky, C. 2010. *Prudes, Perverts, and Tyrants: Plato's Gorgias and the Politics of Shame*. Princeton, NJ: Princeton University Press.

Whitehead, A.N. 1933. *Adventures of Ideas*. New York: Free Press.

Winnicott, D.W. 1965. *The Maturational Processes and the Facilitating Environment: Studies in the Theory of Emotional Development*, edited by M. Khan. London: Hogarth and the Institute of Psycho-Analysis.

Winnicott, D.W. 1971. *Playing and Reality*. London: Routledge.

Winnicott, D.W. 1984. *Deprivation and Delinquency*, edited by C. Winnicott, R. Shepherd, and M. Davis. London and New York: Routledge.

Winnicott, D.W. 1986. *Home Is Where We Start from: Essays by a Psychoanalyst*, edited by C. Winnicott, R. Shepard, and M. Davis. New York: W.W. Norton.

Winnicott, D.W. 1989. *Psychoanalytic Explorations*, edited by C. Winnicott, R. Shepard, and M. Davis. Cambridge, MA: Harvard University Press.

Žižek, S. 1989. *The Sublime Object of Ideology*. London and New York: Verso.

Žižek, S. 2007. *How to Read Lacan*. First American Edition. New York: W.W. Norton.

2

EXPERIENCE, FAILURE, AND THINKING

In *Jokes and Their Relation to the Unconscious*, Sigmund Freud relates G.C. Lichtenberg's witticism that "experience means experiencing what one does not wish to experience." Freud praises the form of the joke, what he calls the "joking envelope," for deceiving us about its content. On first hearing, "we are bewildered and think we have learnt a new truth," but in time we realize that the joke merely disguises the familiar sayings: "Injury makes one wise," and, "Adversity is the best teacher" (1960, 109–110).

In order for Freud to transliterate the joke as he does, he splits the idea of "experience," rendering it as a self-contradictory term. The first instance of "experience" is taken to refer to something self-evidently good, something desirable, something valuable. It is the kind of experience we *want*. On the other hand, "what one does not wish to experience" suggests "injury," "adversity," pain, or suffering. This is experience we *do not want*. What seems to be funny about the joke is that, if it is correct, what we want and what we do not want are the same.

If there is truth concealed in the joke, or in the adages refashioned by the joke, then enduring what is antithetical to our wishes yields wisdom, makes us learned, offers something of value. The joke tells us that what might be thought of as 'bad' experience (i.e., adverse, injurious, or painful experience) is actually 'good' (i.e., desirable, redeeming, valuable experience). The joke implies that we have been, at least at certain moments, utterly mistaken about what is truly good and what is truly bad, since we did not wish to experience that which we ought to have wished to experience.

To be more precise, the joke directs our attention to those moments when our understanding of 'good' and 'bad' undergoes a radical change. At first, what we wanted or did not want, what was 'good' or 'bad,' might have seemed straight-forward enough, perhaps referring simply to what was pleasing or displeasing. But then, rather abruptly, 'good' and 'bad' come to refer to a perspective that is more complicated, one that is "beyond the pleasure principle" (Freud 1920), to say the least, such as when "the best teacher" delivers adverse and injurious experience that also makes us "wise." The supposedly 'good' experience that is delivered is experienced as 'bad' *until* the experiencer identifies more fully with the perspective of the "teacher" than with her original estimation of her own experience.

It is this shift, this process of psychological and ethical realignment, that the joke condenses into a single phrase and a single instant. Although Freud makes no such observation, it is likely that part of the humor of the joke derives from the ambivalence we feel about this 'learning process,' which is, ultimately, a collision of two moral worlds: In the first world, the bad is bad; in the second world, the bad is good. This collision may be reminiscent of adverse childhood experiences involving parents, caretakers, or other authorities, especially if those authorities injured, deprived, or abandoned the child while telling him that such adversity, injury, deprivation, or victimization were actually 'for his own good.'

The sort of experience being described here is relational: It is experience *between*, and typically between those unequal in power, such that one (for instance, a parent) may say to the other (for instance, a child) that what she is experiencing as neglect and abuse is actually care and love. A child put into this position will very quickly lose touch with her ability to sense what is desirable or undesirable, needed or unnecessary, good or bad, on her own terms. What is more, she will quickly lose the ability even to perceive that there is a coercive bargain in place by which she has been asked to transform her 'bad' experiences into 'good' experiences at the cost of contact with her (potential) self.

It is true that, in order for children to mature into adults, they must contend with the "reality principle," which involves the recognition that, in addition to a subjective inner world, we inhabit a world of objects, a social world.[1] Acceptance of the reality principle, however, need *not* overturn our authentic estimations of the good. Rather, as D.W. Winnicott reminds us, while the reality principle is a disappointment and even a terrible "insult" to the child's belief that his wishes determine reality (1986, 40), if the child's caretakers have helped him to 'know' his inner world – in the sense described below – then he may navigate the challenges and obstacles associated with reality without losing all connection with himself. The adversities sometimes presented by natural and social realities, that is, need not obliterate the self, nor need they be transfigured from adversities into illuminations in order for a shred of self to survive. Rather, given 'good-enough' circumstances, the self may cope with the introduction of reality as an "insult," and need not internalize it as a permanent "injury."

If, however, the caretaking environment and subsequent influential environments force a child to choose between (a) preserving contact with authentic impulses, desires, and feelings and (b) relating in the objective world, then the child's experience will be, by definition, adverse and injurious, since losing contact with her self will appear to be the only means of relating, which, for a child, is a matter of life and death. That is, her self will have to die in order for others to return to her a vestige of her life according to their schedule. In order not to be utterly destroyed by reality – and in order not to destroy others out of rage at their apparent assault – such children are forced to internalize the most injurious lesson that could ever be 'taught': that authentic impulses, desires, and estimations of experience must be suppressed in order to be 'good.'

The displacement of authentic early experience and judgment with an alien standard of evaluation is, typically, a coerced collusion by which the child accepts the imposition of harsh restrictions upon itself. It may be understood in Winnicott's language of the replacement of the "true self" with a "false self" (1965), where the false self is compliant, attuned primarily to the needs of others. The false self system involves an implicit social contract or bargain by which the self gives itself up in order to receive from others a modicum of safety, attention, approval, and a refracted sense of its value.

If "adversity" and "injury" are "teachers," *what* precisely do they teach? Do we not call adversity and injury teachers primarily because they teach us how to endure adversity and injury? Adversity and injury teach us that adversity and injury are inevitable, and therefore must be endured by 'learning' to see our 'bad' experience as 'good.' If adversity and injury ask us to change our orientation toward the 'good' and the 'bad,' they do so by 'teaching' us that if we do not accept the 'bad' as 'good,' we cannot survive in a relational reality, which is to say, we can never be 'good.' What is more, the teachings of adversity and injury include the lesson that without adverse, injurious, painful experience, we would be naïve, empty, and foolish, hence: 'bad.' The ability to experience "injury" and "adversity" as 'good' betokens the ability to maintain more extensive relational and social contracts in which the greatest 'good' would be complete identification with 'reality' and its teachings, meaning the complete abandonment of the self.

The dark side of Lichtenberg's joke, then, is not merely its advocacy of travail and injury, but its gallows humor regarding the self: The self seems doomed to have experiences that destroy the self, doomed to learn to embrace its own inevitable destruction. Although we may learn from our mistakes, and although many worthwhile experiences do involve hardship, it is fair to say that Lichtenberg's is a *cruel* joke, a joke whose delight involves elements of violence, sadism, and masochism, qualities Freud remarked at the heart of several types of joking.

The compromise offered by joking is to disguise forbidden thoughts and impulses within permissible forms, allowing us to avoid rebuke from others and from our own critical faculties, while the "joke work," as Freud called it, reshapes the unacceptable material into the form of a joke, permitting the joke-maker and the joke-audience to share in experiences otherwise unattainable owing to the threat of internal (or external) punishment. Beneath the most conscious layer of the joke, we find aggression and cruelty directed at the self – both the self within and the self in others. The degree to which this aggression and cruelty "works" in the joke to produce humor depends upon the extent to which we have *already* suffered the kinds of experiences that have inured us to the necessity of self-loss, experiences in which the 'bad' was mystified and misrepresented as the 'good,' in which the self's authentic impulses, desires, feelings, and judgments were displaced by alien objects or organizing principles. These losses and displacements, of course, may be acknowledged more safely in jokes or other guises, where they are to some degree removed from the emotions that might otherwise attend them.

The truly forbidden material of the joke, if we are to be precise, is the recognition of the cruelty implicit in delivering and receiving injurious experience while presenting it as good. This is a cruelty with which some are already well acquainted, a cruelty that re-transmits itself in the telling of the joke, and perhaps even in a chapter of a book analyzing the telling of the joke. The joke permits the teller and the audience to share and re-experience, for a moment, the pain of such adverse and mystifying experience.[2] There may be, in the sharing of the joke, a discovery of sadistic pleasure, since the joke recalls experiences of injury and self-loss, while at the same time presenting this recollection as socially valuable, as a 'good' joke. It may even be that in sharing his suffering with others in a joke or anecdote, the 'student' of adversity solidifies his identification with the 'teacher,' who would undoubtedly approve of the joke.

Finally, we see in Freud's interpretation of Lichtenberg's joke a fantasy that Freud himself never remarks. The fantasy is that if we remove wishing and willing from our experience, then, in return, a 'good' thing will be provided. The fantasy suggests that real and valuable experiences happen *to us*, only passively, only in opposition to our wills, only in ways that we cannot desire or create for ourselves. If we wish them, will them, design them, or create them, then we cannot 'experience' them fully, cannot profit from their wisdom, cannot come to possess their goodness, or, perhaps, cannot even count them unto our experience.

This strange logic would imply that she who creates her own experience is actually empty of experience, or is empty, at least, of the sort of experience that has value. Experience is only worthwhile, on such a view, if it involves self-absence, displacement, or abandonment of the self, relinquishment of the authorship of experience to an alien force. In many ways, what is celebrated about experience is the *failure* of the self not only to authentically desire, feel, or judge its own experience, but to initiate, design, and realize its own experience.

To express it more simply: Many of our most venerated experiences would seem to be experiences of failure. 'Failure,' here, means the failure of the self to retain contact with itself in its experience, the failure of the self to hold onto its authentic estimations of what is meaningful and valuable – to insist, for example, that a 'bad' experience was actually 'bad' – and the failure of the self to create, contribute to, change, or resist its experience. Nietzsche's famous maxim in *Twilight of the Idols*, that "what does not kill me makes me stronger" (1990, 33), makes him something of an ideologist of experience in this regard. That is, while perhaps a comforting thought, many who have suffered injury or illness against their wills find the opposite to be true: that these experiences have made them weaker.[3] What is more, this lesson Nietzsche claims to have assimilated "from the military school of life," from life conceived as a 'school' of war, and from experiences of non-lethal defeat conceived as its 'teachings.'

The late Randy Pausch's best-selling book and widely broadcast talk entitled *The Last Lecture: Really Achieving Your Childhood Dreams* derived much of its popularity by returning to Nietzsche in so many words, echoing the widespread belief in the value of agonizing experience and of the failure to resist or overcome it. Pausch, a beloved computer science professor suffering from terminal pancreatic cancer, concluded: "Experience is what you get when you didn't get what you wanted. And experience is often the most valuable thing you have to offer" (2008, 157).

The fortification of experience

Michael Oakeshott once cautioned that since "'experience,' of all the words in the philosophic vocabulary, is the most difficult to manage," those "reckless enough to use the word" must make it their primary aspiration to "escape the ambiguities it contains" (1933, 9). While Oakeshott's warning was partly aimed at himself, it is indicative of a sense of danger surrounding investigations of experience, as if a misstep in this domain might bring disaster. Since it is difficult to think critically and creatively amid such fear and caution, one of the unconscious objectives of expressing trepidation about examining experience is to make thinking about experience treacherous, less frequent, and less successful.

Similarly, it is not uncommon in the classroom or in the course of conversation to hear someone say, 'If you have never experienced what I have experienced, then you can't understand.'[4] This claim is not merely intended to inform the listener about the limits of her knowledge. It is meant to admonish the listener for attempting to think about the speaker's experience. When such a statement is made, we may infer that the experience in question involves something central to the speaker's sense of identity. Not coincidentally, it often relates to the speaker's sense of deprivation or victimization, past, present, or future. The listener is urged to stand back and to abandon attempts at thinking, because doing otherwise is perceived to be a potentially destabilizing assault on the speaker's inner world, a world where the experience in question has come to play a central role.

Of course, what is *transmitted* to the listener in the speaker's refusal to communicate is an experience of exclusion, rejection, and suppression: The listener is silenced, denied, shot down. And exclusion, rejection, and suppression often form important parts of the very experiences of deprivation or victimization that the speaker seeks to hide. Thus, as in so many cases involving experiences of trauma, failure, and deprivation, the refusal of conscious communication succeeds in *transmitting* something of the painful experience in question. The experience is *not* communicated but, rather, is both hidden and shared, a dynamic we will encounter again in the following two chapters, on traumatic experience and repetition, respectively, and in Chapter 7, on the deprived and depriving isolation of *hikikomori*.

While threats to our experience may seem to arise from the world outside, it is really our precarious hold on our experience that is highlighted when we defend it so rigidly. The fear of having one's experience thought or comprehended – 'comprehend' comes from the Latin *com + prehendere*, meaning to grasp or seize – by others derives from a confusion by which we imagine that others may seize our experience and destroy it with thought, leaving us with nothing. More likely, we struggle with an internal dilemma in which our own thinking is feared to destroy our own connection to experience and its objects, in which we fear our own thoughts and must project them outward into a world perceived to assault us with thoughts but where we *must* not think if our experience is to survive.

Thinking about experience must be avoided if thinking leads to questioning or doubt of experience's necessity, inevitability, and goodness. To question or doubt would be to risk upsetting the bargain whereby the self replaced its own estimations of what was 'good' and 'bad' with injurious and adverse experience. To control the threat posed by thinking about experience, the act of thinking is split off both from the self and from its relationship to its experience. It is projected onto others, particularly onto easy or at least "suitable targets of externalization" (Volkan 1985), which include knowledge- and expertise-based institutions and groups, which are imagined to be interested in greedily devouring individuals' experience. As we shall continue to see in the chapters that follow, the psychic projection of repressed doubts, authentic estimations of experience, and genuine needs and desires often results in exaggerated perceptions of the power and destructiveness of such others, institutions, and groups.

Consider American poet and essayist Bill Holm's summary of the relationship between experience and power in his book *The Music of Failure*:

> Sacredness is unveiled through your own experience, and lives in you to the degree that you accept that experience as your teacher, mother, state, church. … One of power's unconscious functions is to rob you of your own experience by saying: we know better, whatever you may have seen or heard. … We are principle, and if experience contradicts us, why then you must be guilty of something. Power – whether church, school, state, or family – usually does this at first in a charming way while feeding you chocolate cake, bread and wine, advanced degrees, tax shelters, grant programs, and a strong national defense. Only when contradicted does it show its true face, and try to kill you. Instead, kill it inside you fast, and do it whatever damage seems practical in the outer world. Next, put your arms around everything that has ever happened to you, and give it an affectionate squeeze.
>
> *(2010, 15–16)*

According to Holm and his intellectual forebears, powerful institutions "rob" us of our experience, threaten us with the authority of "principle," and bribe us to collude in our own deprivation. If these methods fail to loosen our grip on our experience, "power" shows "its true face" – one of persecutory violence – and tries "to kill" us. Therefore, our survival, which here means the survival of our experience in our inner worlds, requires that we destroy not primarily external powerful institutions but their internal psychic representative: knowledge. It is knowledge that we must "kill inside [us] fast."

Without conversing directly with the post-structuralist tradition, Holm's argument is not entirely dissimilar to Michel Foucault's well-known concept of "power/knowledge," the alignment of normalizing, disciplinary, and technocratic knowledge with political power spread in "capillary" fashion throughout society (1975; 1980). To kill power/knowledge "inside [us] fast," we make a substitution: Any authority originating in institutions such as the "church, school, state, or family" must be replaced with a consecration of our experience, that is: "everything that has ever happened to [us]." We must "put [our] arms around" our experience as our *new* "teacher, mother, state, church." Institutions and their authority must be remade not exactly in our own images but in the images of our past and *passive* experiences (i.e., "everything that has ever happened *to* [us]"). These past and passive experiences must become our new internal "sacred" objects, if we hope to escape destruction by the "power" of knowledge.

Christopher Bollas has famously suggested the category of "the unthought known" to describe that which is never cognitively processed but nevertheless becomes an individual's basic orientation to self and to life, referring specifically to the internalized operational logic of parents and even the introduction of the reality principle (1987, 277–283). It may be more appropriate to name it the "unthought experienced," since Bollas does not intend to invoke the usual understanding of "knowledge" as a product of conscious, mental representation.[5] Using the example of a child forced to bear a family's grief and loss, Bollas writes: "Containing the other's projective identification seems life-defining; grief, in this last example, feels like the essence of the person; it is not to be thought – it cannot be; it is *lived*" (1987, 281, emphasis added). The child Bollas describes is forced to *live* grief because thinking about it would be to doubt it, and to doubt it would be to challenge it, just as experiencing himself or being *a* self, as opposed to being a container for the family's grief, would be to challenge his role and provoke chaos, punishment, or catastrophe.

Georges Bataille, famed, radical French philosopher and "father of post-modernism" (see Drury 1994, 123), would agree that, instead of thinking, "one must *live* experience" (Bataille 1988, 8, emphasis in original). Indeed, this simple yet consequential assertion has resounded in academic and conventional wisdom for centuries, where what has been *lived*, particularly when what has been lived involves suffering, must never be thought or known, lest it lose its connection to reality, its normative force, or its historical importance.

Claude Lanzmann has rather famously declared that "there is an absolute obscenity in the very project of understanding" the Holocaust (1995, 204), for reasons which are not fundamentally different from Albert Camus' disparagement of "the sin of wanting to know" (1955, 49). What is threatening about thinking about experience to these men is that if we were to understand experiences of horror, or even of 'absurdity,' we might become incapable of *living out* the roles that such experiences demand of us, roles deemed politically and morally necessary. In this light, we see how emphasizing *lived* experiences reflects not an interest in knowing how experiences are actually lived, but the opposite: an interest in *not* knowing experience, so that individuals, groups, or institutions whose psychic survival has come to depend upon the unthought, unquestioned *living out* – and *re-living out* – of experience can continue to perform.

Many public commemorations of atrocity or disaster, such as the memorial of the attacks on the World Trade Center in New York City on September 11 and the Holocaust Memorial Museum in Washington, D.C., are designed to be interactive, 'living' experiences for visitors, some of whom find them moving, others of whom find them overwhelming and intolerable. Visitors to such memorials are typically encouraged to identify with victimizers while sharing in the experience of the victim (see Levine 2003), an ambivalent and uncomfortable set of demands that generates psychic tension most readily relieved in fantasies of redeeming the victims by victimizing the victimizers and all that resembles them in visitors' inner and outer worlds.

The effort to generate in visitors powerfully ambivalent identifications with both victims and victimizers, along with emotions of shame and rage, is effective in displacing thought while binding visitors to the experience of suffering in question. Such commemorations make thinking about, learning about, and communicating about such events psychically threatening and significantly more difficult, which may imply that the stated purposes of education, reflection, and contemplation which these memorials often advertise as their missions may be at least partly dishonest.

It is no coincidence that the kind of extreme and traumatic experiences with which postmodern cultural, political, and literary theorists have been preoccupied of late have been declared both "literally" true and inherently "unknowable" (Caruth 1996, 57–62). Even some of the sagest commentators find themselves surrendering to the imperative to defend experiences, and the roles to which experiences assign us, as sacred things, by protecting them from the reach of thought. Martin Jay, for instance, holds that experience is:

> both a collective linguistic concept, a signifier that yokes together a class of heterogeneous signifieds in a diacritical force field, and a reminder that such concepts always leave a remainder that escapes their homogenizing group ... at the nodal point of the intersection between public language and private subjectivity, between expressible commonalities and the ineffability of the individual interior.
>
> *(2005, 6–7)*

If human experiences are, by definition, "ineffab[le]," "unformulated," or "slip-pery" (Stern 1997, 35), always leaving an unknowable "remainder," then experience becomes an unthinkable 'thing-in-itself.' The combination of the unquestioned "truth-value of experience" (Gadamer 1989, 357) and the putative "obscenity" and "sin" of attempting to intellectually access experience suggests that many champions of experience have built walls around cherished experiences, if you will, walls from which such experiences are not intended to escape.

If attempts to think about experience are imagined to be doomed to fail, then ideologists of experience insist upon *and* create conditions that assure the inevit-ability of this failure. This failure, in turn, transmits an experience of its own, an experience of intellectual failure, which, by a circular sort of logic, confirms the original presupposition that thinking about experience is futile. Put more simply: The failure of thinking about experience is a self-fulfilling prophesy. We may surmise, then, that the experience of the failure of thinking is a desired or desir-able experience, an experience that we wish to repeat and share. Why should anyone wish to repeat or share the experience of failure? Only if this failure meant a kind of success, which is precisely the arrangement described by Lich-tenberg's joke about experience. The failure to feel, think, and authentically judge experience is necessary for the self to imagine that its 'bad' experience is 'good.' And, as we shall see in several subsequent chapters, particularly in Chapter 8, on the state of nature, champions of experience explicitly advocate the trans-mission of failed thought and the failed self as a source of (regressive) psychic liberation and (regressive) political cohesion.

If we must work to protect experience from thought so as to protect and share failure, then it would seem that, contrary to its characterization as powerful, solid, and "sturdy" (Emerson 2009, 314), our relationship to experience is fragile, something that can be dissolved, emptied, destroyed. Cognate with *peril*, the word 'experience' refers, etymologically, to a trial, a danger through which one passes. Now this perilous passage, itself, appears to be imperiled. Indeed, if we believe André Malraux, Walter Benjamin, Giorgio Agamben, Theodor Adorno, R.D. Laing, and others, we modern and contemporary citizens have *already* suffered an extraordinary "impoverish[ment]" of our experience (Benja-min 1999, 735), "an almost unbelievable devastation of our experience" (Laing 1967, 11).

In his short essay "Erfahrung und Armut" (Experience and Poverty), Walter Benjamin famously claims that experience itself has "fallen in value," specifically for the generation of 1914–1918, who "had to experience some of the most monstrous events in the history of the world" (1999, 731). Never before, writes Benjamin, "have experiences been punished [*gestraft*] more severely by lies than strategic experience by the lie of the war of position (trench warfare), economic experience by the lie of inflation, corporeal experience by hunger, ethical experience by those with power" (quoted in Leslie 2000, 84):

> A generation that had gone to school in horse-drawn streetcars now stood in
> the open air, amid a landscape in which nothing was the same except the
> clouds and, at its center, in a forcefield of destructive forces and explosions,
> the tiny, fragile, human body.
>
> *(Benjamin 1999, 732)*

What Benjamin describes is akin to trauma on a collective scale: traumatic
experience that leaves us naked, without a recognizable self or world, without the
ability to narrate our lives from past to present or to make connections with those
before or after us, without the capacity to make meaning or to teach lessons that
carry authority. "Where has it all gone?," Benjamin asks. "Where do you still
hear words from the dying that last, and that pass from one generation to the next
like a precious ring?" (1999, 731). If the war has left a generation unable to
communicate, this, for Benjamin, is only a part of the "new ... barbarism" that
threatens to engulf all of "human experience" (1999, 732).

What is fascinating about such accounts is that it is experience, itself, that has
"been punished ... severely" by world events. Much of the critical-theoretical
tradition begins with this very presumption that we must recognize the degree to
which our experience has been impoverished, or to which our "experience
has ... been expropriated" (Agamben 1993, 16). By this, of course, Benjamin and
Agamben mean that "we have been "deprived of effective experience" and have
been even "bereft of the capacity for experience" (Agamben 1993, 16), but here,
again, if it is not experience itself that suffers, then the human being has been
robbed of experience in the most passive of ways. If we have been "stripped of
experience," "bereft of humanity," and "stripped of our deeds," these vital possessions have been "taken out of our hands like toys from the hands of children"
(Laing 1967, 13). Thus, modern painters like Klee and Loos are said to have
rejected "the traditional, solemn, noble image of man," to "turn instead to the naked
man of the contemporary world who lies screaming like a newborn babe in the
dirty diapers of the present" (Benjamin 1999, 733).

Benjamin's explicitly infantilized depiction of the contemporary human,
Laing's allusion to the snatching away of a child's toy, and the passive construction of phrases describing the deprivation of our experience all suggest that
experiences of psychic devastation have left us in a confused condition, where the
relationship between experience and experiencer is muddled and often tilted
toward the former, and in a childlike condition, precarious and vulnerable before
obscure and almighty forces that can return us to desolation at their will.
Benjamin and Agamben, for their parts, do also write of a more active
"rejection of experience," particularly among the young (Agamben 1993, 14–16),
but this seemingly active repudiation turns out to be little more than the last
remaining "legitimate defense" against the prior, utter destruction of experience
in society, suggesting that this "rejection" is not active or creative but reactive and
defensive.

If, as I have proposed, the powerful, terrible, yet nebulous agents of our devastation may be understood as external representations of the internal process of thinking, which is perceived to be destructive to the experiences we *have had* and must *live* and *re-live* without thinking, in order not to foment crisis in our inner worlds, then the alternative to destruction, which is also the alternative to thinking about experience, is the "hypertrophic development of the apparatus for projective identification" (Bion 1988a, 112). Fear, badness, anxiety, and the threat posed by thinking must be contended with by turning to an "evacuative discharge" of internal elements (Grinberg, Sor, and de Bianchedi 1977, 58).[6] Thinking, itself, is specifically avoided in projective discharges because the objects of experience *must* become 'unthinkable,' larger than life, "indistinguishable from … thing[s]-in-[themselves]" (Bion 1988, 112). For this reason, projects undertaken in the name of experience, protected from thought or rational inspection and addressed to incomprehensibly *lived* moments, create conditions averse to the kinds of thinking, relating, and communicating required for the development and sustenance of mature selves and groups.

Thinking and selfhood

The orientation described above may be contrasted with an ideal of selfhood, an ideal which is perhaps never *absolutely* attainable, but which, for the purposes of this book, consists of at least three significant elements, as outlined in Chapter 1: the capacity to think in the sense defined here, the capacity to act creatively and not compulsively or compliantly, and the capacity to be alone, which is also the capacity to relate ethically with others. These three aspects of self may be found in the enjoyably non-technical language of Isaiah Berlin in his famous essay on liberty:

> I wish to be a subject, not an object, to be moved by reasons, by conscious purposes, which are my own, not by causes which affect me, as it were, from the outside. I wish to be somebody, not nobody; a doer – deciding, not being decided for, self-directed and not acted upon by external nature or by other men as if I were a thing, or an animal, or a slave incapable of playing a human role, that is, of conceiving goals and policies of my own and realizing them. … I wish, above all, to be conscious of myself as a thinking, willing, active being, bearing responsibility for my choices and able to explain them by references to my own ideas and purposes.
>
> *(1969, 131)*

To be a self means to be not a 'given' thing, just as it means to be not 'given' to others as their property, nor to be 'given over' either to instinctual reactivity or to the pressures of conformity in one's thoughts, feelings, and activities. To be a self is not to be determined by causes or forces arising from outside the metaphorical 'area' delineated by the self, which includes both the human being's biological impulses and forces exerted by others.

As discussed in Chapter 1, the idea of a self requires the (sometimes misleading but nonetheless necessary) imagination of a boundary. Along with this boundary, selfhood requires the ability to control the borders, to be able to "limit access" to internal experience, for instance, so as to safeguard an inner world that is one's own (Levine 2003, 60–61). For similar reasons, selfhood also requires the ability to "control … the initiation, maintenance, termination, and avoidance of social contact" (Stern 1985, 21–22). Certainly, individuals are profoundly influenced by others, by groups, by institutions, and their internal complements. The literatures of critical theory and social construction, not to mention psychoanalysis, attest to this fact. But the extent to which we may speak about selves and not automata or slaves is precisely the extent to which we may speak about the freedom with which a self can think its own thoughts, create and act upon its own designs, and even retreat into itself to be alone.

In this chapter, I am particularly concerned with the first of these three aspects of selfhood: the way that the capacity to be a self derives from the activities of "thinking," "knowing," and "being known" by a nurturing parent or caretaker. "Thinking," for Wilfred Bion, a student of Melanie Klein, means approaching experiences and objects, even those that frustrate or enrage us, as "problem[s] to be solved" (1988a), which requires resources in the nascent self and in the environment that facilitate frustration-tolerance and containment. The development of these resources, in turn, depends upon "knowing" and "being known," which refer here not to intellectual knowledge but to communications between parent and child in which one contains and ameliorates the experiences of the other. A parent's ability to "know" her child involves the ability to recognize anxiety in the child, to moderate it by psychologically containing it, and to successfully convert it into something less fearsome: a word, a smile, a gesture of sympathy, a touch, a feeding, some form of relief.

In this process, the child is permitted to "know," by internalizing the actions and affects of his caretakers, a manageable version of himself and his own feelings, initially by "reintroject[ing] a mitigated or modified emotional experience" provided by the parent (Grinberg, Sor, and de Bianchedi 1977, 57). If all goes reasonably well, eventually the child develops the ability to take on the role of both child and parent, mitigating and moderating his own experiences by "thinking" through them, by "knowing" and "being known" by his self, which is to say: by tolerating, relating to, and maintaining contact with his self. From repeated experiences of thinking, knowing, and being known in this way, the child is able to construct a psychological landscape containing a whole, safe, and valued self as well as whole, safe, and valued others (see Bion 1988b).

Thinking, then – as in its more standard usage – describes an attempt to know. But, in a more profound sense, thinking describes the attempt *to be*, to *be* a self in a world of others selves who *are*. We may recognize, in the above description, an apparent similarity to the conversion of 'bad' experience into 'good' experience, discussed in the context of Freud's re-telling of Lichtenberg's joke. But, really, the two processes are radically opposed. In the relationship described immediately above, 'bad' experience is contained and modified within dyadic relationships and then within the self, through the processes of thinking, knowing, and being known. In Lichtenberg's joke, 'bad' experience must become 'good' immediately, *without* ever having been mediated or moderated by thinking or knowing. It must be swallowed *tout entier*, accepted without question, *just as it is*. In fact, in something of a frustrating contradiction, the 'bad' experience referred to in Lichtenberg's joke must be internalized as if it were 'good,' which is to say, it must be accepted both *just as it is* and as if it were *not just as it is*.

The only way to manage this dilemma is to turn to the "apparatus for projective identification," which means an "evacuative discharge" of elements that threaten to disrupt the precarious state of *not* thinking and *not* being. Just as the child of an abusive or narcissistic parent may find her self de-centered, with a false and compliant self in its stead, both projections of threatening forces and repetitions of 'bad' experiences may come to hold more central and more powerful places in the inner world than they might if the mediating and moderating influences of thinking, knowing, and being known had not been thwarted.

Since the child cannot *be*, and yet cannot avail herself of the most appropriate target for her rage, rage at *not being* is turned inward, just as the object of 'bad' experience is imagined to be the 'teacher' of a valuable experience. Here, we see part of the emotional logic that results in the reification of experience, affording experience the status of an independent and powerful subject, while reducing the self to an object. There is a dynamic here partly reminiscent of Ronald Fairbairn's notion of "moral defense," articulated in his paper "The Repression and the Return of Bad Objects" (1952). Also named "the defense of the super-ego" and "the defense of guilt," Fairbairn argues that the moral defense is driven by experiences that signal that the objects on which the child depends are not good but bad. The moral defense splits off the bad experiences from the good object, taking responsibility for them by internalizing them, and so attempting to assure that the object remains 'good,' such that "outer security is thus purchased at the price of inner insecurity" (65). The aim of the moral defense is, of course, "the conversion of an original situation in which the child is surrounded by bad objects into a situation in which his objects are good and he himself is bad" (68).

But, although, as Fairbairn famously writes, "it is better to be a sinner in a world ruled by God than to live in a world ruled by the Devil" (67), the internalization of badness is not the end-point of the defense, for the bargain at the heart of the moral defense hinges on the transformation of unconditional badness into conditional badness, which can be later expelled through self-punishment, merging with 'good' objects purged of their bad aspects, or finding external targets into which to project bad qualities. These latter processes may be explained by mixing psychoanalytic metaphors and turning briefly to Heinz Kohut's notion of "selfobjects" (1971).

A selfobject, for Kohut, is an object put in the service of holding part of the self that, for one reason or another, the self cannot contain. A selfobject may be a security blanket, a parent, a god, or a psychoanalyst who comes to hold alienated aspects of the self. Kohut posited various types of selfobject transference, of varying degrees of importance, but all of which are means of forging connections to narcissistic ideals. The idealization of a selfobject may be the first step to merging with that object, so as to partake in its greatness and perfection. For instance, a mirroring selfobject may be used to reflect an idealized version of the self, and is likely subjected to the demand that the object affirm grandiose aspects and fantasies about the self.

Imagining some of experience's favored objects – such as 'Fate,' 'the People,' 'Nature,' or even, as we shall see momentarily, 'Plague' – as selfobjects may help us better understand the type of relationship undertaken with objects of experience, even or especially with the vast and amorphous objects that so readily contain grandiose aspects and fantasies. If Nature, for instance, comes to serve as an idealizing selfobject, then one finds in Nature all of one's "ambitions and ideals" (Alford 1991, 26). One strives to merge with Nature in experiences that endow one with a portion of Nature's perfection. If Nature is a mirroring selfobject, then Nature will be the subject/object in whose presence the self feels affirmed and recognized in its loftiest ambitions: Here, Nature may reflect the ideal of naturalness, natural perfection, or natural innocence, such that only in the experience of Nature is it possible to hold on to positive estimations of the self. We return specifically to the idealization of Nature in the following chapter, and I take up one significant permutation of this problem again in Chapter 8, on the idea of the state of nature.

It is important to note that there is nothing inherently pathological about making moderate use of either the moral defense or selfobjects. On the contrary, projection, identification, internalization, and externalization involved are necessary parts of self-development, parts of the process of coming to "know" the self, in the sense described above. Their health or unhealth, maturity or immaturity, is a matter of degree. The important questions are: "Do we seek to merge completely with our ideal selfobject so that nothing is left of the self? Or do we learn to choose and use those idealizable selfobjects that support our chosen projects?" (Alford 1991, 26). The answers to these questions determine the health or pathology of our relationships with experiences and their objects. Are experiences and their objects called upon to replace parts of our selves, to hold all that is valuable such that we can only partake in the good when we are immersed in, or subsumed by, experience? Or can we *use* experience to think, to act, to relate, and to craft an authentic self in the world?

Failures of thought and the body politic

Bill Holm strives to articulate what is "sacred" about the "failures" of struggling individuals and communities, praises his own "immigrant culture that ... succeeded at failure" (2010, 96), and imagines a glorious history of failure that, instead of the history told by the victors, would be a more 'real' and 'honest' history of human defeat. Holm argues that, "since 1945, self-building has become a matter of life and death for the whole planet. We have now reached the point in human history where some cure is absolutely necessary, some embracing of wholesome failure" (100–101).

Holm's fear of "self-building" and his insistence that the history of the failed is more real than the history of the successful links him to the extensive tradition of anti-subjective contemporary ethical theory. The fear and rejection of the self or subject as dishonest and dangerous has everything to do with the contention, supposedly confirmed in the terrors of the twentieth century, that subjectivity cannot be maintained as an ideal without also idealizing an unacceptable level of real and symbolic violence.

The modern and contemporary subject is supposed to have an innate desire for recognition or a *désir d'être tout* (desire to be all), an inability to stop himself from abusing, incorporating, or consuming others. Thus, a central project of contemporary and postmodern ethical thought has been to dismember the subject as a "self-identical substance" (see Blackman et al. 2008), and to find respite from fear and shame about the dangers subjects pose. Of course, those who embrace the discourse of the "death of the subject" hope that, once the subject is dispensed with, our "self-differential selves" will flourish: For Jean-François Lyotard, among others, subjective death means nothing less than the possibility of the revival of genuine experience (see Terada 2001; 2010, 151).

In Georges Bataille's celebration of *supplice*, the experience of vulnerability to a superior affirms one's powerlessness and precariousness, negating one's will to be and do. *Supplice* preserves the human being's exposure to an overwhelming object of experience that continually ruptures, dominates, and violates, in a way that presages our understanding of traumatic violation (see Bataille 1988, 33–61). For Bataille, that we fail to achieve autonomy, integrity, and self-sufficiency, that we break down and *dysfunction*, that we become *inoperative* (*inoperosità*) – to use Giorgio Agamben's language (2005) – is key to achieving the fullest human experience.

Bataille expresses the fantasy that experiences of vulnerability, incapacitation, boundary-loss, and trauma are pre-eminently real, and are, therefore, the only real foundations for social being. If all are thoroughly traumatized, violated, and penetrated in a torturous, Sade-istic communion, no member of a community could possess autonomy, agency, identity, or any other correlate of subjectivity or selfhood, and without these qualities, this argument goes, no one would be capable of abusing anyone or doing anyone any harm. Of course, faced with Bataille's "strange ethics of horror" (Botting and Wilson 1997, 27), we may reasonably ask: If each is so traumatized and incapacitated that no harm can befall any other, what harm would be left to be done?

It is important not to mistake the destructive aims of this discourse of anti-subjectivity: The self must fail, must fail to think, must fail to be, in order for the experience of failure to take up a central place and organizing function in the outer life of the community and in the inner lives of its members. A moral community founded upon failure is permitted only by breaking open the would-be self, by uniting human beings via experiences of trauma, and by developing a shared "point of identification with suffering itself" (Butler 2004, 30; see also Haraway 1990; Jay 1993; Lauro and Embry 2008; Levinas 1998).

Bill Holm's prose is simpler than Bataille's, yet similar in its objectives. Holm claims:

> There is a certain pleasure that comes from swallowing your own failure. ... [H]umor grows out of these indigestible lumps of history. Nothing that is itself can conceivably be termed a failure by the transcendental definition. But things must acknowledge and live up to their selfness. This is fairly effortless for a horse or a cow, more difficult for a human being. ... When it happens occasionally, as I argue that it did in the case of the Icelanders, it creates a rare wonder, a community that has eaten its own failures so completely that it has no need to be other than itself.
>
> *(2010, 100)*

So, we must first fail, and then swallow our failures, to become ourselves, where becoming ourselves means becoming our failures. Holm's phrase, "nothing that is itself can conceivably be termed a failure," is absolutely inconsistent with his overall argument, which is really, on the contrary, that 'nothing that fails completely can conceivably be termed itself.' To eat or swallow failure, within Holm's logic, means to embrace it, and, although it is "indigestible," to attempt to sustain oneself upon it.

To swallow failure is to internalize failure, supplanting other objects and aspects of the inner world. It is to establish failure as a locus of identity, primarily, for Holm, a locus of the *community's* identity, in which all community members partake. When all community members have swallowed their individual and collective failures, then the community "has no need to be other than itself." Another way to say this would be: 'The community is the collective result of all members' failed attempts at being selves. The community has no need to be anything other than this, since the community understands its function *not* to be that of redeeming individual selves but, rather, that of assuring members of their place in a community of equally failed selves.'

It is by this investment of value in the idea of failure that we arrive at the curious idea that internalizing self-failure both destroys and returns to us our lost selves. As in the self hypostatized in Caruth's and others' theories of trauma, discussed in the following chapter, the premise of Holm's notion is that the self is necessarily unreal and, in that respect, 'bad.' The self that fails and the self that is lost must have been unreal because they were incapable of containing the unquestionable reality imputed to experience. In other words, on this line of thought, experiences that incapacitate or destroy the self prove the self's unreality. At the same time, the experience of failure binds one to the failures of others and to the community of failed selves that remains in contact with its collective failure as a matter of solidarity or community-identity. While accepting such an attitude toward self-failure is, in its own way, *traumatic*, it represents another piece of the psychic social contract by which a self-destructive attitude toward experience is the price of entry into the moral community.

A common interpretation of Albert Camus' famous allegorical novel *The Plague* is helpful in illustrating this perspective. In Camus' novel, the plague is not merely a disease but a representation of a trauma inflicted upon the *body politic* of Oran. Indeed, interpretations of plagues as metaphors for breakdowns of political bodies or communities have often, and rightly, been applied to the earlier literary plagues of Thucydides and Defoe, among others. But what Camus and his late modern and postmodern readers, particularly those influenced by the well-known commentaries of Shoshana Felman, make of the plague in Oran is unique.

For Camus and Felman, what is good about the plague, if we may so speak, is that it is impossible to conceive of it as an individual disease. The plague transforms individual cases of disease into a collective, shared disease, thereby transforming individual bodies into sites of moral and political collapse for the entire community (see Bowker 2014). Just as one individual does not contract the plague without sharing the disease with others, one cannot combat the plague without sharing what might be called the 'plague experience' with the community, a community now united by a "shared vulnerability to tragedy" (Irwin 2002, 24).

"We all have plague," Jean Tarrou tells Bernard Rieux, in one of the most important dialogues in the novel. Thus, "we can't stir a finger in this world without the risk of bringing death to somebody" (Camus 1991, 252). In times of plague, one person's symptoms may affect others, such that a stir of a finger may indeed infect or kill. But Tarrou speaks of plague not literally, but as a metaphor for thinking and knowing, a plague that, he argues, tempts us to legitimize and participate in violence as "rational murderer[s]" (253). In a grim irony, the actual plague epidemic presents the citizens of Oran with the opportunity to rid themselves of the plagues of thinking and selfhood. Instead, they must internalize the plague as a lesson in the failure of thinking and selfhood, and must learn to experience the plague and its attendant failures as members of a shared, traumatized body.

The people of Oran must resist the temptation to think, for thought or "abstraction" is defined as the most cowardly means of escaping the reality of the 'plague experience,' contravening one's duties to the suffering communal body. Even physical departure would be more acceptable than intellectual abstraction, for Camus finds the latter incompatible with the necessary moral identification with the community, while the former need not be. Throughout the novel, one character charges another with "abstraction" the way one might accuse a criminal: "You can't understand," Raymond Rambert alleges of Dr. Rieux, "you're using the language of reason, not of the heart; you live in a world of abstractions"

(1991, 87). And Rieux, for his part, declares his primary mission to be to "fight abstraction" (91). This mission is especially important when "an abstraction sets to killing you" (83), which is how Camus seems to interpret not the plague but what the plague represents: ideologies of conquest, authoritarianism, Nazism.

Jennifer Cooke is correct to claim that, for Camus, "abstraction is not … just a matter of language … but in fact a sort of parasitic state of mind which must be resisted and fought off, much as Rieux talks heroically about fighting plague" (2008, 31). The problem with abstraction seems to be that it comprehends violence, whereas the body (and the shared body), as unthinking organs, can only experience and endure it. When Camus has Father Paneloux preach to his congregation that the plague is a punishment for sin, these words are meant to be as scandalous to the reader as the actual disease. When later, Father Paneloux dies from a "doubtful case" of plague, it represents not so much a defeat of his faith or of God but of abstraction, an inevitable failure to think the plague, and, therefore, a sort of victory for the shared suffering body that has endured and even preserved the 'plague experience,' never turning away from it toward intellectualization or abstraction.

Tarrou joins in the fight against the plague, just as he claims to refuse abstraction and therefore to refuse to "join forces with the pestilences" (1991, 254). But in order to avoid being a "rational murderer," Tarrou also refuses for himself "a place in the world of today." By quarantining himself in a metaphorical "exile that can never end," by "leav[ing] it to others to make history," Tarrou spends a good deal of his energy fighting not the plague disease but the possibility that the plague of thinking and selfhood will infect his moral center. Instead, he has resolved only to say that:

> there are pestilences and there are victims; no more than that. If by making this statement, I, too, become a carrier of the plague-germ, at least I don't do it willfully. I try, in short, to be an innocent murderer. You see, I've no great ambitions.
>
> *(253–254)*

Tarrou's preoccupation with rationalized murder and his assumption of personal responsibility for even the most distant acts of violence derive, he confesses, from the experience of witnessing his father prosecute a defendant in a capital case, in which his once kindly father suddenly "spewed out long, turgid phrases like an endless stream of snakes" (1991, 248), culminating in "that foul procedure whereby dirty mouths stinking of plague told a fettered man that he was going to die" (252). Of course, judges, revolutionaries, military commanders, political leaders, even doctors also participate in uttering "death sentences," and this realization causes Tarrou to become obsessed with the notion that the entire "social order … was based on the death sentence" (252). For Tarrou, any form of action grounded in thought or reasoned calculation, as opposed to experience, is tantamount to uttering a "death sentence," a phrase that conveniently unites the act of killing with the acts of thinking, speaking, and writing.

The real danger of the plague, we learn, is not that it will return, for its return is inevitable. In a sort of encomium to the plague, the final lines of Camus' novel read: "Joy is always imperiled" for "the plague bacillus never dies or disappears for good." Eventually, "the day would come when, for the bane and the enlightenment of men, it would rouse up its rats again and send them forth to die in a happy city" (1991, 308). The plague is not just our bane but our enlightenment, and the repetition of its trauma is inevitable. Whatever lessons may be learned are lessons given through experience, the experience of uniting with the shared suffering body of the town of Oran. That is, we must accept the inevitability of the plague, and what it represents – the necessary failure of the self to escape through thought and abstraction, the return to immediate experience, and the moral orientation to the group – in order to profit from it.

Shoshana Felman claims:

> What there is to witness urgently in the human world ... is always fundamentally, in one way or another, the scandal of an illness, of a metaphorical or literal disease; and that the imperative of bearing witness, which here proceeds from the contagion of the Plague – from the eruption of an evil that is radically incurable – is itself somehow a philosophical and ethical correlative of a situation with no cure, and of a radical human condition of exposure and vulnerability.
>
> *(1995, 16)*

For Felman, what the novel teaches is that what is most important to experience, witness, and testify to in the world is evil, illness, and disease, suggesting, along the lines of Judith Herman's argument, that every instance of traumatic injury "is a standing challenge to the rightness of the social order" (quoted in Shay 1995, 3). As we will discuss more extensively in the following chapter, on this line of thought, what the plague teaches us is that the scandalous, evil, and traumatic condition of the plague is in fact the *human* condition, a condition with "no cure," and, therefore, a condition that must be experienced, witnessed, shared, and even preserved as part of our heritage, and not reasoned away.

Since, for Felman, to witness is not to analyze or understand but to transmit that which is not entirely communicable by thought and language, a real danger presented by plagues is that we will cease witnessing them and start thinking about them, that we will yield to the "sin of wanting to know," which would mean becoming morally infected by the plague of abstraction, rather than preserving the incomprehensible experience of plague in our bodies, in our communal bodies, and in the shared corpus of human history.

Instead of being ideologists of reason, we are urged to be ideologists of illness, plague, and evil, insisting that inexorable, "incurable," experiences of horror stand at the center of human life and must remain there. They must not be abstracted, thought about, or known, lest we diffuse or dislodge their necessary badness, necessary perhaps so that we may continue to adopt a posture of scandalized outrage, which, somewhat conveniently, leaves us morally unaccountable for evil in the world while permitting us to transmit our traumatic experiences to others under the aegis of "bearing witness" (see Bowker 2014). Perhaps we may now see why popular cultural entertainments are so replete with fantasies of seemingly horrifying experiences of persecution, victimization, apocalypse, inhuman monsters, and supernatural evils: because these scenarios reinforce the psychic organization demanded by the ideologies of experience in which the destruction of the self is inevitable and thinking otherwise is the real outrage.

Notes

1 Here, and throughout this book, I employ the word 'object' in its psychoanalytic sense, to refer to other persons and to internal representations of persons, groups, and abstractions, including even a "country, liberty, [or] an ideal" (Freud 1957, 243) with which one may relate. My use of the term is guided by object-relations theory, but the term itself arose out of Freud's terminology of drives and their 'objects.' For object-relations theorists, objects are others, internal representations of others, and even parts of others and of the self. "People react to and interact with not only an actual other but also an internal other, a psychic representation of a person which in itself has the power to influence both the individual's affective states and his overt behavioral reactions" (Greenberg and Mitchell 1983, 10). The history, dynamics, and patterns of an individual's relationships with internal and external objects are, in some sense, the very content of the individual's psychic experience of her inner and outer worlds.
2 The masking work of the joke is accomplished via the repetition of the word 'experience,' a repetition which de-familiarizes the term (see Bowker 2012; Brecht and Bentley 1961; Shklovsky 1991), distracting us from the fact that we are already familiar, although perhaps not consciously, with the perspectival shift from 'bad' to 'good' that it implies and with the cruel bargain at its core. The repetition of the word "experience" is confounding enough that we chuckle at the semantic puzzle set before us, even as the material of the joke may call up memories of suffering and self-abandonment.
3 The testimonies of survivors of atrocity, such as those recorded in the Fortunoff Archive for Holocaust Testimonies, analyzed to powerful effect by Fred Alford (2009), should be enough to at least cast doubt upon Nietzsche's claim. Upon returning from a period of relatively dangerous and unsanitary work in Benin, West Africa (Bowker 2015), I myself met casually with others who worked in equally difficult conditions, at home and abroad, some of whom had suffered, or continued to suffer, the effects of physical and psychic trauma, physical injury, heightened anxiety and depression, and fears both general and specific about the body's fragility. We shared a joke – it is important to recognize that this, too, was a 'joke' – that, *contra* Nietzsche, 'What didn't kill us made us much, much weaker.'
4 I am grateful to David Levine for relating some memorable examples of this phenomenon from his own teaching experience.
5 For one thing, this would avoid some confusing phrasing, i.e., "How will [the analysand] know what he knows?" (Bollas 1987, 281). For another, it would permit us to see more clearly why "lived" experience can seem more profound, more essential to the person than anything thought or known.

6   Although derived from a different domain of the psychoanalytic tradition, that associated with the work of Melanie Klein, projective identification may be considered in terms commensurable with Kohut's idea of selfobject transference, in that what is sought is not communication or relation between a whole self and whole objects but an unconscious transmission of psychic material across the boundaries of self and other, a process which, precisely because it is unthought, leads individuals and groups to expel, exaggerate, identify, and merge with objects in a nearly automatic fashion.

References

Agamben, G. 1993. *Infancy and History: Essays on the Destruction of Experience*. Translated by L. Heron. London: Verso.

Agamben, G. 2005. *State of Exception*. Translated by K. Attell. Chicago, IL: University of Chicago Press.

Alford, C.F. 1991. *The Self in Social Theory: A Psychoanalytic Account of its Construction in Plato, Hobbes, Locke, Rawls, and Rousseau*. New Haven, CT: Yale University Press.

Alford, C.F. 2009. *After the Holocaust: The Book of Job, Primo Levi, and the Path to Affliction*. New York: Cambridge University Press.

Bataille, G. 1988. *Inner Experience*. Translated by L.A. Boldt. Albany, NY: State University of New York Press.

Benjamin, W. 1999. "Experience and Poverty." In *Selected Writings, Volume II, 1927–1934*, edited by M. Jennings, H. Eilans, and G. Smith, 731–736. Translated by R. Livingstone. Cambridge, MA: Belknap/Harvard University Press.

Berlin, I. 1969. *Four Essays on Liberty*. Oxford: Oxford University Press.

Bion, W.R. 1988a. "A Theory of Thinking." In *Melanie Klein Today: Developments in Theory and Practice. Volume I: Mainly Theory*, edited by E. Spillius, 178–186. London: Routledge.

Bion, W.R. 1988b. "Attacks on Linking." In *Melanie Klein Today: Developments in Theory and Practice. Volume I: Mainly Theory*, edited by E. Spillius, 87–101. London: Routledge.

Blackman, L., J. Cromby, D. Hook, D. Papadopoulos, and V. Walkerdine 2008. "Creating Subjectivities." *Subjectivity* 22: 1–27.

Bollas, C. 1987. *The Shadow of the Object: Psychoanalysis of the Unthought Known*. New York: Columbia University Press.

Botting, F., and S. Wilson, eds. 1997. *The Bataille Reader*. Oxford: Blackwell.

Bowker, M.H. 2012. *Ostranenie: On Shame and Knowing*. New York: Punctum Books.

Bowker, M.H. 2014. *Rethinking the Politics of Absurdity: Albert Camus, Postmodernity, and the Survival of Innocence*. Series: Routledge Innovations in Political Theory. New York: Routledge.

Bowker, M.H. 2015. *Escargotesque, or, What is Experience?* New York: Punctum Books.

Brecht, B., and E. Bentley 1961. "On Chinese Acting." *Tulane Drama Review* 6(1): 130–136.

Butler, J. 2004. *Precarious Life: The Powers of Mourning and Violence*. London: Verso.

Camus, A. 1955. *The Myth of Sisyphus and Other Essays*. First Vintage International Edition. Translated by J. O'Brien. New York: Vintage.

Camus, A. 1991. *The Plague*. First Vintage International Edition. Translated by S. Gilbert. New York: Vintage.

Caruth, C. 1996. *Unclaimed Experience: Trauma, Narrative, and History*. Baltimore, MD: Johns Hopkins University Press.

Cooke, J. 2008. "Writing Plague: Transforming Narrative, Witnessing, and History." In *The Tapestry of Health, Illness, and Disease*, edited by P. Valitzkus and P. Thowig, 21–42. Amsterdam: Rodopi.

Drury, S. 1994. *Alexandre Kojève: The Roots of Postmodern Politics*. New York: St. Martin's.

Emerson, R.W. 2009. "Experience (1844)." In *The Essential Writings of Ralph Waldo Emerson*, edited by B. Atkinson, 307–326. New York: Random House.

Fairbairn, W.R.D. 1952. *Psychoanalytic Studies of the Personality*. New York and London: Tavistock and Routledge.

Felman, S. 1995. "Education and Crisis, or the Vicissitudes of Teaching." In *Trauma: Explorations in Memory*, edited by C. Caruth, 13–60. Baltimore, MD: Johns Hopkins University Press.

Foucault, M. 1975. *Discipline and Punish: The Birth of the Prison*. Second Vintage Books Edition. Translated by A. Sheridan. New York: Vintage.

Foucault, M. 1980. *Power/Knowledge: Selected Interviews and Other Writings (1972–77)*, edited by C. Gordon. New York: Pantheon Press.

Freud, S. 1920. "Beyond the Pleasure Principle." In *The Standard Edition of the Complete Psychological Works of Sigmund Freud, Volume XVIII*, edited and translated by J. Strachey, 7–64. London: Hogarth.

Freud, S. 1957. "Mourning and Melancholia." In *The Standard Edition of the Complete Psychological Works of Sigmund Freud, Volume XIV*, edited and translated by J. Strachey, 243–258. London: Hogarth.

Freud, S. 1960. *Jokes and Their Relation to the Unconscious*. Translated by J. Strachey. New York: W.W. Norton.

Gadamer, H.-G. 1989. *Truth and Method*. Second Revised Edition. Translated by J. Weinsheimer and D. Marshall. New York: Crossroad.

Greenberg, J., and S. Mitchell 1983. *Object Relations in Psychoanalytic Theory*. Cambridge, MA: Harvard University Press.

Grinberg, L., D. Sor, and E. de Bianchedi 1977. *Introduction to the Work of Bion: Groups, Knowledge, Psychosis, Thought, Transformations, Psychoanalytic Practice*. Translated by A. Hahn. New York: Jason Aronson.

Haraway, D. 1990. "A Manifesto for Cyborgs: Science, Technology and Socialist Feminism in the 1980s." In *Feminism/Postmodernism*, edited by L. Nicholson, 190–233. New York: Routledge.

Holm, B. 2010. *The Music of Failure*. First University of Minnesota Press Edition. Fesler-Lampert Minnesota Heritage Series. Minneapolis and London: University of Minnesota Press.

Irwin, A. 2002. *Saints of the Impossible: Bataille, Weil, and the Politics of the Sacred*. Minneapolis, MN: University of Minnesota Press.

Jay, M. 1993. *Force Fields: Between Intellectual History and Cultural Critique*. New York: Routledge.

Jay, M. 2005. *Songs of Experience: Modern American and European Variations on a Universal Theme*. Berkeley, CA: University of California Press.

Kohut, H. 1971. *The Analysis of the Self: A Systematic Approach to the Psychoanalytic Treatment of Narcissistic Personality Disorders*. Chicago, IL: University of Chicago Press.

Laing, R.D. 1967. *The Politics of Experience*. New York: Routledge and Kegan Paul.

Lanzmann, C. 1995. "The Obscenity of Understanding: An Evening with Claude Lanzmann." In *Trauma: Explorations in Memory*, edited by C. Caruth, 200–220. Baltimore, MD: Johns Hopkins University Press.

Lauro, S., and K. Embry 2008. "A Zombie Manifesto: The Nonhuman Condition in the Era of Advanced Capitalism." *Boundary 2* 35(1): 86–108.

Leslie, E. 2000. *Walter Benjamin: Overpowering Conformism*. Translated by E. Leslie. London: Pluto Press.

Levinas, E. 1998. *Of God Who Comes to Mind.* Translated by B. Bergo. Stanford, CA: Stanford University Press.

Levine, D.P. 2003. *The Living Dead and the End of Hope: An Essay on the Pursuit of Unhappiness.* Denver, CO: Broken Tree Press.

Nietzsche, F. 1990. *Twilight of the Idols and The Antichrist.* Translated by R. Hollingdale. London: Penguin.

Oakeshott, M. 1933. *Experience and Its Modes.* Cambridge: Cambridge University Press.

Pausch, R., with J. Zaslow 2008. *The Last Lecture: Really Achieving Your Childhood Dreams.* New York: Hyperion.

Shay, J. 1995. *Achilles in Vietnam: Combat Trauma and the Undoing of Character.* New York: Simon and Schuster.

Shklovsky, V. 1991. *Theory of Prose.* Translated by B. Sher. Normal, IL: Dalkey Archive Press.

Stern, D.B. 1997. *Unformulated Experience: From Dissociation to Imagination in Psychoanalysis.* Hillsdale, NJ: The Analytic Press.

Stern, D.N. 1985. *The Interpersonal World of the Infant: A View from Psychoanalysis and Developmental Psychology.* New York: Basic Books.

Terada, R. 2001. *Feeling in Theory: Emotion after the "Death of the Subject."* Cambridge, MA: Harvard University Press.

Vermeulen, P. 2010. "Upstaging the Death of the Subject: Gertrude Stein, the Theater, and the Self-Differential Self." *Arcadia: International Journal for Literary Studies* 45(1): 150–165.

Volkan, V. 1985. "'Suitable Targets of Externalization' and Schizophrenia." In *Toward a Comprehensive Model for Schizophrenic Disorders*, edited by D. Feinsilver, 125–153. New York: Analytic Press.

Winnicott, D.W. 1965. *The Maturational Processes and the Facilitating Environment: Studies in the Theory of Emotional Development*, edited by M. Khan. London: Hogarth and the Institute of Psycho-Analysis.

Winnicott, D.W. 1986. *Home Is Where We Start from: Essays by a Psychoanalyst*, edited by C. Winnicott, R. Shepard, and M. Davis. New York: W.W. Norton.

3

THE INCORPORATION AND TRANSMISSION OF TRAUMATIC EXPERIENCE

The construct of psychic trauma and the diagnosis of Post-Traumatic Stress Dis-order (PTSD) have been profoundly influential in shaping contemporary ideas about the nature and extent of psychological injury. Trauma has come to signify a diverse range of human experiences of suffering, loss, victimization, and both physical and psychological violence. At least within certain fields, the idea of trauma has undoubtedly impacted the way we conceive of the possibility and meaning of subjectivity, the relationship between psyche and soma, and the place of the individual in society. In spite of areas of disagreement, contemporary trauma discourses offer a relatively stable normative foundation for the recogni-tion of trauma victims (see, e.g., Fassin and Rechtman 2009). That is, trauma victims, along with non-victims' relations to them, are invested with moral and epistemic meaning, meaning related to ideological assumptions about the experience of trauma.

Trauma as truth

Primary among the qualities attributed to the experience of trauma is its putative ability to grant privileged access to truth. It is the "truth of traumatic experience," writes the best-known trauma theorist in the humanities, Cathy Caruth, "that forms the center of its pathology or symptoms." The "overwhelming occurrence" of trauma returns insistently to the traumatized individual, although in delayed and incom-plete forms, yet remains "absolutely true to the event." Therefore, the pathology of trauma "is not a pathology ... of falsehood or displacement of meaning, but of history itself." Trauma is "a symptom of history," and "the traumatized ... carry an impossible [yet true] history within them, or they become themselves the symptom of a history that they cannot entirely possess" (1995, 5).

The marriage of cognitive neuroscience with literary and cultural studies in the 1990s and 2000s has produced an ideology of trauma that both laments and celebrates some of the most extreme, violent, and destructive moments of human life and human history. As will be discussed below, it has resulted in some curious conceptions of the body, its affects, and their relation to the psyche and the self. In speaking of the 'literal truth' and 'historical reality' of traumatic experience, our discourses of trauma resemble those valorizations of injurious and adverse experiences discussed in the previous chapter, in which bad experiences were incorporated without mediation or moderation, and in which the attainment and preservation of their 'goodness' or value relied upon the deployment of primitive and defensive stratagems aimed at suppressing the self.

Widespread agreement about the truth and reality of traumatic experience seems difficult to distinguish from acceptance of trauma victims' understandings of events, particularly of the events held responsible for generating post-traumatic symptoms, which are often considered to contain a "literal" truth. Caruth, for instance, understands trauma as inherently "unknowable" (1996, 57–62) and inherently "latent" (1995, 4–11), while at the same time defining post-traumatic experience as "absolutely literal" (1995, 4) and "the literal return of the event" (1996, 59).

In her meticulous genealogy, Ruth Leys describes the dramatic shift in trauma theory that compelled researchers to reject the construct's murky intellectual origins and the "mimetic dimension" of trauma symptoms (2000, 40). Since the end of the Vietnam War, and in light of the psychiatric ratification of PTSD in the DSM-III (*Diagnostic and Statistical Manual of Mental Disorders*, Third Edition) in 1980, clinical, medical, literary, and philosophical communities have located the traumatic quality of trauma, as it were, in the experience of an overwhelming thing-in-itself that leaves an uncognizable imprint on an increasingly physical conception of the psyche, piercing its boundaries, shattering its integrity, disrupting contact with itself, and precluding its capacity to function, attach, and relate. Leys describes this conceptual shift in language that is, itself, reminiscent of the well-known trauma symptom of exteriorization:

> The antimimetic turn … is simultaneously the moment when emphasis tends to shift from the notion of trauma as involving a mimetic yielding of identity to identification to a notion of trauma as a purely external cause or event that comes to an already constituted ego to shatter its autonomy and integrity. Passionate identifications are thereby transformed into claims of identity, and the negativity and violence that according to hypothesis inhere in the mimetic breaching of the boundaries between the internal and the external are violently expelled into the external world, from where they return to the fully constituted, autonomous subject in the form of an absolute exteriority. The result is a rigid dichotomy between internal and external such that violence is imagined as coming to the subject entirely from the outside.
>
> *(2000, 37)*

The turn Leys helpfully describes involves our understanding not merely of the nature or process of traumatization, but of the status of a self that *must have existed* in order to be traumatized. That is, the corollary of the process of exteriorization is the creation of an 'inside' undertaken in bad faith. Contemporary notions of trauma create a self, a 'straw self,' if you will, that is inevitably lost, constituted in order to be destroyed at the moment of trauma. "In trauma," writes Caruth:

> the outside has gone inside without any mediation. ... There is an incomprehensible outside of the self that has already gone inside without the self's mediation, hence without any relation to the self, and this consequently becomes a threat to any understanding of what a self might be in this context.
>
> *(1996, 59, 132n)*

There must be an "inside," a self, and a boundary in order for there to be an obliteration of the same in a traumatic experience that occurs "without any relation to the self."

Henry Krystal has wisely noted that the traumatized experience life as originating almost entirely from the outside, from the not-self:

> Much of the psychic representation of the "enemy" or "oppressor" or even impersonal elements such as "fate" and clearly personal attributes like one's own emotions come to be experienced as outside the self-representation. Thus, the post-traumatic state is characterized by an impoverishment of the areas of one's mind to which the "I" feeling of self-sameness is extended, and a hypertrophy of the "not-I" alienated areas.
>
> *(1995, 85)*

Recent trauma theory, in this sense, recapitulates trauma symptomology, and may even be thought to involve theorists, writers, and intellectuals in dynamics similar to those undergone by the traumatized. That contemporary theories of trauma presuppose a self, then assert trauma's activity to be that of penetrating, disintegrating, and taking up residence where the self lives no longer, makes traumatic experience a curious thing, a kind of experience without an experiencer, arising from an absolute outside, yet left indelibly "inside," lodged somewhere between the (lost) self and the (lost) world. Trauma is present, all-too-present, for the traumatized, yet, as it is deemed unthinkable and unknowable, can only be expected to find its place in the body, such that the body that expresses trauma's paradoxically "literal" presence has become trauma's privileged locale.

'Body studies,' the sociological and anthropological 'turns to corporeality,' and the 'affective turn' have all problematized the idea of 'molar bodies,' such that bodies are no longer conceived as simple, material things, but as 'processes' and even 'organizers' of "diverse practices and areas of experience." Bodies are "open, relational, human and non-human, material and immaterial, multiple, sentient, and processual" (Blackman 2008, 2849–2851; see also Clough 2007).

On one hand, the psyche has been physicalized in psychological and philosophical discourses over the past several decades, in no small part due to the influence of trauma theory. Teresa Brennan's work on the "transmission of affect" (2004) goes so far as to declare that:

> the psyche is, of course, also a physical or embodied thing. This has to be so if one accepts the premise that the psychical actually gets into the flesh, whether it is manifest as the inertia of depression, or as an actual psychosomatic illness, or in other ways, such as anger. It is these embodied psychical urges, these constellations of affects, that lead us to eat the wrong way, do the wrong things, push ourselves for the wrong reason, and so forth.
>
> *(156)*

On the other hand, the body seems to be no longer a thing at all, but an ironically abstract 'organizing process.' In order to understand bodies, we must not "start with bodies as a key focus," but with "concerns about lived experience, sleep, marching, dance, identity, eating disorders, technologies, the placebo effect, communication, body language, performance, emotion, twinning and cloning, the senses, the mouth and health and illness" (Blackman 2008, 2847–2849). Amid this odd assortment of experiences and phenomena, the body is always:

> *in process* and is assembled and made up from the diverse relays, connections and relationships between artefacts, technologies, practices and matter which temporarily form it as a particular kind of object. However, even the term "it" implies a form or shape that can be easily recognizable as a body. What is clear … is that talk of the body extends to talk of body assemblages that might not resemble the molar body in any shape or form.
>
> *(2849–2855, emphasis in original)*

Contemporary bodies, apparently, may not resemble bodies at all, not only because bodies are now imagined as organizers and processes, but because bodies "always extend and connect to other bodies, human and non-human, to practices, techniques, technologies and objects which produce different kinds of bodies" (Blackman 2012, ix–x). That is, parallel to the endeavor to demonstrate the permeability and inter-dependence of subjects, the body, too, has become that which is not individually possessed but shared, ever exposed to experiences transmitted and disseminated by or through other bodies. Since "bodies are processes," bodies are "articulated and articulate through their connections with others, human and non-human" (Blackman 2008, 2857–2858). What truly defines bodies, then, is their "capacity to affect and be affected" (Blackman 2012, x).

Perhaps the physicalization of trauma is not entirely surprising, for if traumatic experience cannot be thought or known, neither can the body. If what defines the body is its constant contact with other bodies, then it may be imagined to receive and transmit truth more reliably than other human faculties. 'Body language,' to take a rather mundane example, is often taken to be more a real and 'honest' form of expression than the spoken or written word (see Csordas 2008). As the renowned American dancer Martha Graham averred, "the body never lies" (see Burt 1988, 34). Later, Alice Miller (2006) would borrow her famous dictum to title her study of the physical manifestations of childhood abuse. To suggest that "the body never lies" is to suggest not only that the body can hold the unknowable truths of experience, but that the body can safeguard experience from the distortions of thought.

Indeed, it may be fruitful to conceive of the contemporary understanding of the body as that which is not material but real, or, more precisely, real *only* because of its connections with other bodies, only because of its "capacity to affect and be affected." If this is true, then the body is real because the body is not thought or known.[1] In several ideologies of experience, the unthinkability of the body is equated with its reality, with the sum of "artefacts, technologies, practices and matter" that form reality, which can only be reliably incorporated and transmitted through the body's experience.

R.D. Laing has objected that scientific authorities often dismiss experience by regarding it as a "psychosis of matter ... another countable aberration in the universe that knows nothing of it, and gets on its own way apparently without it" (Laing and Kirsner 2013, 367). On the face of it, Laing's objection seems to be that scientists (and presumably clinicians) unfairly dismiss experiences that should be recognized as real and significant (i.e., as things that "matter") in "the universe." But what is interesting about Laing's argument is his presumption that even those who discount or ignore experience would agree that experience is material, that experience is a type of "matter," albeit 'psychotic matter.' It would seem more likely that those whom Laing targets would reply that experience is not "matter" at all.

Ironically, of course, Laing's jab at the scientific outlook borrows something of its humor from the fact that, according to the same scientific paradigm he critiques, "matter" is incapable of behaving psychotically. If "psychosis" refers to a loss of contact with shared reality, most of us find it difficult if not impossible to imagine a "psychosis of matter" precisely because, to the modern and contemporary mind, matter – that ill-defined term that nevertheless signifies the most fundamental property shared by physical objects – *is* reality. In this way, Laing's defense of the materiality of experience also indirectly accuses those who disagree with his perspective of being, themselves, 'psychotic,' since it is they, he argues, who ignore the material 'reality' of experience and retreat into an insular universe that "gets on its own way ... without it."

In a related metaphor, for Bill Holm, "the divine" is an example of something that is "entirely abstract, a series of slogans said but not believed in. ... Since the divine has *no body*, it needs no place to live." On the other hand, "the world is only real estate, and can be filed at the court house" (Holm 2010, 162–163, emphasis added). What Holm means, of course, is that, having no body, the divine cannot be *experienced*, and therefore cannot be trusted to be *real*. On the contrary, things of "the world," by which Holm means not merely physical objects but bodies, experiences, failures, and the like, make themselves 'at home' in reality, in "real estate." These real things with bodies and earthly homes are what can be "believed in." Here, we might expect that Holm intends to refer not to the sort of belief that requires thought or imagination, but to one that may be located in the body, perhaps in our 'gut feelings.'

Both Caruth's and Leys' accounts imply that theorists' location of the violence of trauma "outside" the self intends to protect something of the self's constitution, perhaps even to protect the traumatized self from irremediable harm. But if trauma has come to be defined as the intrusion of an overwhelmingly violent and overwhelmingly real 'thing-in-itself,' it is not, as Leys claims, because we inhabit a culture in which "the therapist demand[s] that the patient be a subject" (2000, 37). Rather, this understanding of trauma identifies traumatic experience as the experience that can only be experienced in the body, which, again, is conceived to be not the same kind of body as it once was, but, rather, a body whose reality is established and realized in its connection with other bodies. This body, or these bodies, come to hold a moral and epistemic authority that serves primarily to protect not selves from traumatic experience, but traumatic experience from selves, from distortion by the self's immaterial and unreal thinking. This discourse of trauma is reminiscent of earlier philosophical and literary discourses of experience, in which an intellectual submission to overwhelming experiences and their objects is conceived to be the surest path to a physical, unknowing truth and wisdom that even the most gifted of writers found it (not surprisingly) difficult to articulate.

At a collective level, the vision of trauma with which we live suggests that we inhabit, or that we ought to inhabit, a "post-traumatic century" (Felman 1995, 13), which means that our historical truths are preserved not in thoughts or writings but in bodies and their experiences. If this is so, then some have extended the argument so far as to claim that we must "understand history [itself] as the history of trauma" (Caruth 1996, 60), that "history," itself, "is precisely the way we are implicated in each other's traumas" (24), and that we must approach all "history as holocaust" (Felman and Laub 1992, 95). While some, like Reinhart Koselleck (2002), have merely challenged the conventional wisdom that history is written by the victors by claiming that "historical gains in knowledge stem in the long run from the vanquished," because "the history of the vanquished … offers a more truthful expression of 'the experience of history'" (Fassin and Rechtman 2009, 16), others have returned to orientations guided by a fascination with physical violence and terror, such as Walter Benjamin's famous claim that "to articulate the past historically does not mean to recognize it 'the way it really was'," but rather "to seize hold of a memory as it flashes up at a moment of danger" (2003, 391). Benjamin's assertions seems *prima facie* absurd, yet the ideological proposition of the unquestionable and unknowable truth of traumatic experience remains in force, and, as I now hope to show, has been in force in philosophical treatments of experience undertaken well before trauma's heyday.

Humility, self-occlusion, and failure

Our contemporary approach to trauma is linked not only to anti-subjective trends in postmodern philosophy and contemporary literature, but to longstanding and widespread ideologies of experience that reflect a sustained effort to locate moral, cultural, and epistemological authority in a state of unthinking self-occlusion.

Michel de Montaigne

For the celebrated Renaissance essayist Michel de Montaigne, the great virtue of experience is its humbling quality. Experience, for Montaigne, is the antidote to overreaching, to the sin of pride. The learned and inexperienced reach for "lofty and inaccessible heights," thinking "supercelestial thoughts" and indulging in "transcendental humours" which, of course, lead only to "subterrestrial conduct." The humble path of experience, on the contrary, does not so tempt its followers "to get out of themselves and to escape from the man" (1993, 405).

Pride, according to Montaigne, persuades us that we are superior to experience. Much of his famed "Apology for Raymond Seybond" is dedicated to recounting the danger of this idea. In the section entitled "Man's Knowledge Cannot Make Him Good," Montaigne writes:

> The simple and ignorant, says Saint Paul, raise themselves to heaven, and take possession of it; and we, with all our learning, plunge ourselves into the infernal abyss. ... The urge to increase in wisdom and knowledge was the first downfall of the human race; it was the way by which man hurled himself into eternal damnation. Pride is his ruin and his corruption; it is pride that casts man aside from the common ways, that makes him embrace novelties and prefer to be the leader of an erring troop that has strayed into the path of perdition, prefer to be a teacher and tutor of error and falsehood, rather than to be a disciple in the school of truth, led and guided by another's hand, on the straight and beaten path.
>
> *(1965, 367–368)*

Montaigne, although learned enough to quote Quintilian in saying "learning makes difficulties" (1965, 816), offers his own essays as "simple," "natural," and "naked" accounts of life (1993, 23), "present[ed] ... pure, not at all corrupted or altered by art or theorizing" (1965, 826). Setting himself up as a disciple of the "common ways," Montaigne relies on his own experience and occasionally, and perhaps ironically, upon the testimony of others, when those others are clearly artless (1993, 151–152; see also Frisch 2009, 182). If there is one over-arching theme of his entire collection of essays, it is the theme of rejecting intellectual pride, and, along with it, trust in one's ideas about the world.

The specific danger of the intellect, for Montaigne, is the mind's tendency to distort reality to suit its own preferences. The mind treats each of its objects "not according to the nature of the thing, but in accordance with itself. Things in themselves perhaps have their own weights, measures, and states; but inwardly, when they enter into us, the mind cuts them to its own conceptions" (1993, 131). For Montaigne, the prideful, vain mind, like Narcissus, falls in love with its own reflection and drowns in its own image. Finding nothing so engaging as its own reflection, in attempting to possess itself the mind is emptied of reality.

Montaigne's metaphors for the mind's activity typically emphasize this inward, draining, drowning quality. For instance:

> The mind … does nothing but ferret and search, and is all the time turning, contriving, and entangling itself in its own work, like a silk-worm; and there it suffocates, "a mouse in pitch." … Its case is much like that of Aesop's dogs who, seeing something like a dead body floating in the sea, and being unable to get near it, set about drinking up the water to make a dry passage, and choked themselves.
>
> *(1993, 347–348)*

Here, the mouse suffocates in its own activity, just as Aesop's dogs choke to death, not only in pursuit of something lifeless, but by attempting to drink up the sea, an exercise in futility.

If we are to humble the mind and to resist its morbid temptations, to what resource shall we turn for truth about 'things-in-themselves?' For Montaigne, "events and outcomes depend, for the most part … on Fortune, who will not fall in line and subject herself to our reason and foresight." Indeed, Montaigne declares that "our counsels and deliberations depend just as much on Fortune" as on reason, for "[Fortune] involves our reason also in her confusion and uncertainty" (1965, 209).

Although Montaigne is perhaps best known as a champion of "individual experience" (see, e.g., Gossin 2002, 289), it is not the experience that belongs to the individual that Montaigne truly celebrates. Rather, the individual's experience is false if she refuses to recognize the exteriority and superiority of the objects that shape our experience, such as Fortune, and, more importantly, Nature. Nature and Fortune, Montaigne's primary idealized (self)objects, which work in tandem, are to be revered as "great and mighty" (1965, 109), mysterious, lying "beyond" our awareness, and nevertheless in a position to command and rule, "bend[ing] us to [their] laws" (209).

Learning from experience, for Montaigne, means quieting the mind and attending, instead, to experience's objects. Put another way, attending to experience's objects means humbling ourselves before them. According to Montaigne, "to learn [from experience] that one has said or done a foolish thing … is nothing." Rather, "one must learn that one is nothing but a fool, a much more comprehensive and important lesson" (1993, 355). To learn that one is "nothing but a fool" is crucial because internalizing the self-attribution of fundamental nothingness cements a self-occlusive relationship with experience's objects, in which the mind will not dare to pridefully "cut" things "into its own conceptions" but will accede to the given reality of 'things in themselves.'

The "lesson" we learn by humbling ourselves in this way is that we are empty, powerless, and, in a sense, unreal, at least when we are not attached to an object of experience. The truth Montaigne is after is the truth of our utter foolishness, our inevitable nothingness. Learning from experience, therefore, demands that we pay particular attention to experiences that highlight this truth: experiences of failure. These experiences directly demonstrate the impotence of the mind. They assist us in accepting our humble place vis-à-vis Nature and Fortune, which we must refrain from resisting, just as we must learn not to "kick against natural necessity" if we are to avoid "the foolishness of Ctesiphon, who tried a kicking match with his mule" (1993, 374).

When, in "On Experience," Montaigne famously describes the kidney stones that plagued his later years, he details his physical suffering, his eating, sleeping, and defecatory habits, and his experience of his body, using his personal example to inveigh against medical, legal, and political authorities and their prescriptions. Although he cites Plato's argument that doctors ought to personally suffer from any illnesses they would treat, he radically departs from Plato's teaching by using medicine as a metaphor for the danger of relying on reason to address what ails our bodies and bodies politic.

Instead, Montaigne emphasizes the necessity of habituating himself to whatever afflictions come his way, all of which must be "quietly put up with" (1993, 373), for "we must learn to endure what we cannot avoid" (1965, 835). Montaigne is especially content that his ailment asks him mainly to endure, without engaging his mind, for like Camus' protagonists in *The Plague* (1991), he strives to resist the temptation to *think* about his illness. He resolutely rejects "medical consultation and diagnosis," speculation about the "causes, states, and progress" of his condition, and the urge to "follow so many different arguments and opinions" like those whom "the imagination plagues … when the body is sound" (1993, 380–381). Consider the following remarkable passage:

> It has happened again that the slightest movements force the pure blood out of my kidneys. What of it? … It is some big stone that is crushing and consuming the substance of my kidneys, and my life that I am letting out little by little, not without some natural pleasure, as an excrement that is

henceforth superfluous and a nuisance. Do I feel something crumbling? Do not expect me to go and amuse myself testing my pulse and my urine so as to take some bothersome precaution. ... I judge of myself only by actual sensations, not by reasoning. What would be the use, since I intend to apply only waiting and endurance.

(1965, 831–840)

Montaigne's experience of his illness seems to have convinced him that the blood from his kidneys, along with his life, itself, are *excrements*, waste products to be let out little by little, and "not without some natural pleasure." Montaigne's way of embracing his experience demands judgment without "reasoning," and includes, instead, thanking "Fortune" for teaching him how not to protest his pain, by "assailing me so often with the same kind of weapons. She fashions and trains me against them by use, hardens and accustoms me" (1965, 837). In this spirit, Montaigne also praises "the first lesson" Mexican parents purportedly give their children: "When they come forth from the mother's womb, their elders greet them with these words: 'Child, you have come into the world to endure. Endure, suffer, and be silent'" (1993, 373).

This capacity for "suffering," "waiting and endurance," for resisting reason, protest, and even action, becomes, for Montaigne, a central virtue. It is a central virtue because suffering is taken to be inevitable, and its inevitability is mistaken for an essence. That is, suffering is not merely incidental to the purpose of human life: It is its essence. A child is not merely born into a world that incidentally includes suffering and demands endurance, but she is born *in order to* suffer and endure. Suffering, enduring, and effacing the self become the human being's *raison d'être*. This odd philosophy may be applied to the life of the individual, as well as to political communities, in which "humility, fear, obedience, and affability, which are the principal things that support and maintain human society, require an empty and docile soul, and little presuming upon itself" (1887, 12).

But why should human beings accept such a state? Why should they give up, at birth, the hope of achieving their own aims and ends? Is it the will of God, of Nature, of Fortune? While Montaigne never answers these questions directly, his dedication to, and identification with, the self-negating objects of experience are starkly revealed in his short essay "On Democritus and Heraclitus," where we encounter a surprising advocacy of self-loathing, scorn, and shame.

Although the two ancient Greek philosophers Democritus and Heraclitus agreed that the human condition was "vain and ridiculous," Heraclitus is said to have wept unceasingly at this misfortune, while Democritus "never appeared in public except with a mocking and ribald expression." In considering these two responses, Montaigne declares that he prefers Democritus' attitude:

not because it is pleasanter to laugh than to weep, but because it expresses more contempt and is more condemnatory of us than the other. I do not think we can ever be despised as much as we deserve. Wailing and commiseration imply some valuation of the object bewailed; what we mock at we consider worthless.

(1993, 132–133)

For Heraclitus, our inadequacies and relative powerlessness in relation to Nature and Fortune are agonizing. They drive him to despair. For Democritus and for Montaigne, however, our condition is only lamentable if we value ourselves. If we embrace our worthlessness, then reflection upon our condition occasions only the (emotionally dissociative) responses of self-mockery and laughter. What is truly ridiculous, according to Democritus and Montaigne, is that we should somehow think ourselves worthy of *not* suffering, that we should *think of or imagine an alternative* to experiences of failure or pain. Instead, we are asked to find pleasure in scorning ourselves and in ridiculing our vain thoughts and wishes.

Ironically, we rediscover in Montaigne's and Democritus' emotionally distant, self-scornful laughter a departure from the experience of the genuinely suffering human being and an identification with the object or objects of experience that cause suffering. As in the final lines of the Book of Job, the restoration of the relationship between God and Job, which is hardly a relationship at all, owing to their absolute incommensurability – this incommensurability being very much the point of the Book – is consummated only when Job "abhors himself in dust and ashes" (42:6, AV; see also Bowker 2014, 28–34). Likewise, for Montaigne, self-devaluation is a necessary part of the reconciliation between the human being and almighty Nature and Fortune, who have seen fit to make human beings ludicrous. Indeed, Montaigne compares Job to one of his primary heroes, Socrates, whose famously humble declaration of ignorance Montaigne takes as evidence of human absurdity and emptiness:

> At last [Socrates] concluded that he was not distinguished from others, nor wise, but only because he did not think himself so. ... The sacred word declares those miserable among us who have an opinion of themselves: "Dust and ashes," says it to such, "what hast thou wherein to glorify thyself?" And, in another place, "God has made man like unto a shadow," of whom who can judge, when by removing the light it shall be vanished! Man is a thing of nothing.
>
> *(1887, 12)*

Contrary to all critical interpretations of Montaigne of which I am aware, it is possible to understand his *oeuvre* as an attempt – an *essai* – to buttress the experiential devaluation of the self, to explore, indulge, and even insist upon the self's failure in order to secure a more self-effacing relationship to experience's objects. Much as the early mimetic theories of trauma conceived of trauma as an identification with a traumatizing object or scene, Montaigne conceives of suffering, self-failure, and even the physical trauma of deadly illness as pathways to unite with, perhaps to belong to, experience's objects: Nature and Fortune.

Montaigne's well-known idiosyncrasies, his willingness to portray his 'personality,' his self-contradictions, factual errors, and repeated failures to arrive at reasoned treatments of his subjects, too, may be more than marks of his undeniable charm, intellect, and wit.[2] They may represent a ritual of intellectual failure, consciously or unconsciously intended to realize the futility of thinking about or resisting the overwhelming forces imagined to drive experience.

Ralph Waldo Emerson

Almost three centuries later, Ralph Waldo Emerson's 1844 essay "Experience" would recapitulate Montaigne's fundamental teaching: "If we will take the good we find, asking no questions," Emerson declares, "we shall have heaping measures. The great gifts are not got by analysis. Everything good is on the highway" (2009, 315). If Montaigne's mind was "a mouse in pitch," a dog choking on sea water to satisfy a morbid curiosity, for the Emerson of "Experience," contemplation is a form of suicide: "If a man should consider the nicety of the passage of a piece of bread down his throat, he would starve" (313).

Emerson and Montaigne both accuse mental activities of interfering with the unreflective and self-effacing attitude required to 'take in' or 'swallow' experience. Our ability to sustain ourselves via experience, then, relies on a minimalization of, or even disappearance of, the self, in order to give place to experience's object. Emerson urges:

> Do not craze yourself with thinking, but go about your business anywhere. Life is not intellectual or critical, but sturdy. Its chief good is for well-mixed people who can enjoy what they find, without question. Nature hates peeping, and our mothers speak her very sense when they say, "Children, eat your victuals, and say no more of it." To fill the hour, – that is happiness; to fill the hour, and leave no crevice for a repentance or an approval.
>
> *(2009, 314)*

For Emerson, it is not that we fill ourselves with experience's object, nor that we take in or enjoy "the hour." Rather, experience's object must be filled *by us*, and, more precisely, *by our emptiness*. Here, time or "the hour" represents experience's object, and "to fill the hour" means "to fill" the object by emptying the self. To fill the object, and then to partake secondarily or vicariously in the object's plenitude, requires that we give ourselves to the object fully, without leaving the slightest "crevice for a repentance or an approval."

How odd it is that repentances and approvals are figured not as subjective additions to experience but as destructive subtractions, "crevices," cuts or gashes in the object, as if our expressions of thought, feeling, or spontaneity might tear, break, or empty the object that contains the 'good.' To avoid tearing, breaking, or emptying the object, of course, we must tear, break, and empty ourselves.

Thinking, for Emerson, disrupts the process of finding and taking in experience, which is 'the good.' Thinking – and with it 'peeping' and questioning and doubting and other activities associated with curiosity, reflection, and being a self – represent withholding the self from experience's object, failing to give the self 'fully' to the object of experience. This withholding, in turn, contains the forbidden suggestion that the self possesses some of 'the good' in itself, and therefore is not completely empty in the absence of the object. This suggestion is what Montaigne would call "pride."

Thinking – and related activities that healthy selves engage in – can only starve the human being by denying absolute power and goodness to an object of experience that might have nourished us. Activities appropriate to selves, on this account, might even be imagined to offend or outrage the object of experience, by implying that the self possesses something of worth on its own. Since being our selves is abhorrent to the objects of experience that nourish us, our selves must appear to us as 'bad.' Apparently, the self's relationship to experience's objects is similar to a child's relationship to a narcissistic parent, in which the child may receive only unpredictable and transitory experiences of 'the good,' not according to her needs or designs but only in passing or "on the highway," and only if the parent is attended to first and fully, such that the parent's value, reality, and autonomy are upheld in the same instant that these qualities in the child are dismissed or repudiated.

To be commanded to "eat your victuals" while being forbidden to speak may be to be physically nourished, but it is to be emotionally and intellectually starved. To accept this starvation of self as 'the good' that life bestows, to return once again to Holm's metaphor, is one way 'to swallow our failure.' It is also one way to be traumatized.

Let us push further and say that to advocate for a kind of nourishment that is actually an evacuation of the self is to become a *center of trauma* or a "site of trauma" (Caruth 1995, 11), rather than a "center of initiative" (Kohut 1977, 99) or site of authentic being and doing, thinking, creating, or relating. The traumatized individual may be said to be engaged in an object-relationship that involves emptying his self and incorporating, instead, the traumatic experience that has been suffered. Of course, since unthought or unthinkable experience cannot be contained within the self, and since the self, itself, has been devastated by its overwhelming encounter with experience's object, attempts to 'hold onto' or 'possess' such experience can only be physical and affective, and can only mean repeating and returning to the experience and its object again and again.

Perhaps this is what Caruth means when she suggests that, while, on one hand, the traumatized carry "the symptom of a history that they cannot entirely possess," on the other hand, "to be traumatized is precisely to be possessed by an image or event" (1995, 4–5): that an experience may possess the traumatized human being by usurping the self's place in the inner world. But Caruth does not seem to argue, as I am arguing, that the goal for the traumatized should be for the self to recapture its place. Absent this objective, it would seem that repeated moments of traumatic experience, or repeated expressions of one's possession by trauma, are mistaken for a connection to truth and reality.

Traumatic transmission

In *The Interpretation of Dreams*, Freud tells of a mourning father, whose recently deceased son comes to him in a dream and asks, "Father, don't you see I'm burning?" Upon waking, the father sees a glare in the child's room and rushes in to find that the body of his deceased child has been burned by a fallen candle. Freud's explanation of the dream is that the father is able, in the dream, to experience the child as alive once again, and therefore, even given the horrible circumstances, the dream represents a wish. Indeed, Freud writes that:

> here we have the most general and the most striking psychological char-acteristic of the process of dreaming: a thought, and as a rule a thought of something that is wished, is objectified in the dream, is represented as a scene, or, as it seems to us, is experienced.
>
> *(1950, 534)*

Caruth, following Lacan, sees in the dream, instead, a traumatic repetition and a "traumatic awakening" in which the father finds that his self "is bound up with, or founded in, the death that he survives" (1996, 92). In fact, Caruth claims that:

> what the father cannot grasp in the death of his child ... becomes the foun-dation of his very identity as a father. In thus relating trauma to the very identity of the self and to one's relation to another ... the shock of traumatic sight reveals at the heart of human subjectivity not so much an epistemological, but rather what can be defined as an ethical relation to the real.
>
> *(1996, 92)*

By this logic, since the death of his child is a trauma, and since the self is not, according to Caruth, present in trauma, then the father could not have been present to witness his child's death: The father failed to see it. For a father to dream that his living child demands that he see the child burning, for Caruth, becomes an insistence that the father see his own failure to see, to see his own "repeated failure to respond" (103).

"The awakening" that results from the dream and that occurs, on a metapho-rical level, within the dream, "embodies an appointment with the real," writes Caruth, again echoing Lacan. And "the real" here is identical to the "awakening [that] is itself the site of trauma, the trauma of the necessity and impossibility of responding to another's death" (1996, 100). That is, "the real" is always "the site of trauma," which escapes us. On this line of thought, 'real' experiences and traumatic experiences can *never* be experiences of the self's reality, only of the self's "inevitable" yet "necessary" *failures* to be, to think, to see, and to act in reality. Caruth claims that it is these experiences of failed being, thinking, seeing, and doing that cannot be imagined or represented but that also "demand" to be shared or transmitted, meaning that, in their sharing, the witness or listener also must fail to be present. "The repeated failure to have seen in time," Caruth continues, "can be transformed into the imperative of a speaking that awakens others"; awakens them, no doubt, to "the appointment with the real" that consists not of the trauma itself but of the "missing" of it (108).

There are only minor differences between such claims and ontological-existential claims that conceive of "failure as 'the Real'" (Oprisko 2014; see also Žižek 1989, 2008), where the Real is "a kind of ontological 'collateral damage' of symbolic operations: the process of symbolization is inherently thwarted, doomed to fail, and the Real is this immanent failure of the symbolic" (Žižek 2012, 959).[3] Both of these types of claims, as Žižek himself admits, are difficult to distinguish from moral demands that elements of trauma ought to remain central parts of our shared experience. Thus, within debates about witnessing and representing trauma, and in spite of the well-known difficulties in communicating traumatic narratives, one often discovers the assumption that trauma *should be* transmitted and shared.

"In order to be diffused," Nossery and Hubbell argue, "trauma must move beyond isolation and be shared with participants willing to engage in the victim's torment. ... The [transmissive] encounter could be beneficial for both the victim and the addressee, *as it merges the two parties' experiences*" (2013, 11, emphasis added). The assumption that a merger of experience is desirable, and perhaps even superior to a relationship between selves and a communication of experiences, is discussed in greater detail in subsequent chapters. A substantial part of the logic of such an assumption is derived from the belief that experience, even vicarious experience, can rescue selves from their inevitable isolation, vanity, and destructiveness.

If, in Shoshana Felman's words, we are obliged by "the imperative of bearing witness" (1995, 16), if it is necessary to share our traumatic history, this sharing remains problematic, since trauma must remain "referential precisely to the extent that it is not fully perceived as it occurs ... grasped only in the very inaccessibility of its occurrence" (Caruth 1996, 18). In spite of the urgency with which we are exhorted to transmit trauma, what can be transmitted is only a confounding experience, an experience of incomprehension, perhaps even an experience of *not being, not being* in relation to the individual bearing witness, *not being* in contact with the self, *not being* in relation to the not-self of the traumatized. A malformed missive, a message that 'self-destructs' upon arrival, traumatic experience occludes thinking about trauma, just as transmitting trauma seems to involve a traumatic failure of thinking, communicating, and being.

Dori Laub claims that the witness to trauma or traumatic narrative:

> come[s] to be a participant and a co-owner of the traumatic event: through his very listening, he comes to partially *experience* trauma in himself. The relation of the victim to the event of the trauma, therefore, impacts on the relation of the listener to it, and the latter comes to feel the bewilderment, injury, confusion, dread and conflicts that the trauma victim feels.
>
> *(1992, 57–58, emphasis added)*

If what must be transmitted, according to Walter Benn Michaels, is "not the normalizing knowledge of the horror but the horror itself," then this "horror itself" is not even the horror of the traumatic event but the horror of failing *to be* in its presence (quoted in Leys 2000, 268).

Since we cannot – and must not – think or know experience, we can only share traumatic experience in the breakdown of language and reason, in the "failure of witnessing or representation," which is to say: in the active destruction of the knowledge of experience and of our presence of being in experience. Attempts at thinking, relating, communicating, or other expressions of self-being would distort the traumatic truth, for if trauma is a "symptom of history," then "it is a symptom which must not ... be cured but simply transmitted, passed on" (Leys 2000, 268–269).

Discourses of trauma, literatures of atrocity and the Holocaust, 'traumatized texts' of contemporary literature, and insistences that we protect traumatic objects from corruption by thought form the core of an ideology of trauma. This ideology sets forth an ethical demand that we surmount our 'crisis of truth' by undertaking a deliberate "infection," "contaminat[ion]" (Leys 2000, 268), and "contagion" (Caruth 1995, 10; Terr 1988) of traumatic material across persons and groups. To blend our discussion of Camus from the last chapter with our discussion of Felman and Caruth here, we might say that the ethical imperative yielded by the ideology of trauma is to transmit a homeopathic 'plague experience' in order to inoculate the population against the plagues of thinking and selfhood.

It is likely that the valorization of transmitting trauma both eases the burden of the traumatized victim – by making use of projective identification to witness one's trauma in others – and sustains the fantasy of a future community of victims in which the self has "depart[ed]," a community united by trauma, strengthened by immediate connections to traumatizing objects and experiences. "In a catastrophic age," Caruth writes, "trauma may provide the very link between cultures ... as our ability to listen through the departures we have all taken from ourselves" (1995, 11).

In his short paper entitled "Communicating and Not Communicating Leading to a Study of Certain Opposites," Winnicott discusses an "incommunicado element" of self, a "secret self" or sacred core that must be protected from the world of objects, lest it be adjusted or altered (1965, 187). But if we are possessed by an ideology of trauma, then instead of generating the feeling of reality in the self by making contact with this secret incommunicado element, we may turn to traumatizing objects to replace non-communicative elements of the self.

The dynamic I have in mind is not precisely the "mimetic dimension" of trauma to which Leys draws our attention (2000, 18–40), but one in which experiences of trauma, failure, and deprivation, along with the objects that are imagined to deliver such experiences – be they Nature, Fortune, God, Chance, the Law, the Nation, or the Community – supplant a part of the self. Now it is the traumatic experience and its object that must be protected, just as if they were the "secret self," and it is the traumatic experience and its object that must be nourished and contacted in order to find feelings of aliveness and reality. The attributions of unknowability and unthinkability we ascribe to both experience and trauma, then, reflect the same need to protect what are taken to be the most sacred elements of our psyches against being found or altered.

Of course, in spite of what we are told by celebrants of trauma and experience, the internalization of objects of traumatizing experience cannot succeed in providing sought-after feelings of reality and aliveness. Ambivalent desires to both hide and transmit our experiences derive from this failure. Traumatic experiences are hidden because they are confused with the secret, non-communicative element of self, having substituted an identity with an identification. They are transmitted and re-transmitted because, having failed to issue in the feelings of value, vitality, and reality for which we had hoped, we mistake our task to be that of confirming our inner traumatic experience in the world outside, by provoking or instilling it in others. In the following chapters, I discuss how both of these tendencies may become repetitive, compulsive, and profoundly destructive.

Early in this chapter, I suggested that our current discourse of trauma recapitulated fundamental dynamics of traumatic experience, itself. Specifically, a 'straw self' is presupposed in order to be traumatized, making the self an inevitably lost object. This lost self, however, was fundamentally flawed, false, morbid, even dangerous, at least if we are persuaded by ideologists of experience such as Montaigne and Emerson, who teach us that the activities appropriate to selves, such as thinking and knowing, interfere with the natural process of experiencing to which we ought to be entirely attuned. Thus, to lose this flawed self is no great loss, for what is gained is experience, its devastating wisdom, and the opportunity to identify with experience's objects, which, even if injurious, are grander than the self could ever be.

At this point, it is possible to advance the thesis that our preoccupation with trauma, and with experiences of failure, deprivation, and suffering in general, may represent a need to demonstrate to ourselves and others the impossibility of *ever having established a real, vital self.* This demonstration serves the purpose of reassuring ourselves that the exchange of selfhood for identification with traumatizing objects and experiences is 'good.' What is more, if a real, vital, thinking, relating, creative self is impossible to begin with, then we may be absolved of feelings of guilt, not only at having failed to achieve this ideal for ourselves, but for our impulses to share our own traumatic experiences with others.

Notes

1 I am grateful to David Levine for our conversations about the notion of the body as the unthought.
2 "If I knew myself less well," Montaigne writes, "I should take the risk of treating some subject thoroughly. But, since I scatter a word here and a word there, samples torn from their piece and separated without plan or promise, I am not bound to answer for them" (1993, 131).
3 Although this book does not deal with Žižek's (or Lacan's) philosophy directly, it may be worthwhile to note that while Žižek's notion of "the Real" has changed substantially over the past twenty-five years, the Real has always been defined as that which is not symbolized nor symbolizable. Žižek himself notes that: "Although I still stand by the basic insights of *The Sublime Object*, it is clear to me, with hindsight, that … it basically endorses a quasi-transcendental reading of Lacan, focused on the notion of the Real as the impossible Thing-in-itself; in so doing, it opens the way to the celebration of failure: to the idea that every act ultimately misfires, and that the proper ethical stance is heroically to accept this failure" (2008, xi–xii).

References

Benjamin, W. 2003. "On the Concept of History." In *Benjamin: Selected Writings, Volume IV: 1938–1940*, edited by H. Eiland and M. Jennings. Translated by E. Jephcott et al. Cambridge, MA and London: Belknap/Harvard University Press.

Blackman, L. 2008. *The Body: The Key Concepts*. Kindle Edition. Oxford: Berg.

Blackman, L. 2012. *Immaterial Bodies: Affect, Embodiment, Mediation*. London: Sage.

Bowker, M.H. 2014. *Rethinking the Politics of Absurdity: Albert Camus, Postmodernity, and the Survival of Innocence*. Series: Routledge Innovations in Political Theory. New York: Routledge.

Brennan, T. 2004. *The Transmission of Affect*. Ithaca, NY and London: Cornell University Press.

Burt, R. 1998. "Dance, Gender and Psychoanalysis: Martha Graham's 'Night Journey'." *Dance Research Journal* 30(1): 34–53.

Camus, A. 1991. *The Plague*. First Vintage International Edition. Translated by S. Gilbert. New York: Vintage.

Caruth, C. 1995. "Introduction." In *Trauma: Explorations in Memory*, edited by C. Caruth, 1–12. Baltimore, MD: Johns Hopkins University Press.

Caruth, C. 1996. *Unclaimed Experience: Trauma, Narrative, and History*. Baltimore, MD: Johns Hopkins University Press.

Clough, P., ed., with J. Halley 2007. *The Affective Turn: Theorizing the Social*. Durham, NC and London: Duke University Press.

Csordas, T. 2008. "Intersubjectivity and Intercorporeality." *Subjectivity* 22: 110–121.

Emerson, R.W. 2009. "Experience (1844)." In *The Essential Writings of Ralph Waldo Emerson*, edited by B. Atkinson, 307–326. New York: Random House.

Fassin, D., and R. Rechtman 2009. *The Empire of Trauma: An Inquiry into the Condition of Victimhood*. Princeton, NJ: Princeton University Press.

Felman, S. 1995. "Education and Crisis, or the Vicissitudes of Teaching." In *Trauma: Explorations in Memory*, edited by C. Caruth, 13–60. Baltimore, MD: Johns Hopkins University Press.

Felman, S., and D. Laub 1992. *Testimony: Crises of Witnessing in Literature, Psychoanalysis, and History*. New York: Taylor and Francis.

Freud, S. 1950. *The Interpretation of Dreams*. Translated by A. Brill. New York: Modern Library.

Frisch, A. 2009. "Cannibalizing Experience in the *Essais*." In *Montaigne After Theory: Theory After Montaigne*, edited by Z. Zalloua, 180–201. Seattle, WA: University of Washington Press.

Gossin, P. 2002. *Encyclopedia of Literature and Science*. Westport, CT and London: Greenwood.

Holm, B. 2010. *The Music of Failure*. First University of Minnesota Press Edition. Fesler-Lampert Minnesota Heritage Series. Minneapolis, MN and London: University of Minnesota Press.

Kohut, H. 1977. *The Restoration of the Self*. Chicago, IL: University of Chicago Press.

Koselleck, R. 2002. *The Practice of Conceptual History: Timing History, Spacing Concepts*. Translated by T. Presner et al. Stanford, CA: Stanford University Press.

Krystal, H. 1995. "Trauma and Aging: A Thirty-Year Follow-up." In *Trauma: Explorations in Memory*, edited by C. Caruth, 76–99. Baltimore, MD: Johns Hopkins University Press.

Laing, R.D., and D. Kirsner 2013. "'Human, All Too Human': Interview with R.D. Laing." *Psychoanalytic Review* 100(2): 361–372.

Laub, D. 1992. "Bearing Witness, or the Vicissitudes of Listening." In *Testimony: Crises of Witnessing in Literature, Psychoanalysis, and History*, edited by S. Felman and D. Laub, 57–74. New York: Taylor and Francis.

Leys, R. 2000. *Trauma: A Genealogy*. Chicago, IL: University of Chicago Press.

Miller, A. 2006. *The Body Never Lies: The Lingering Effects of Hurtful Parenting*. New York: W.W. Norton.

Montaigne, M. de. 1887. *Essays of Michel de Montaigne*, edited by W. Hazlitt. Translated by C. Cotton. www.gutenberg.org/files/3600/3600-h/3600-h.htm. Accessed December 17, 2015.

Montaigne, M. de. 1965. *The Complete Essays of Montaigne*. Translated by D. Frame. Stanford, CA: Stanford University Press.

Montaigne, M. de. 1993. *Essays*, edited and translated by J. Cohen. London: Penguin.

Nossery, N., and A. Hubbell 2013. "Introduction." In *The Unspeakable: Representations of Trauma in Francophone Literature and Art*, edited by N. Nossery and A. Hubbell, 1–20. Cambridge: Cambridge Scholars.

Oprisko, R. 2014. "Failure as the Real: A Review of Slavoj Žižek's *Less Than Nothing: Hegel and the Shadow of Dialectical Materialism*." *Theoria and Praxis* 1(2): 1–4.

Terr, L. 1988. "What Happens to Early Memories of Trauma? A Study of Twenty Children Under Age Five at the Time of Documented Traumatic Events." *Journal of the American Academy of Child and Adolescent Psychiatry* 27(1): 96–104.

Winnicott, D.W. 1965. *The Maturational Processes and the Facilitating Environment: Studies in the Theory of Emotional Development*, edited by M. Khan. London: Hogarth and the Institute of Psycho-Analysis.

Žižek, S. 1989. *The Sublime Object of Ideology*. London and New York: Verso.

Žižek, S. 2008. *For They Know Not What They Do: Enjoyment as a Political Factor*. London and New York: Verso.

Žižek, S. 2012. *Less Than Nothing: Hegel and the Shadow of Dialectical Materialism*. London and New York: Verso.

4

MISUNDERSTOOD AND REPEATED EXPERIENCE IN *LE MALENTENDU*

Albert Camus' early three-act play *Le Malentendu* (*The Misunderstanding*) borrows thematic elements from classical tragedy, alludes explicitly to Gospel narrative, references structural and character elements from the Renaissance *commedia dell'arte*, and propels its action in ways reminiscent of situation comedies modernized by Shakespeare but perhaps most familiar to contemporary audiences via televised serials.

The plot of *Le Malentendu* is rather simple: Jan is a wealthy, married, middle-aged man who, on hearing of his father's death, returns after twenty years of absence to the small Moravian inn where his mother and sister live and work. Jan is not immediately recognized by his family, due, in part, to his extended absence and, in part, to his mother's and sister's habit of sparing attention to guests whom they intend to rob and murder. Jan also takes care to hide his identity from them, ostensibly in order to gather information about them, to gain "a better notion of what to do to make them happy" (Camus 1958, 84), and to set up a joyful surprise when he eventually reveals himself.

Jan's ruse is protested by his wife, Maria, who accompanies him but whom he sends away for his first night at the inn. Jan's mother and sister, Martha, mistaking him for a wealthy solitary traveler, murder him and dump his body in the river before his identity is revealed. Upon realizing what she has done, his mother drowns herself in the river where she and Martha killed January Martha, now alone and in despair, will hang herself. Maria in agonizing grief, pleads for help and mercy but is heard only by an aged, taciturn servant, who replies, simply: "No."

Performances of the play were not terribly successful in the eyes of critics, but the play itself has retained a great deal of influence in the context of Camus' broader philosophical and literary project. A few of Camus' contemporaries were quite fond of it. Jean-Paul Sartre, who would soon cease admiring Camus' work, claimed that the play attained mythic proportion in that its central misunderstanding *"peut servir d'incarnation à tous les malentendus qui séparent l'homme de lui-même, du monde, des autres hommes"* (embodies all the misunderstandings that separate man from himself, from the world, and from others) (1973, 62–63). Written in the early 1940s, in a time of terror, moral outrage, and physical illness for Camus, *Le Malentendu* is typically read as modern, absurdist tragedy, its central theme being that of "revolt against death and the arbitrary, irrational nature of man's fate" (Brée 1964, 150).

Beyond associations with Camus' absurd philosophy, there are two main 'moral' conclusions scholars have derived from the play. The first is that Jan's quest for recognition, for his identity to be seen and known by his family, is impossible and, thus, destined to bring disaster. Jan, on this account, suffers from a sort of Hegelian *hubris*, believing he can be recognized and that his family's recognition will bring him infinite happiness, erasing the pain of their long estrangement. Certainly, such an interpretation seems to fit Camus' philosophical project, which asks us to recognize that our "sin[ful]" desire to know and our "wild longing for clarity" are unfulfillable, impossible, and destructive (1955, 21). To chase after understanding and recognition seems, in some of Camus' writing, to lead only to violence and death, whereas internalizing the inevitability of failure – as in our fundamental "absurdity" – permits us to survive (see Bowker 2014).

The second, and nearly opposite, interpretation is that the play proclaims the ethical necessity of open dialogue and communication, while condemning silence and obfuscation (see, e.g., Matherne 1971, 74–77; Willhoite 1968, 64–66). This conclusion was advanced by Camus himself after his play suffered a poor reception: It is:

> a play of revolt, perhaps even containing a moral of sincerity. … If a man wants to be recognized, one need only tell him who he is. If he shuts up or lies, he will die alone, and everything around him is destined for misery. If, on the contrary, he speaks the truth, he will doubtless die, but after having helped himself and others to live.
>
> *(Quoted in Todd 2000, 186)*

This extremely facile interpretation, although offered by the author himself, is confounding and perhaps backward, for recognizing a person surely means something other than "tell[ing]" that person "who he is." In the best of cases, this interpretation would flatten an already bare drama, making *Le Malentendu* the simplest of cautionary tales.

Indeed, such an interpretation closely resembles the simplistic conclusion reached by Meursault when Camus places a prototype of the story of *Le Malentendu* in *The Stranger*. Here, Meursault describes the idea of hiding one's identity from one's family as "a joke" (*plaisanterie*) (Camus 1988, 80). If, as alluded to in

Chapter 2, "nothing distinguishes jokes or jests more from other psychological structures than their double-sidedness or duplicity" (Freud 1960, 213–214), then jokes must always conceal or confound their own expression, must "muddle" their true intentions (Camus 1958, 83), and, in this sense, must always miscommunicate and must always be misunderstood.

Of the story, Meursault concludes: "On the one hand it wasn't very likely. On the other, it was perfectly natural. Anyway, I thought the traveler pretty much deserved what he got and that you shouldn't play games" (Camus 1988, 80). While Meursault is not always the keenest observer of human emotion, he is right that Jan's gambit is like a joke and a game because it appears to be a species of play, play being a form of creative experimentation where impulses are heeded and where some departures from the rules of reality are tolerated, as in the dramatic medium called the *play*.[1] On the other hand, more sophisticated understandings of the concept of playing, such as Winnicott's (1971), would suggest that there is something lacking in Jan's play, perhaps even in his capacity to play.

It may seem callous to discuss a drama full of violence and tragedy in relation to jokes or games. But there is something to be learned in this comparison. First, it reminds us that Jan's actions express impulses and perhaps fantasies that may belong to the periods of life in which playing is of the greatest import: infancy and childhood. Second, Jan does not play *well*, not only because the consequences of his playing are disastrous, but because he is unable to enact or realize his play in the space between his subjective imagination and his objective interactions with his mother and sister. This makes his playing frustrating and agonizing, to him and to Maria, who strenuously objects to his ruse on precisely these grounds, insisting that "there's something … something morbid about the way you're doing this" (Camus 1958, 83).

Contrary to the two 'moral' conclusions cited above, the real tragedy of *Le Malentendu* derives from Jan's unconscious desire to re-experience his family's misrecognition and neglect, a traumatic experience he suffered years ago, which he re-lives by undertaking an elaborate deception. An important clue about the unconscious motivations of Jan's actions comes when he describes his ruse as the inevitable result of his "dreams," by which he seems to mean both dreams experienced in sleep and hopes of a happy reunion with his family, upon which depends his ability to "find his true place in the world" (1958, 87). Jan's dedication to his unlikely 'dream' of resolving twenty years of estrangement and psychological suffering by orchestrating a surprise announcement of himself remains strong even as he begins to realize the potentially devastating outcomes of his actions. This inflexible pursuit of his 'dream,' in spite of his family's clear inability to respond in the way he had hoped, also tells us something about Jan's unconscious motivations and, therefore, about one of the subtler *malentendus* in the play.

Recognition, relation, and identification

What really compels Jan to play this trick on his family? Why does he not heed his wife's advice to announce himself immediately? Maria over-simplifies things but is not entirely wrong in suggesting that, "on such occasions one says, 'It's I,' and then it's all plain sailing." It is "common sense," she argues, that "if one wants to be recognized, one starts by telling one's name. ... Otherwise, by pretending to be what one is not, one simply muddles everything" (Camus 1958, 83). It would seem sensible for Jan to introduce himself, as Maria instructs him, to say: "I'm your son. This is my wife. I've been living with her in a country we both love, a land of endless sunshine beside the sea. But something was lacking there to complete my happiness, and now I feel I need you" (84).

But, of course, for Jan, and for Camus, and likely for many others, relating to one's family is not "so simple as all that" (1958, 84). Jan's first line of defense against the idea of openly communicating is to suggest that he has played no part in the deception. When he is "given a glass of beer, against payment," "received ... without a word," and "looked at, but ... [not] *seen*" (82–83, emphasis in original), he claims to be stunned, deciding only at that moment to remain silent and "let things take their course." Maria correctly objects, however, that there is no 'thing' to take its course, that, instead, the 'thing' to which Jan refers is actually "another of those ideas of yours." To this comment Jan retorts: "It wasn't an idea of mine, Maria; it was the force of things" (83).

Jan's denial of his part in fabricating the deception, a denial of his own free will, suggests that he is once again silenced by his family's treatment of him, that he finds himself paralyzed, perhaps re-experiencing the moment when his mother sent him off so coldly twenty years before. "My mother didn't come to kiss me," Jan recalls, tellingly. "At the time I thought I didn't care" (Camus 1958, 82). This withholding of affection, this non-existent farewell by Jan's mother, involves the rejection of him at a precarious moment of separation, at the very moment when he literally separated himself from his family.

Jan's mother's rejection of him at this moment expresses her rejection of him as a separate self, her refusal or inability to relate with him as someone other than a member of the family. This event, and what it likely reflects about a pattern of behavior in Jan's family, appear to have been to some degree traumatic for Jan, not only because of their lasting effects on his emotional life and his inability to be happy, but in the 'latency' or delay (*nachträglichkeit*) of their impacts: "At the time I thought I didn't care."

Jan does not *feel* that he has a choice. His deception appears as necessary to him, but he must assign responsibility for his choices to forces outside of himself. Imagining one's choices to be necessary consequences of forces outside of the self is one way of misunderstanding oneself, of remaining unaware of one's true intentions, and of pursuing aims about which one must remain unconscious. It is also common in repetitive and ritualized behavior, particularly that associated with the compulsive element in traumatic repetition: the feeling that one is not in control, that one is 'forced' to re-visit a traumatic scene either literally, in dreams, or in obsessive behaviors that express or reflect traumatic material. An absence of will and choice is also, as we have seen, an important component of several ideologies of experience: Experience leads us where it will, Emerson might say, while we are only along for the ride, hoping to find a passing good somewhere "on the highway."

While little is offered by Camus on the subject of Jan's childhood, conversations between his mother and Martha suggest that in his family – as was likely the case in Camus' own family – one is either 'in' or 'out.' Even when 'in,' of course, one is not recognized as a unique or separate being but merely as a family member. Incredibly, Jan's mother fully admits as much, saying she "might have forgotten her daughter [Martha], too," if Martha hadn't "kept beside me all these years ... probably that's why I know she is my daughter" (Camus 1958, 95). Martha is only known by her mother, only recognized, because she is literally beside her mother. She is only known and recognized as a mother's daughter, not as an individual, and certainly not as a self.

The mother's rejection of Jan at the moment of his physical departure therefore seems to reflect a dilemma of relating that pre-dated it, a dilemma in which relatedness with family members across difference or distance was impossible. Faced with such a dilemma, Jan would have had to choose between being absolutely exiled and, in some sense, 'dead' to his family, and being permanently "beside" his family only to receive acknowledgment as a family member. In other words, in such a family as Jan's, there is *no* relatedness. Instead, there is a schizoid *either/or*, whereby one either exists in an immersive co-presence with the family, or, if one attempts separation in any of its forms, one does not exist at all. Once Jan decides to leave his family, he ceases to exist. Thus, for his mother, there was, in some sense, no one there to kiss farewell.

Children raised in conditions similar to these are forced to make a terrible choice at a young age: to identify with a parent's or the family's needs and to serve those needs as a family member, or to face emotional exile by heeding the child's need to explore and discover something authentic and unique within himself (see, e.g., Miller 1997; Winnicott 1965). Of course, since the child is both physically and emotionally dependent upon the parent and the family, the choice is really no choice at all, as such children must almost instinctively learn to repress not only their needs but their awareness of them, for any outbursts of emotion reflective of their discomfort – for instance, rage at those who demand self-negation, or grief at the loss of self-expression – would only provoke retaliation from the family in the form of further neglect, deprivation, or abandonment.

These dynamics are readily apparent throughout the play, particularly when Jan speaks about his sense of "duty" toward his family (Camus 1958, 84–85), a rather mysterious duty, presumably neglected for twenty years, by which he must now make a conscious effort to procure the family's "happ[iness]" (84), while at the same time refusing to announce his true identity, and while misrecognizing and repressing his own needs in relation to his family. "I don't need them," he insists, "but I realized they may need me" (84).

Jan does admit a desire to "find his true place in the world" (Camus 1958, 87), and the play asks us to imagine that he strives to establish this place by returning to his family and "making happy those I love. ... I don't look any farther" (87). But, of course, Jan's act of concealing his identity succeeds neither in making his family happy nor in bringing him closer to finding his "true place." The "true place" Jan seeks is really a regressive *experience*, an experience meant to substitute for a genuine "place" for himself amidst his family, which he knows to be impossible. This regressive experience Jan seeks is, in many ways, the opposite of finding a "place," for he unconsciously desires not to be recognized but to be misrecognized, not to be welcomed but to be rebuffed, not to find joy and reunion but to re-encounter his rage and grief at his unfeeling expulsion from the family.

To understand these claims, we must recall that although Jan has clearly designed his charade in advance, telling Maria that her unexpected presence at the hotel "will upset all [his] plans" (Camus 1958, 82), when he enters the inn, he says that he "expected a welcome like the prodigal son's" (83). Why, we may wonder, would Jan consider playing his trick if he sincerely expected such a joyous reception? Since this is not the sole reference to the story of the prodigal son in the Book of Luke – later, Jan raises the cup of poisoned tea to his lips and calls it "the feast of the returning prodigal" (109) – and since that story is, itself, full of ambivalence, misrecognition, and resentment between members of a family, it is worth a moment to analyze this reference.[2]

In Luke, the prodigal son, having wasted his inheritance "with riotous living," now in fear of starvation, returns to his father, saying: "I have sinned against heaven, and in thy sight, and am no more worthy to be called thy son" (15:21, AV). The ashamed son plans to offer himself as a servant to his father's household, as he feels assured that he no longer deserves recognition even as a member of the family (15:19, AV). But the prodigal son's father rejoices that "this my son was dead, and is alive again" (15:24, AV), giving him fine robes and preparing a lavish feast in his honor. Such treatment arouses jealous rage in the elder brother, who complains that, while he has toiled and served beside his father his whole life, he has never been given such gifts nor inspired comparable joy in his father. In reply, the father attempts to reassure the elder son of his indelible membership in the family: "Son, thou art ever with me, and all that I have is thine" (15:31, AV).

Jan's reference to this story and his self-identification as the prodigal son, then, suggest several things about his feelings and intentions regarding his family. Although he has not wasted his family's fortune on debauchery, he feels ashamed. He is likely aware of the possibility of a negative or unsatisfying reception. He may fear, in particular, the reaction of his sister Martha, who has remained by her mother's side and, in so doing, has not enjoyed the same freedom, travel, romance, or fortune as he has. He may feel or anticipate guilt at the contrast between his seemingly separate existence and his sister's lifelong enmeshment with their mother and their home. Jan's mother's treatment of Martha is similar to that of the father toward the elder son in the story of the prodigal: The father's reply to the elder son does not directly address the elder's son's complaint that he has never been 'recognized' as special or worth celebrating. Instead, the father offers an erasure of boundaries between the son, the father, and all that belongs to the family: The elder son's unique self is still overlooked, while, in returning from 'the dead,' the prodigal son seems to have found a form of loving recognition.

Like the prodigal son, Jan fears announcing himself and incurring the rejection of his family because he has at least partly internalized his family's insistence that his separateness is tantamount to his being "dead." While the prodigal son in Luke feared his own literal death by starvation, if Jan has internalized the equation of separateness with death, then Jan may feel psychically "dead" while separated from his family. Unlike the prodigal son however, Jan cannot bring himself to announce that he has returned. He cannot make himself "alive again."

Jan says he expected a welcome like the prodigal son's, but his ruse assures that he will receive exactly what the prodigal son feared: an experience of indifference from the family and treatment as an outsider. Indeed, after Jan's mother admits she "might have forgotten her daughter" had she left her side, she adds, "if a son came here, he'd find exactly what an ordinary guest can count on: amiable indifference, no more and no less" (1958, 96). Just as the prodigal son imagines that he may be forced to take on the identity of a servant to the family, rather than being a member of the family, Jan assumes a second identity when he pretends to be a mere lodger. Both a servant and a lodger can be expected to elicit, if not indifference, something far less than familial intimacy. As in the prodigal son's offer to make himself a servant in penance for his sins, Jan seems to heap emotional punishment upon himself by pretending to be a mere stranger.

According to Jan, his desire to return home is derived from the fact that, in his separation from the family, he and his family have been lost or dead to each other. He desires to revive his connection, however, with a family that offers only self-occluding family membership or nothing. While he pretends to seek recognition from and a mature relationship with his family, he must be at least partly aware that his family is incapable of recognizing and relating with him as a separate self. Thus, if he does seek to revive a relationship with his family, it can only be one based on immediate presence, family membership, and de-subjectified reunion. In this light, it is a matter of some importance that Maria offers him a more profound and more complete loving recognition of his self. "I've always loved everything about you, even what I didn't understand, and I know that really I wouldn't wish you to be other than who you are" (1958, 85). Tragically, Jan forsakes this apparently mature, loving relationship to re-enact a drama of silence, loss, and death with his family.

Rage and reunion

Jan tells Maria that one of his aims in concealing his identity is to "take this opportunity of seeing [his mother and sister] from the outside" (Camus 1958, 83), to become informed about how to make his family happy. But it is not clear why Jan should expect his family to be more revealing or honest when standing before a stranger than before a son. Furthermore, to see others "from the outside" by making them naïve about one's identity risks exposing them to embarrassment, registered by a hidden 'eye' (a hidden 'I') of which they are unaware.

Jan's aim to hide, then reveal, his identity is a type of deception that manipulates the emotions of his family, and perhaps his own emotions as well. Jan has made the family naïve about an important piece of information. To make someone naïve, as in practical jokes, may lead the naïve person to speak or act in a way that is inappropriate, humiliating, or shocking to those privy to the withheld information. The 'practical joke,' as it were, is 'on' the naïve person because she is not 'in' on the joke. The victim of such a joke is 'unmasked' when she who once loomed large is revealed to be flawed or ridiculous. As in satire, a portion of the pleasure of joking lies in depicting those who are exalted (*erhaben*) as vulgar or stupid (Freud 1960, 248).

For Freud, in joking, in satire, and in deceptions, we experiment with aggressive impulses, in which we discover a way to inflict suffering upon others without excessive guilt. More specifically, deceptions and jokes of this nature impose upon their victims experiences resembling the helplessness of childhood (Freud 1960, 280–284): The naïve subject of the joke is exposed in a moment of childlike confusion, ignorance, humiliation, or anxiety, particularly when provoked into losing control or unwittingly transgressing social or moral norms. This aggressive impulse to provoke, then witness, helplessness in others likely arises in connection with the instigator's own experiences of helplessness, although such experiences are not always consciously recalled. In this way, such deceptions may actually be attempts to *transmit* painful or traumatic experiences onto others via projective identification, to re-experience them through others, and even to forge renewed connections with others based upon a suffering now shared.

It is important, in the context of *Le Malentendu*, to ask how Jan's family members could be expected to feel after having been seen 'from the outside' treating their own son and brother as a perfect stranger, selling him beer and making up his room. Although Jan's mother is devastated at having taken part in his murder, it is not precisely her killing of Jan that she laments most profoundly. Rather, she is deeply aggrieved by her mistaking of January "When a mother is no longer capable of recognizing her own son," she claims, "it's clear that her role on earth is ended" (Camus 1958, 120). Even had Jan not been murdered, it is certain that his ruse would have succeeded in making his mother's misrecognition of him all too clear. It seems likely, therefore, that Jan's aim is not to happily surprise his family by exposing his identity, but to expose his family's failure to recognize him. Of course, Jan succeeds in exposing this failure, and thereby re-experiences the earlier traumatic instance of this failure, all too well.

Jan's odd yet carefully crafted deception permits him to re-experience something of his original rage and grief while inflicting pain and humiliation upon his family. At the same time, he protects himself from the possibility of further trauma and protects his family from his resentment and anger. He pursues his deception in a way that leaves his family a way out, an absolution from responsibility for this instance of misrecognition, since it is, after all, his deception and not their hateful indifference that misleads them *this* time. His ruse, therefore, partly protects his mother and sister, which expresses an underlying identification with his family, with those who abandoned him, rather than with his self, which felt and which continues to feel abandoned. Indeed, it is fair to say that Jan, rather than being able to make himself "alive again" before his family, has made himself a stranger to them, which suggests that his action may also express his desire to take responsibility for the loss associated with separation.

To summarize, Jan's deception allows him to hold on to his conscious estimations of his feelings and intentions – that he is happy, that he does not 'need' his family, and that he wishes to make his family happy – along with his unrealistic hope for a loving reception by his family. It permits him to safely recall an otherwise dangerous and anxiety-provoking rage and grief while 'muddling' those feelings with the pretenses of his ruse. It permits him to internalize responsibility for his family's rejection of him while protecting his family from the punchline of his joke, as it were. Perhaps most importantly, it succeeds in replaying *the very experience* that he both dreads and needs, the experience that set him apart from his family for twenty years, the experience of standing before his family as a separate person and being unrecognized, unseen, unknown. By repeating this traumatic experience, Jan finds a way to identify with his family and their extreme demand that one either belong or die, that one be in or out. He, therefore, seems to seek not loving recognition for himself, but only a "morbid" repetition of a traumatic experience from his past.

Loss and melancholia

While the repetition of Jan's experience of misrecognition reminds us of the repetition-compulsion suffered by victims of trauma, an equally illuminating analogy for his attempt to hold on to connection with an object, protecting it while raging against it, all while repeating the experience of suffering or loss associated with it, is the experience of melancholia, as defined by Freud and developed by many of his followers.[3]

In his famous essay "Mourning and Melancholia," Freud claims that the normal work of mourning involves reality-testing which helps the individual to see "that the loved object no longer exists, and [to proceed] to demand that all libido should be withdrawn from its attachments to that object" (1957, 244), while melancholia is a "mental constellation of revolt" against loss, a refusal to mourn (248). As opposed to the process of mourning, in melancholia a connection to the lost object is sought in extreme and destructive ways.

The work of mourning consists in accepting the loss of the object – in this case, the loss of Jan's family – and in adjusting to a world where that object, or that object-relationship, is absent. The lost object is unmourned in melancholia because its disappearance and, more importantly, the loss of the quality of feeling in connection with the object are too difficult to bear. In a largely unconscious effort to retain connection with the lost object, the melancholic person identifies with the object's bad aspects and grapples with this badness by punishing the self and the representation of the object in the self forged via identification. Freud famously referred to this process as one in which "the shadow of the object [falls] upon the ego" (1957, 249). By punishing the self and the object-in-self, the melancholic individual finds a certain sadistic pleasure as well as the possibility of communion with the lost object:

> If the love for the object ... takes refuge in narcissistic identification, then the hate comes into operation on this substitutive object, abusing it, debasing it, making it suffer and deriving sadistic satisfaction from its suffering. The self-tormenting in melancholia, which is without a doubt enjoyable, signifies ... a satisfaction of trends of sadism and hate which relate to an object, and which have been turned round upon the subject's own self.
>
> *(Freud 1957, 251)*

While much more could be said about melancholia and its vicissitudes, it is sufficient to note that in melancholia a regressive fusion is established with an object in tandem with the hatred and rage occasioned by the loss. This fusion is powered by the desire to identify with the lost object, rage against the object for the broken relationship, and rage and shame directed at the self for still desiring the object. The melancholic individual prefers this form of fusion – even with all of its torment – to mourning the loss, since mourning implies separation from the object and 'moving on.'

In much postmodern ethical theory, this melancholic preference for fusion has been valorized as a sort of moral revolt against loss. For Jacques Derrida, the impossibility of mourning becomes nothing less than an ethical injunction never to erase the other. Derrida argues that mourning must fail because when it fails, it succeeds in leaving the other intact: It is then "a tender rejection, a movement of renunciation, which leaves the other alone, outside, over there, in his death, outside of us" (Derrida 1989, 35). In her essay on Emmanuel Levinas and Julia Kristeva, Ewa Ziarek draws out the logical conclusion to Derrida's argument by claiming that the melancholic's inability to heal from grief must be recognized as a valiant moral refusal, undertaken with "unusual sobriety," resulting in "a powerful critique of the desire to master alterity through the order of representation" (Ziarek 1993, 73).

But these accounts fundamentally (and tellingly) misunderstand the ideas of mourning and separateness. To refuse to complete mourning, to refuse to represent a lost friend or to reconcile oneself with mere memories of him, is to refuse to let go of the friend. To reject our interiorizations and imaginations of the friend (see Derrida 2001) does not "leave the other alone," but holds on to the friend as a now unthinkable thing-in-itself who, although dead, remains present in life precisely to the extent that we cannot think of him as either alive or dead.

In successful mourning, we would be able to admit that the life of our friend is gone, and that the remaining traces of him *cannot* be preserved 'outside of us,' for even if we keep his ashes in an urn on the mantel, the living person is dead and gone, and all we have left of him is interior: our memories, our thoughts, our dreams, which can never be identical to the actual friend. To mourn loss is to permit the self to separate from the object by recognizing that the lost friend is actually lost and can never return, that even if the self keeps the memory of the friend "alive," the self's imaginations will never be the same as the actual lost friend.

The problem with Derrida's, and others', approach is that, in the exhortation to refuse mourning, we find also a rejection of thinking, knowing, and imaginatively relating to others, as these activities come to be associated with forms of rationalized destruction (Derrida 1989; see also Bowker 2014). This danger is expressed in Emmanuel Levinas's account of the threat we pose to others even in encountering them, as we inevitably subsume them in a system of our own design, "making them play roles in which they no longer recognize themselves" (1969, 21). To prevent ourselves from intellectually colonizing others, Levinas recommends what Fred Alford aptly names "hostage-being" (2002, 29), where the self must be the other's hostage, enthralled to the other's demands without relation or comprehension, in any usual sense.

As discussed in Chapter 1, the Levinasian notion of an ethical other-invasion of self, especially as it has been appropriated by postmodern theorists like Jacques Derrida and Judith Butler, makes ethical being the opposite of the ideal of selfhood. Instead of relating to the other, the other must not only be left "alone," but must be given precedence over the self, such that the self's very existence must be put "into question ... by the presence of the other" (Levinas 1969, 43).

This rejection of thinking, knowing, and imaginatively relating resembles what Bion calls "attacks on linking," by which he means repudiations of the potentially healthy emotional links between selves and objects. Attacks on linking blur the boundaries between self and other because the "link" that is attacked is always a "contact barrier" (Grinberg, Sor, and de Bianchedi 1977, 49), a boundary that both separates and connects. To attack the links between self and other is to attack the boundary that permits both self-integration and relatedness between selves, since, in lieu of a boundary, material must be projected and introjected between disintegrated, unreal, and unknowable objects in an attempt to manage anxiety, desire, rage, fear, and badness. In the end, attacks on linking lead to a kind of disintegration of both self and object, for without separateness or relatedness, there can be neither an 'I' nor a 'you.'

To be sure, the condition in which there is neither an 'I' nor q 'you' has been championed by many of the celebrants of experience, cited in Chapter 1 and throughout this book, as a desirable state of (non-)being, a foundation for a political community without selves and therefore without the capacity for self-ishness or rationalized violence. As such, the valorization of melancholy experience, the refusal to mourn, and the rejection of separateness and relatedness in modern and postmodern thought represent an attack on the separate self. In particular, they represent an attack on the capacity of selves to get out from under the shadow of experience's object.

If these refusals and rejections attack the self by undercutting its capacities for integration, separateness, and relatedness, they also encourage individuals to discover a substitute for selfhood in agonizing fusion with experience's object. Members of a family or group who find their "place" only in proximity and belonging are in some sense united by melancholic experience because thinking, relating, and communicating as separate selves have become impossible.

On this note, it is helpful to conclude by considering a more recent play about deception and communication. In John Guare's *Six Degrees of Separation*, based largely on real events, wealthy Manhattan art dealers Flan and Ouisa Kittredge take in a young conman, Paul, who presents himself as the child of Sidney Poitier and a friend of their children at Harvard. He is invited to stay for dinner and the night and quickly develops affectionate connections with those he meets. Much of the action takes place within private residences, while the Kittredges relate their shocking and perhaps even traumatizing experience at parties and social gatherings. The relation between public communication and the intimate, although deeply distressing, experience of Paul is at the very heart of the drama. Indeed, in what may be the most important moment of the play, Ouisa blusters that they are turning their experience with Paul:

> into an anecdote to dine out on. Or dine in on. But it was an experience. I will not turn him into an anecdote. How do we fit what happened to us in life without turning it into an anecdote with no teeth and a punch line you'll mouth over and over years to come. "Tell the story about the imposter who came into our lives −" "That reminds me of the time this boy −." And we become these human juke boxes spilling out these anecdotes. But it was an experience. How do we keep the experience?
>
> *(Guare 1990, 115)*

Here, Ouisa is protesting relating their story about Paul, arguing that in communicating her traumatic experience she will lose it, that in making it known, recognized, or recognizable to herself or to others, she will no longer possess it.

Ouisa also fears that by turning Paul, whom Ouisa has come to love, into an anecdote, endlessly and perhaps compulsively repeated, she and her husband are losing their humanity, that they have become mere "human juke boxes."

Ouisa seems to feel that she must "fit what has happened to [her] in life" the way one fits into a suit or cocktail dress. That is, even if the experience does not suit her, she must fit into it. Would simply not communicating about Paul allow Ouisa to "fit" her experience, to "keep the experience" intact and, so, to keep him intact? Why must she continue to be connected with her agonizing yet enthralling experience of him?

Ouisa's fear of transforming her experience and the object of her experience, Paul, and his intimate violation of her trust and her family, into an anecdote with no "teeth," just a "punch line," suggests that, for her, the telling of anecdotes diffuses a deep, inner, perhaps even secret or "incommunicado" experience stored somewhere between her self and the outside world. She hates the notion of turning her experience into something she and others can "dine out on," preferring, instead to keep this experience to herself, perhaps somewhere in her body, in that unknowable area referred to in Chapter 3, neither inside or out. This holding on to traumatic experience permits her to remain connected to her experience and to the individual who tormented her, but it alienates her from her family and friends, and, very likely, from herself, in that it will be difficult for her to be herself in light of this experience, to act and relate with others in ways that are not disrupted by frequent feelings of unreality, confusion, or despair.

Winnicott's idea, discussed in the previous chapter, of an "incommunicado element" of self, which must be protected from the world of objects lest it be adjusted or altered (1965, 187), seems to come into play in the case of both the repetition of traumatic experience, as in the case of Jan, and its hiding, a subject to be explored in greater detail in Chapter 7, on the experience of *hikikomori*. If Jan's experience shattered the integrity of his separate self, and if the Kittredges' experience with Paul broke through the "barrier" or "protective shield" (Caruth 1996, 61) surrounding their home and their private lives, then it would seem that traumatic experience sets itself up both inside and outside the self, as an object around which both Jan's and Ouisa's lives now revolve.

This is but another way of stating what has been set forth in Chapter 3 as the hypothesis that trauma may be less about the *après-coup* effects of shock or incursion than about the adoption of experience's objects as a seemingly essential yet ultimately unsatisfactory element of identity. As discussed earlier, if traumatic experience cannot be held or contained within the self, but must be introjected and pro- jected *ad nauseam*, then attempts to 'possess' such experience as part of the self's identity can only mean repeating and returning to experience, over and over again. Thus, seeking to derive feelings of reality not from an authentic "little fragment of living substance" (Freud 1920, 27), nor from a "secret self" protected from the world, but from the repetition of traumatic experience and melancholy reunion with experience's objects, leads to a dilemma from which there is no easy escape.

Notes

1 Freud considers play to be "the first stage of jokes" (1960, 156–157), and jokes to be forms of "developed play" (222), because jokes and jests pursue aims discovered first in play that nevertheless rely on sophisticated psychological mechanisms in order to find expression.
2 As Jan drinks his poisoned tea at his "feast of the returning prodigal," he says: "The least I can do is to do it honor," he says, "and so I shall have played my part until I leave this place" (Camus 1958, 109).
3 The relationship between trauma and melancholia is substantial and complex. If one examines the underlying fantasies and dynamics of traumatic repetition, one finds many meaningful similarities (see, e.g., Caruth 1996; Freud 1957, 1961; Rauch 1998).

References

Alford, C.F. 2002. *Levinas, the Frankfurt School, and Psychoanalysis*. Middletown, CT: Wesleyan University Press.

Bowker, M.H. 2014. *Rethinking the Politics of Absurdity: Albert Camus, Postmodernity, and the Survival of Innocence*. Series: Routledge Innovations in Political Theory. New York: Routledge.

Brée, G. 1964. *Camus*. Revised First Harbinger Books Edition. New Brunswick, NJ: Rutgers University Press.

Camus, A. 1955. *The Myth of Sisyphus and Other Essays*. First Vintage International Edition. Translated by J. O'Brien. New York: Vintage.

Camus, A. 1958. "The Misunderstanding." In *Caligula and Three Other Plays*. Translated by S. Gilbert, 75–134. New York: Vintage.

Camus, A. 1988. *The Stranger*. First Vintage International Edition. Translated by M. Ward. New York: Vintage.

Caruth, C. 1996. *Unclaimed Experience: Trauma, Narrative, and History*. Baltimore, MD: Johns Hopkins University Press.

Derrida, J. 1989. *Memoires for Paul de Man: The Wellek Library Lectures at the University of California, Irvine*. New York: Columbia University Press.

Derrida, J. 2001. *The Work of Mourning: Jacques Derrida*, edited by P. Breault and M. Naas. Chicago, IL: University of Chicago Press.

Freud, S. 1920. "Beyond the Pleasure Principle." In *The Standard Edition of the Complete Psychological Works of Sigmund Freud, Volume XVIII*, edited and translated by J. Strachey, 7–64. London: Hogarth.

Freud, S. 1957. "Mourning and Melancholia." In *The Standard Edition of the Complete Psychological Works of Sigmund Freud, Volume XIV*, edited and translated by J. Strachey, 243–258. London: Hogarth.

Freud, S. 1960. *Jokes and Their Relation to the Unconscious*. Translated by J. Strachey. New York: W.W. Norton.

Freud, S. 1961. *Civilization and Its Discontents*. Translated by J. Strachey. New York: W.W. Norton.

Grinberg, L., D. Sor, and E. de Bianchedi 1977. *Introduction to the Work of Bion: Groups, Knowledge, Psychosis, Thought, Transformations, Psychoanalytic Practice*. Translated by A. Hahn. New York: Jason Aronson.

Guare, J. 1990. *Six Degrees of Separation*. New York: Vintage.

Levinas, E. 1969. *Totality and Infinity: An Essay on Exteriority.* Translated by A. Lingis. Pittsburgh, PA: Duquesne University Press.

Matherne, B. 1971. "Hope in Camus' 'The Misunderstanding'." *Western Speech* (Spring): 74–87.

Miller, A. 1997. *The Drama of the Gifted Child: The Search for the True Self.* Revised Edition. Translated by R. Ward. New York: Basic Books.

Rauch, A. 1998. "Post-Traumatic Hermeneutics: Melancholia in the Wake of Trauma." *Diacritics* 28(4): 111–120.

Sartre, J.-P. 1973. "*Forger des Mythes.*" In *Un Théâtre de Situations*, edited by M. Contat and M. Rybalka, 55–67. Paris: Gallimard.

Todd, O. 2000. *Albert Camus: A Life.* Translated by B. Ivry. New York: Carroll and Graf.

Willhoite, F. 1968. *Beyond Nihilism: Albert Camus's Contribution to Political Thought.* Baton Rouge, LA: Louisiana State University Press.

Winnicott, D.W. 1965. *The Maturational Processes and the Facilitating Environment: Studies in the Theory of Emotional Development*, edited by M. Khan. London: Hogarth and the Institute of Psycho-Analysis.

Winnicott, D.W. 1971. *Playing and Reality.* London: Routledge.

Ziarek, E. 1993. "Kristeva and Levinas: Mourning, Ethics, and the Feminine." In *Ethics, Politics, and Difference in Julia Kristeva's Writing*, edited by K. Oliver, 62–78. New York: Routledge.

5

EXPERIENCE AND CONTROL IN HIGHER EDUCATION

Today, two contradictory discourses reign in American higher education. The first is the *pedagogical discourse of experience*, by which, for approximately the past four decades, experience has become a principal – if not *the* principal – value guiding the development of teaching methods and pedagogical aims. Best represented by the renewed interest in the work of early twentieth-century American philosopher John Dewey, the pedagogical discourse of experience recommends the application of experiential, collaborative, and problem-solving orientations and methods to virtually all academic disciplines.

There is "no such thing as educational value in the abstract," writes Dewey (1997, 46), stating what must have seemed to him to be a self-evident truth. Having "taken for granted the soundness of the principle that education in order to accomplish its ends both for the individual learner and for society must be based upon experience" (89), what matters, for Dewey, is that students participate in a "process of social intelligence" (72). That is, the processes and outcomes of learning are both experiential and social in character. Indeed, the difference between experience and sociality is intentionally blurred in Dewey's account, as will be discussed below. The Deweyan educator creates socially controlling learning experiences that produce students who will contribute to the betterment of society, which means the betterment of social experiences.

The second is the *discourse of student narcissism*, in some sense an age-old discourse involving the disparagement of the young, but, in this case, a definable new trend in which the vaguely defined generations known as 'millennials,' 'post-millennials,' 'Generation Z,' and, as Jean Twenge calls them, "Generation Me" are characterized as uniquely and dangerously "narcissistic" (Twenge 2006; Twenge and Campbell 2009; see also Bowker 2012; 2015). Unfortunately, most of those who wield accusations of narcissism lack understanding of the concept or its origins, mistaking "narcissism" for excessive self-love, usually thought to be derived from the indulgence of parents, overly tolerant educational cultures, or lax moral standards.

Related diagnoses of American youth as lacking "grit" or toughness have also become increasingly fashionable (see Duckworth et al. 2007). Peter Gray (2015) of Boston College argues that "young people, eighteen years and older, [are] going to college still unable or unwilling to take responsibility for themselves, still feeling that if a problem arises they need an adult to solve it." Citing Dan Jones, past president of the Association for University and College Counseling Center Directors, Gray agrees that students today "don't seem to have as much grit as previous generations."

Calls for increased stouteheartedness and accusations of childishness and narcissism now work together to establish a narrative about education that suggests that 'tough love' and exposure to the realities of experience are needed to prepare young people for the adult world, which is characterized as a world of labor, self-denial, and sacrifice.

These discourses are problematic, contradictory, and at odds with other related trends in higher education. Consider how, even as educators lament the rising egocentrism of students, the ideal of 'student-centeredness' is simultaneously embraced to justify an ever-increasing bevy of personalized services and amenities available on college campuses, including, but not limited to: state-of-the-art dining and athletic facilities; 24-hour Technical Support hotlines; four-year 'graduation guarantees'; personalized 'skills teams' comprising academic, financial, and psychological staff; and myriad opportunities for 'engagement' activities that involve the student in campus and community life. Today's student is encouraged to believe that most, if not all, of her needs, desires, and goals, even those having little to do with formal education, can be met in connection with her learning institution.

So, on one hand, students' expectations of 'narcissistic' gratification are stoked by promises of an immensely stimulating, entertaining, and accommodating college experience. At the same time, the hostile attribution of student 'narcissism' is deployed to justify efforts to break students out of their intellectual 'comfort zones' and to expose them to the tough realities of life in the community, which is the life they will face after college. It has become all but routine for educators in the United States to be entreated – in campus addresses, teaching workshops, 'webinars,' or institutional initiatives – to liberate students from their 'narcissistic' self-orientations, which are thought to be correlated with low levels of "intrinsic motivation" (Deci and Ryan 1985), by connecting learning experiences inside the classroom to experiences outside the classroom, in 'the real world.' These 'real world' experiences are imagined to motivate and prepare students for the type of social labor that awaits them upon graduation (see, e.g., Curtis 2001; and Kolb and Kolb 2009).

Means of connecting so-called 'real world' experiences to college courses have been developed far beyond yesterday's 'field trip.' Today, some students spend a majority of time in a course engaged in a community-service project, while other students find that the 'real world' has overtaken their very classrooms, which are no longer simple assemblages of desks and chairs but are 'interactive learning spaces' and 'collaboratoria,' outfitted with the latest in 'interactive technologies' and designed, often at great expense, to maximize student stimulation and technology-assisted interaction.

Although these trends are familiar to educators and scholars of teaching and learning, in his recent *Atlantic* article, Michael Godsey relates a few truly memorable examples of how "classroom environments that embrace ... dynamic and social learning activities are being promoted now more than ever," to the detriment of students, some of whom are "easily drained by constant interactions with others." For instance, the University of Chicago library announced recently that "in response to 'increased demand,' librarians are working with architects to transform a presumably quiet reading room into a 'vibrant laboratory of interactive learning'" (2015).

Similarly, Dartmouth's Institute for Writing and Rhetoric has challenged its students to "forego passivity in favor of contribution and participation," apparently because, unbeknownst to many writers, writing is "a communal act," not a "private isolated one." Indeed, the site explains, "students must overcome isolation in order to learn to write" (Dartmouth College 2015). Worse, Georgia College's official statement on collaborative learning informs students: "Together is how we do everything here at Georgia College. Learn. Work. Play. Live. Together. ... It's a fact. We're all in this together" (2015). Perhaps Godsey is not wrong to compare this statement to Sartre's famous line from *Huis Clos* (*No Exit*): "*L'enfer, c'est les autres*" (Hell is other people) (1989).

If experience-based approaches are designed in part to enhance students' 'intrinsic motivation' to learn, then it becomes either an ironic or misguided use of the adjective 'intrinsic' when students' motivational levels become the objects of extensive manipulation by educators and administrators. Indeed, too few eyebrows were raised when Dan Berrett, unwittingly echoing Noam Chomsky, titled his popular article in the *Chronicle of Higher Education*: "Can Colleges Manufacture Motivation?" (2012).

As if the confusion over who is motivating whom were not enough, experience-based learning efforts stand in uncomfortable relation to the increasing emphasis on the socio-economic instrumentality of academic work. It is neither "educational value in the abstract" nor learning for its own sake that is advertised in campus brochures, nor underscored in campaign rhetoric about the value of education. Rather, education is now conceived almost exclusively in terms of its economic benefits to the student and to the community.

To take but one example, the educational and political prioritization of what are known as STEM disciplines – disciplines related to Science, Technology, Engineering, and Mathematics – has been clearly embraced by the US government and, subsequently, by both public and private learning institutions. As Gonzalez and Kuenzi outline in their Congressional Research Report, efforts to promote STEM have been officially justified by:

the relationship between STEM education and national prosperity and power. ... [T]oday the economic and social benefits of scientific thinking and STEM education are widely believed to have broad application for workers in both STEM and non-STEM occupations. As such, many contemporary policymakers consider widespread STEM literacy, as well as specific STEM expertise, to be critical human capital competencies for a 21st century economy.

(2012, 1)

One way to understand how these contradictory discourses and practices could all stand side by side is to recognize the financial interests that unite them. The costs of new services and amenities are justified by their relationship to increased enrollment and retention of students: More students apply, more pay tuition, and more are kept satisfied and in good academic standing. Affording students opportunities to forge 'lifelong' identifications with learning institutions also fosters alumni involvement and monetary donations after graduation. Community activities and partnerships may be understood as highly marketable semi-public 'events' that serve publicity functions for learning institutions, functions integral to developing corporate sponsorships and affiliations with community institutions, not to mention both private and public grants available to institutions that can demonstrate their 'social impact.'

But it would be foolish to presume that changes in higher education in recent years have had only financial motives at their root. There are 'true believers' among university executives, administrators, and faculty who, over time, have inaugurated an ideological transformation that transcends financial strategy. In this chapter, I argue that these two discourses, together with their contradictions, may be understood only if we regard the focus on shaping the student's experience as an effort not to liberate the student from his 'narcissism,' nor to afford him opportunities for intellectual growth. Rather, experience-based education represents an effort to correct the putatively self-satisfied subjectivity of the student by coercing him to replace the discovery and pursuit of his authentic needs with activities that promote enmeshment with the educator's, the institution's, and the community's needs.

To put it in a stark light: Many experience-based pedagogies and methodologies aim to destroy the student's self. This aim is motivated partly by hatred and envy, but, most importantly, by a narcissistic dilemma faced not by students but by *educators* in the increasingly deprived and depriving environment higher education has become. This dilemma, one in which academics and academic work are deemed valueless unless they have 'social impact,' has not been resisted by educators, but, surprisingly, has been embraced, perhaps in an attempt to salvage careers, political identities, or modicums of self-respect. Unfortunately, the consequent need to connect academic work to social experience and social impact, in the classroom and out, ends by persuading students to participate in projects and pursuits whose aims and ends are not their own.

Experience: continuous and interactive

In his 1938 *Experience and Education*, among his latest works, John Dewey presents two related principles of experience: (1) *continuity*: that all experiences shape future experiences both by shaping the self that experiences and by changing the world and its objects; and (2) *interaction*: that experience is a bi-directional interplay of objective and internal conditions, a kind of interpenetration of individual and world, one that can and must be managed by those with the benefit of greater experience, such as parents and educators (1997).

Dewey maintains that experiences are naturally continuous, and that the individual who fails to manage experiences so as to preserve their continuity is to blame:

> Different situations succeed one another. But because of the principle of continuity something is carried over from the earlier to the later ones. ... The process goes on as long as life and learning continue. Otherwise the course of experience is disorderly, since the individual factor that enters into making an experience is split. A divided world, a world whose parts and aspects do not hang together, is at once a sign and a cause of a divided personality. When the splitting-up reaches a certain point we call the person insane. A fully integrated personality, on the other hand, exists only when successive experiences are integrated with one another.
>
> *(1997, 44)*

Dewey's defense of continuity puts the onus on the experiencing individual – and, by extension, on the intermediaries of experience, such as educators – to integrate experience as a continuity. It is "the *individual factor* that enters into making an experience" that is responsible for making "the course of experience" either orderly or disorderly, and the person either sane or insane.

Since Dewey also contends that experience is naturally and essentially interactive, that it consists of an inter-connection between internal psychic factors and external objects of experience, then, in order for experience to be continuous, interactive experiencing relationships must be consistent. That experience is "interactive" means, for Dewey, that experience has the power to shape and configure the individual's inner world, principally to determine the individual's desires and values. "Every experience is a moving force," writes Dewey. "Its value can be judged only on the ground of what it moves toward and into" (1997, 38).

The learning experience, if it is successful, should generate in the student a desire for repeated experiences, based largely on the pleasure of controlling, or believing she is controlling, both inner experience and experience in the outer world. When Dewey writes that "the most important thing is to keep student's desire for learning intensified," and that "attentive care must be devoted to the conditions which give each present experience a worthwhile meaning" (1997, 48–49), he specifically rejects the notion that educators should entice students to learn with pleasurable or immediately gratifying learning experiences. Instead, he asserts that the educator's responsibility is to understand the particular "needs and capacities of the individuals who are learning at a given time" (46), and to institute "conditions for the kind of present experience which has a favorable effect upon the future" (1997, 50). That is, the educator arranges experiences such that the student is led down a path of 'discovery,' where the discoveries have actually been pre-arranged to suit the specific needs of each student and pre-assessed so as to have maximally enticing effects upon her.[1]

Since, for Dewey, "all human experience is ultimately social" (1997, 38), the educator must govern educative experiences such that the interactive elements in learning experiences contribute to the continuous growth of a social attitude, an attitude that looks favorably upon future similar educative experiences. The student's experiences must generate in him an unquestioned sociality, a paradigmatic orientation toward social objects and toward the useful and productive interactions he may have with them.

Continuity and interaction, then, are not merely descriptive qualities of experience, but are prescriptions and objectives that determine experience's value. Since "continuity and interaction in their active union with each other provide the measure of the educative significance and value of an experience," these become the "immediate and direct concern of an educator," who must regulate all objective conditions and each learning experience, including:

> not only words spoken but the tone of voice in which they are spoken … equipment, books, apparatus, toys, games played … materials with which an individual interacts, and, most important of all, *the total social set-up* of the situations in which a person is engaged.
>
> *(1997, 44–45, emphasis added)*

The conclusion Dewey draws from the intersection of his two principles is that great attention must be devoted not only to the external, objective conditions of experience, but to the internal states of students, such that their internal experiences are also well regulated, educative, and orderly. How the educator may consistently transform the interior world of the student, then, is the primary question of Dewey's text.

"The ideal aim of education," Dewey writes, "is creation of power of self-control. But the mere removal of external control is no guarantee for the production of self-control" (1997, 64). On the contrary, technologies of "social control" must be improved, made more subtle, even made invisible, so that "self-control" may be instilled without the student ever feeling as if she has been controlled. Needless to say, the solution Dewey proposes to generate this quantity and quality of control over the student is "experience" (51–60).

Technologies of self/social control

"The ordinary good citizen," explains Dewey, "is as a matter of fact subject to a great deal of social control," although this control is not "felt to involve a restriction of personal freedom" (1997, 52). Why is this?, Dewey wonders, and how can this situation be duplicated with young people in the educational environment?

While appearing to liberate students from restrictive, traditional educational methods, the aim of Deweyan education is the unthought acceptance of the controlling effects of experience upon the student's activities and intentions. The educative ideal at which Dewey aims is, in several ways, identical to what Michel Foucault famously critiques as technologies of self-discipline and self-government (1975, 1980), in which individuals internalize frameworks and agents of control, unwittingly recapitulating political power upon and through their thoughts, language, and behavior.

To "guarantee the production of self-control" in the student, Dewey recommends a course of experiential interactions between the student and the social environment, carefully designed by the educator, such that the student comes to believe that she is being guided along by the 'natural' force of her own experience.[2] When there is a "weakness in control" within the student, it arises:

> from failure to arrange in advance for the kind of work (by which I mean all kinds of activities engaged in) which will create situations that of themselves tend to exercise control over what this, that, and the other pupil does and how he does it. This failure most often goes back to lack of sufficiently thoughtful planning in advance.
>
> *(Dewey 1997, 57)*

Dewey sets out three related means of achieving this end: the creation of an illusion of freedom in the student; the diffusion of the locus of control across the social group; and the generation of experiences of fusion that lead to indelible attitudinal shifts.

The illusion of freedom

As discussed above, the "interactive" nature of experience means, for Dewey, that educators must consider not only objective conditions but also internal ones, for the problem with the "traditional education" against which he rails is "not that it emphasized the external conditions that enter into the control of the experiences but that it paid so little attention to the internal factors which also decide what kind of experience is had" (1997, 42). Dewey's call for attention to the "needs and capacities of the individuals who are learning" may seem liberal enough, but the goal of understanding students is *not* to gauge or serve their authentic desires, but to arrange learning encounters that "will function in generating an experience that has educative quality with particular individuals at a particular time" (46).

Indeed, when Dewey recommends that educators heed students' communities – a recommendation that has been used to justify all manner of experience-based, community-based, and service-based learning projects – he does *not* intend this recommendation to mean that students should literally leave their classrooms and learn via community-based experiences. Instead, he urges educators to gather knowledge about students' home lives and communities as tools, granting educators greater access to students' psyches. Better understandings of where students 'come from,' and with what they are familiar, helps the educator ascertain how they will respond to various learning experiences (1997, 39–41). In fact, it would be entirely possible to host a strictly Deweyan 'experiential learning program' wherein students never left the classroom, for Dewey's account of the value of learning about the student's community is as a reconnaissance operation for educators, to gather information that may be used to entice, manipulate, and ultimately mystify the student into believing that he is operating freely in an environment that he has chosen, when, of course, the opposite is the case.

When Dewey asks himself and his readers what ends increased "liberty" in education serves – and he insists quite emphatically that freedom or liberty is only "a *means*, not an end" (1997, 61–62, emphasis in original), he offers three surprising answers. First, a certain degree of freedom afforded to students permits the educator to gain greater knowledge of them. By using the data offered in 'free' divulgences of students' thoughts and feelings and in spontaneous "disclos[ures of] their real natures" (62), the educator may tailor and craft more "educative" experiences. If the educator unwisely restricts students' freedom to such a degree that nothing of their personalities can be known, then "there is only an accidental chance that the material of study and the methods used in instruction will so come home to an individual that his development of mind and character is actually directed" (62).

Second, freedom counteracts passivity and quietude, which represent the most substantial threats to a Deweyan education, since participation- and group-effects are the primary technologies employed to achieve the pedagogical aim of self-control directed toward socially redeeming ends. Passivity and quietude degrade the coercive power of the social situation and threaten to ruin the illusion of total, voluntary, shared participation on which the Deweyan educator relies. To remain apart, alone, or uninvolved now represents not merely an individual withdrawal but an opposition to the scheme of educative control that requires the involvement of the entire learning group. If the freedom of students does not lead to this end, then it "tends to be destructive of the shared cooperative activities which are the normal source of order" (1997, 63).

What is truly fearsome in "the new education" (1997, 18–22) is not a student's excessive freedom or devolution into unpredictable behavior, but agnosticism, separation from the group, aloneness, disinterest, or, worst of all, an "anti-social attitude" (57). When a group's meanings and purposes are held together by shared experience, about which more will be said below, the greatest threat does not arise from those who accept the group as holder of authority, even if they simultaneously behave wildly. The real threat to the learning group is the student who rejects the group experience and seeks to remain distinct from or separate from it. This student shuns the control of the leader, who has diffused her leadership throughout the group structure, the learning situation, and the other group members who have all been coerced so as to internalize her control.

Of course, there are ways of preventing the separation of the student. Paige Wolf (2015), of George Mason University's Business School, recently argued that the primary benefit of their interactive learning program is its incontestable power to break down of the boundaries of the individual student. Everything, from the physical environment to the norms embedded in the culture, means that "students can't hide," she claims. "They feel responsible for participating." In this way, we may not be entirely incorrect to imagine students who might wish to stand apart as those unlucky individuals in Rousseau's social contract who deviate from the general will and so are "forced to be free" (1987, 150).

Third, the student must believe he is "participat[ing]" in "the formation of the purposes which direct his activities ... to secure the active cooperation of the pupil in construction of the purposes involved in his studying" (1997, 67). Of course, the student does not *really* get to participate in defining these purposes any more than he designs the learning experiences, themselves. Dewey never remotely suggests that the student should take part in the creation of either. Rather, he is quite emphatic that the more experienced educator should always determine the aims and designs of all learning encounters (38–40). But the educator must find a way to convince the student that he is freely participating so that the force of the experience can take full effect.

Since Dewey argues that "freedom is ... identical with self-control," being "the power to frame purposes and to execute or carry into effect purposes so framed" (1997, 67), one might think that respect for the student's autonomy would be central to his philosophy. But Dewey here seems to mistake self-control for self-determination, for the capacity to create, think, and act on behalf of authentic aims and purposes. This mistake, I argue here and in the following chapter, derives directly from an over-emphasis on experience, since, according to the logic of experience, higher purposes are always defined by greater experience, such that submitting to experience or its object comes to be mistaken for thinking and acting on behalf of one's potential self (see also Levine 2011).

As "we can be aware of consequences only because of previous experiences," the development of purpose depends, for Dewey, not only on the power of self-control but on the acceptance of the guidance of a more experienced other. And "since freedom resides in the operations of intelligent observation and judgment by which a purpose is developed, guidance given by the teacher to the exercise of the pupil's intelligence is an aid to freedom, not a restriction upon it" (1997, 71).

Mechanical uniformity and rigid external controls are rejected by Dewey *not* because he is interested in facilitating the student's creativity or the pursuit of students' authentic aims. Rather, rigidity and uniformity prevent the educator from divining the idiosyncrasies of each student, and, therefore, from developing stratagems to "direct," shape, and control the mind and character of each student. These differences in emphasis represent important philosophical and psychological differences related to how the student is regarded and treated. Ultimately, Dewey's "freedom … identical with self-control" is reminiscent of the dark side of "positive liberty" or "positive freedom," referred to in Chapter 2 as a common understanding of the meaning of selfhood.

If positive freedom means the fulfillment of the self's aims and goals, many liberals have pointed out, correctly, the risk that this orientation to freedom may be co-opted by more powerful others (Berlin 1969). In such a case, it is not the self that determines its authentic aims and goals but a teacher, leader, or master who defines what the self *should* desire. This risk, of course, does not negate the importance of self-determination in defining both freedom and selfhood. Instead, it reveals that there is a fine and easily obscured line between supporting the freedom and selfhood of students and destroying it.

Dewey is right that:

> there is no intellectual growth without some reconstruction, some remaking, of impulses and desires in the form in which they first show themselves. This remaking involves inhibition of impulse in its first estate. The alternative to externally imposed inhibition is inhibition through an individual's own reflection and judgment.
>
> *(1997, 64)*

But while it is true that managing primitive impulses is an important component in both freedom and self-development, it is also true that organized efforts to restructure students' impulses without their knowledge or consent, and to replace them with experiences aimed at producing qualities of self-control and pragmatic value-orientations, may result in the loss of contact with what is real and authentic in the student. There are more than enough grounds to suspect that a student of Dewey's method would find herself remaking her will not 'freely,' not in accordance with her own higher aims and goals, but, rather, in accordance with the demands of the learning experiences carefully arranged and tailored to induce acceptance of the aims of the educator and learning institution.

Diffusion of the locus of control

Perhaps the most important aspect of Dewey's thought concerning the aim of self-control is, as we have said, that in order to ensure student cooperation and internalization of the educative experience, the student must never experience control as "the manifestation of merely personal will" but as "control … exercised by situation in which all take part" (1997, 54). The ideal is that "control of individual actions is effected by the whole situation in which individuals are involved, in which they share and of which they are co-operative or interacting parts" (53).

Some of the most famous psychological studies, such as Stanley Milgram's obedience experiments (Milgram 1974) and Philip Zimbardo's "Stanford Prison Experiment" (Haney, Banks, and Zimbardo 1973), not to mention historical studies of civilian involvement in the commission of atrocities (see Browning 1998), have demonstrated that the power of the social situation is considerable in shaping individual attitudes and behaviors. Part of the force of the situation resides in the fact that situations can be made to appear given, natural, or inevitable, as if they were not fabricated or constructed by human design. The apparently voluntary participation of members in social situations also contributes to a feeling that certain tasks and limitations are obviously necessary or unquestionable. Dewey argues that the educator must take full advantage of these persuasive qualities of social situations: The "teacher [must] arrange conditions that are conducive to community activity and to organization which exercises control over individual impulses by the mere fact that all are engaged in communal projects." The planning must allow for "individuality of experience" yet be "firm enough to give direction towards continuous development of power" (1997, 58).

The force of the situation derives largely from its shared quality: that it is a situation in which an entire group takes part. The fact of others' participation lends to the activity a sense of legitimacy that is not unrelated to the drive to comply and conform, not to mention the dread of rejection. The Deweyan educator is invited to avail herself not only of the enticements of sociality, but of the threat of isolation, imagined to result from disobedience or withdrawal:

> The primary source of social control resides in the very nature of the work done as a social enterprise in which all individuals have an opportunity to contribute and to which all feel a responsibility. Most children are naturally "sociable." Isolation is even more irksome to them than to adults. ... But community life does not organize itself in an enduring way purely spontaneously. It requires thought and planning ahead. The educator is responsible for a knowledge of individuals and for a knowledge of subject-matter that will enable activity ties to be selected which lend themselves to social organization, an organization in which all individuals have an opportunity to contribute something, and in which the activities in which all participate are the chief carrier of control.
>
> *(1997, 56)*

The problem with traditional schooling was that the school-day did not consist of experiences "held together by participation in common activities" and, consequently, the ideal "conditions of control were lacking." Without this more effective form of control, control had to be exerted by the direct interventions of the teacher as a superior, external will who "as the saying went '*kept* order.' He kept it because order was in the teacher's keeping, instead of residing in the shared work being done" (Dewey 1997, 55, emphasis in original).

Alternatively, when experience guides education, a social group is formed (Dewey 1997, 58). The educator is encouraged to take up a position within this group that disguises his power to make his power appear to be the power of the group. As "the teacher loses the position of external boss or dictator but takes on that of leader of group activities" (59), a significant shift takes place in the learning experience, such that students now face choices involving group participation versus isolation, rather than obedience versus defiance.

Although Dewey pays lip-service to the idea that learning activities should express the student's aims and not the educator's, there is no room in his philosophy for students' authentic purposes to develop or to find expression. Indeed, he seems even to confuse the facilitation of genuinely student-directed learning with the creation of the *illusion* of it, when he argues, for instance, that the educator's:

> suggestion [is] made to develop into a plan and project by means of the further suggestions contributed and organized into a whole by the members of the group. ... The essential point is that the purpose grow and take shape through the process of social intelligence.
>
> *(1997, 71–72)*

"Social intelligence," as it was originally defined by E.L. Thorndike, and likely in the sense in which Dewey used the term while writing in the 1920s and 1930s, meant the "ability to understand and manage other people, and to engage in adaptive social interactions" (Kihlstrom and Cantor 2011, 359). Around the same time, Moss and Hunt defined social intelligence as the "ability to get along with others" and Vernon described it as the:

> ability to get along with people in general, social technique or ease in society, knowledge of social matters, susceptibility to stimuli from other members of a group, as well as insight into the temporary moods or underlying personality traits of strangers.
>
> *(Kihlstrom and Cantor 2011, 359–360)*

Participating in a "process of social intelligence," then, requires not only a high degree of "susceptibility to stimuli from other members of the group," but the ability to cooperate with others in projects that Dewey prefers to describe as games. The language of 'games,' is actually a fruitful one for our purposes, for games may describe not just the games of school-children but the more complex social and symbolic games played by both children and adults.

The "controlling feature" of all games is that the rules are embedded within the game-structure such that they ultimately become identical with the game, and, to a great extent, incontestable:

> The rules are a part of the game. They are not outside of it. ... As long as the game goes on with reasonable smoothness, the players do not feel that they are submitting to external imposition but that they are playing the game. ... Those who take part do not feel that they are bossed around by an individual person or ... subjected to the will of some outside superior person.
>
> *(Dewey 1997, 52–53)*

Just so in learning experiences, where the diffusion of power across the social group may be continually relied upon, since it is "not the will or desire of any one person which establishes order but the moving spirit of the whole group. The control is social, but individuals are parts of a community, not outside of it" (54).

Even in competitive games, there is a fundamental "sharing in a common experience," which is, in fact, inseparable from the common experience of internalizing the rules of the game as if they were something like natural law. Indeed, players of games tend to identify with the rules of the game so profoundly that they become upset not at the arbitrary exigencies and limitations built into the game, but, rather, at the suspicion that someone has violated or exceeded those exigencies and limitations, that is, that someone has broken the rules. Breaking the rules of the game, of course, is akin to breaking the shared experience that is the unspoken bond uniting the group.

Thus, objections to rule-breaking may be understood as objections to the attempted assertion of separate selves or independent wills over and against the shared experience of the group, which is its law. The experience of the group and its law are, of course, not as naturally or freely developed as a student might think, since they are meticulously designed in advance by the educator. It is in moments of game-playing, then, that students may *feel* free and unencumbered but are, in fact, confused about where the game ends and where they begin; confused, in a sense, about the nature of their own experience.

Fusion with experience's objects

Dewey, along with other empiricist-pragmatists of his day, is known for objecting that, when we try to speak about our experience, we end up speaking about ourselves, about our act of experiencing instead of about the object of experience. If we try, for instance, to describe our experience of a chair, we end up describing how we think about the chair, or the color we perceive in the act of seeing the chair. In our intellectual vanity, we erase experience's object: the chair. Of course, there is nothing objectionable about taking our perception of the chair as an 'object' of study for scientific or phenomenological analysis, although this 'object' of inquiry must be recognized as a secondary and reflective object, whereas the natural reality of the chair remains primary (Dewey 1929, 17–19). When we fail to remember the difference between "crude primary experience" and experience of second-order objects like thoughts or perceptions, when "reflection does not return to primary experience, when it fails to come back to earth, its proceedings become obscure, and lose contact with everyday affairs" (Earls 2012, 52–53).

For Dewey, in order for reflection upon experience not to "lose contact" with experience's objects, it must return to a primary experience that is not reflective. Experiencing a chair in this unreflective way means experiencing no separation between the chair and the individual sitting in it. What counts is not the experience of considering sitting in the chair, nor the experience of remarking how comfortable or uncomfortable the chair is, but, rather, the crude experience of it. It is when the human being and the chair are mixed up in an unreflective unity that we may speak of primary or 'ordinary' experience in Deweyan language. In object-relations language, such experience might be called 'undifferentiated,' 'contiguous,' or even 'fused.'

Following William James, Dewey's view of experience is "double-barreled," meaning that "it recognizes in its primary integrity no division between act and material, subject and object, but contains them both in an unanalyzed totality," whereas "'thing' and 'thought'… are single-barreled; they refer to products discriminated by reflection out of primary experience" (1929, 10–11). Dewey means that experience, itself, refers to moments of undifferentiation or fusion, where differences between subject and object, thing and thought, are not perceived. The goal is for both primary and secondary objects to "get the meaning contained in a whole system of related objects," to be "*rendered continuous* with the rest of nature and [to] take on the import of the things they are now *seen to be continuous with*" (1929, 8, emphasis added).

This philosophical contention directly informs Dewey's vision of the power of experience in education, where learning experiences render students "continuous" with the meanings and purposes of the educator and her broader educative paradigm, without the educator ever having to make such things explicit. Since, as we have noted, "the formation of enduring attitudes, of likes and dislikes" (1997, 47–48) – most importantly the attitude of sociality and the "creation of power of self-control" (64) – are the primary goals of education for Dewey, we may say that experience-based learning is not about learning to think, but about learning to return to unthought moments, to internalize seemingly natural experiences and their embedded values as touchstones to which to return throughout life.

Practitioners of experience-based pedagogies would respond to such accusations by referring to the 'reflective' moments Dewey advocated and the 'reflective practices' now associated with many experience-based learning projects (see, e.g. Kolb and Fry 1975). It is held that offering 'reflective periods' after or between experiential encounters provides students with opportunities to take up critical or higher-order judgments about their experiences. In practice, however, these periods often become occasions to strategize better means of managing or controlling the next experience (see Bowker 2012). Reflection on experience fails in part owing to the attractive nature of experiences designed for students, and in part owing to the enticements of unthought, unanalyzed experience. The pragmatic and instrumentalist foundations of experience-led education also reveal themselves here, for it is to the *use* of the object and to the *experience* of future objects that periods of reflection are dedicated much more often than to a paradigmatic critique of the framework of the experience or the situation or community in which it is embedded.

Dewey, himself, writes that "the intimate coordination and even fusion of these [immediately felt] qualities [of experience] with the regularities that form the objects of knowledge … characterize intelligently directed experience" (1929, xvi–xvii). That is, even in moments of 'reflection,' we design our next attempts at "intelligently directed experience" and remain "fus[ed]" with the felt qualities of experience. Reflection upon experience, especially 'guided reflection,' may even become an instrument "to render [experience] more secure … by ability to control the changes that intervene between the beginning and end of a process" (xvi). Intelligently directed experience, such as we aspire to in experience-based learning, may only further serve the end of linking the learner, the educator, the object of experience, and its instrumental functions (xvi).

If experience teaches the learner how to accomplish something, it also instills the value of practical achievement, gives an uncognized weight to the methods and purposes imbricated in the instrumental approach, and distinguishes worthwhile and "genuine aims" from "merely emotional and fantastic ideals" (1929, xvi). Dewey's program, as we have already shown, centers upon the instillment of a social and pragmatic orientation in the student, the adoption of the goals and purposes of the educator as the student's own, and the development of what Dewey calls "the basic characteristic of habit," which "covers the formation of attitudes, attitudes that are emotional and intellectual; it covers our basic sensitivities and ways of meeting and responding to all the conditions which we meet in living" (1997, 35). If experience is to be a driver of education, it is so that students will meet their conditions of living not as "intellectuals," at "the mercy of every passing breeze" (1997, 51, 85), but as experienced re-actors, well habituated to the rules of the governing social games and the techniques needed to gain control of themselves in response to – in reaction to – their environments.

The Ivory Tower and the attribution of narcissism as a technique of control

Against this vision of education stands the image of the Ivory Tower. We might say that, in reinvigorating curricula and 're-branding' themselves as experience-oriented practitioners, American institutions of higher education have found it necessary to address the 'Ivory Tower Problem.' The 'Ivory Tower Problem' contends that 'traditional' approaches to learning, classroom-based, text-based, and reflection-based methods of learning, along with conceptions of colleges or universities as entities separate from the social, political, and economic communities in which they are embedded, no longer prepare students to serve the needs of employers, communities, fellow citizens, and the state. In their place, efforts to reimagine the learning institution as a "community-partner" and to dramatically increase connections between students' education and community-based, service-based, and experience-based activities have become widely popular (see Bowker 2012, 2015; Mooney and Edwards 2001; Ruben 1999).[3] Few are the voices defending the idea that a separation should be preserved between the learning institution and the community, or between the individual and the social functions of education (Bowker 2012). That students, faculty, and academic institutions should engage community needs, partake in community affairs, and develop themselves in order to serve real and virtual communities is, in many areas of scholarship and practice, taken to be an obvious point.

The advantages of this blurring of the private and the public, the student and the society, are often expressed in terms that can only be described as grandiose fantasy, fantasy in which it is claimed, for instance, that:

> there is *literally* no end to the benefits of integrating cooperative learning strategies into your pedagogy. … Cooperative learning is a way to integrate the social with the academic; but what's more, cooperative learning strategies harness the greatest part of human evolutionary behaviour: sociality. If humans are anything, we are social animals. So *whether you are taking-down a woolly mammoth or trying to study for the mid-term*, humans are always more successful when they exercise cooperation.
>
> *(Haynes 2015, emphasis added)*

If there is to be no distinction, in higher education, between "taking down a woolly mammoth" and "studying for a mid-term," then surely the concepts of students as selves and education as an intellectual project have been lost.

While there are no clear theoretical distinctions separating experience-based, community-based, and service-based pedagogies, these loosely defined orientations inform a number of popular contemporary educational practices, including problem-based learning, experiential learning, service learning, pedagogies of social justice, academic learning communities, collaborative learning, and academic programs focused on the development of values such as 'leadership,' 'stewardship,' and 'citizenship.' Such programs often reveal surprising attitudes toward education, its place, and its meaning.

Consider, first, learning institutions' statements of their own priorities, which frequently center upon the promise that the institution will prepare the student for the day when he will finally enter "the real world" (Barack, Mintz, and Emba 2014; Svetlik 2007) that lies "beyond the campus walls" (Courtney 2009; Moore 2015). One advertising slogan of a college in New York state proclaims to its students: "*When you're here, you're almost there*" (D'Youville 2015). This notion, that when a student is "here," at the college, he is, in effect, *nowhere*, reminds us how even an aspirational slogan may become complicit in producing a vision of the learning institution as a non-place, outside of 'real life,' existing in a liminal dimension from which one can only hope to escape.

Metaphors depicting educational institutions as 'Ivory Towers' or 'non-places,' surrounded by "campus walls," emphasize the desolation of the learning environment, portraying it as a sort of prison. Although relatively few American campuses actually feature high walls or towers, these metaphors ask us to imagine that the traditional university keeps its members shut away from real life and freedom, away from the meaningful and vital activities of others. At the same time, these metaphors express hostility and perhaps envy toward the *esoteric* (i.e., exclusive) functions of towers and walls.

Ivory Towers, and those within them, seem to exist for themselves alone, occupying themselves with ancient philosophies, devising theories full of abstract speculation, even dressing and behaving in manners somewhat out of touch with fashions known in the "real world." The walls and towers that symbolize traditional methods of teaching and learning, therefore, threaten to keep students and educators 'out of touch' and 'inexperienced,' cloistered, surrounded by stale, old books or dry, dead theories. The campus is depicted as sterile and empty to the extent that it is abstinent from inter-penetration with the community. If educators accept such attributions, then we can only conceive of ourselves as infertile, impotent, or, in a more common metaphor, engaged primarily in the non-reproductive act of 'intellectual masturbation.' Such infertility and emptiness are often imagined to be the result of centuries of scholars' greedy solitude, in which we inhabited the esoteric chambers of our minds and, instead of engaging with the world around us, indulged in a sort of incestuous intellectual relationship with ourselves, sometimes creating monstrous theories that would only wreak havoc if applied in the "real world."

In an age where educational objectives are frequently defended with reference not to students' intellectual gains but to the financial benefits of holding degrees or to the vivifying economic effects education can bring – as in the discourse of STEM discussed above – it is not surprising that the Ivory Tower would be condemned as reactionary and purposeless. Indeed, the relationship between community and educator in which the former confers meaning and value on the work of the latter is likely reinforced by changing economic realities according to which educational institutions, particularly smaller ones, are, in fact, increasingly dependent upon community members to assure their financial survival in the form of grants, donations, corporate gifts, and sustained student enrollment.

All of this is to suggest that educators and learning institutions now face a narcissistic dilemma of their own, one in which they seem no longer capable of generating their own value. At the heart of this narcissistic dilemma is a damaging attribution, an attribution that is not always recognized and that is coped with in destructive ways. The attribution is that institutions of learning, faculty members, administrators, and students are all in danger of succumbing to an isolation that threatens our destruction, a threat from which we may be saved only by engaging in a process of "social intelligence," only by re-orienting our aims to match those of society.

That experience-based pedagogies have been embraced by many American educators suggests that they have come to accept self-attributions of emptiness and their implicit imperative to locate the value of academic work in its capacity to serve the needs of society, to have 'social impact,' be it local, regional, national, or global. The basic meaninglessness of 'abstract' academic work can only be redeemed, on this account, if we can break down "campus walls" and forge a (re)productive relationship with the community, if we can "learn to serve and serve to learn" (Hurley 2013), if we can blur or erase any differences between the students' goals, the educator's demands, and the needs of the community.

If contact with the community is what safeguards us from sterility or emptiness, then educating a student means developing in that student skills and attitudes endorsed by social groups and community institutions. The student is educated, as it were, on behalf of society. We have abandoned the notion that, while in college, a student should be permitted to indulge in inhabiting an ivory tower, a sort of adolescent holding environment, protected to some degree from relating to objects in the real world and, thus, protected from impingement and undue external demand. Instead, we insist upon a fundamental identity of interests, shared by educators, students, and the community to which the student must adapt.

Students who wish to gain favor with their professors and their institutions are encouraged to accept this identity of interests and to collude, as it were, in their own enmeshment with the goals and values of the community. Of equal importance, the educator who offers up her students to community experience may become identified with the community's idealized value. Community organizations now 'need' the educator, thank the educator for her 'service,' nominate the educator for awards, and praise her for training young people to serve 'social' ends. Most dangerous about this dynamic is the possibility that students' subjective needs become secondary to the achievement of a desired identification between educator and community, even to the extent that the student's education and the educator's teaching practice are transformed into a ritualized sacrifice of the student's self to the community.

By accepting the premise that separation from the community leaves both educators and students without meaning or value, today's student has met with attributions, not unlike 'narcissism,' once reserved for inhabitants of the Ivory Tower. Although many students are willing to orient their educations toward the attainment of qualifications for careers and toward other exigencies of the "real world," students – or faculty – who resist the social control exercised via experience-oriented pedagogies may be viewed as depriving or dangerous, since they threaten the new source of institutional value and, quite possible, the foundation of institutional financial survival. Such students may find themselves facing hostile attributions or other forms of official or unofficial discipline for being 'narcissists' who must take more seriously the learning experiences that will engender the attitudinal and behavioral shifts necessary to serve the needs of the educator. In this way, we may see in educators' fervent desire to tear down the Ivory Tower an expression of hatred of the student's self (see Bowker 2012, 2015).[4]

Experience and the social order

Dewey's pragmatic philosophy entails the premise that experiences are valuable only if they are useful in shaping future useful experiences, useful not only for the individual but for others: Experiences are valuable if they "promote the enriched growth of further experience" in the student (1997, 73), but the "growth of further experience" also has a pragmatic and utilitarian meaning. This principle is applied with considerable enthusiasm in the late chapters of *Experience and Education*, where Dewey presents experience-led scientific education as the crux of a renewed social order.

Dewey begins with a fairly reductive account of human experience, whereby:

> existing experience in detail and also on a wide scale is what it is because of the application of science, first, to the processes of production and distribution of goods and services, and then to the relations which human beings sustain socially to one another.
>
> *(1997, 80)*

Thus:

> it is impossible to obtain an understanding of present social forces (without which they cannot be mastered and directed) apart from an education which leads learners into knowledge of the very same facts and principles which in their final organization constitute the sciences.
>
> *(80–81)*

Put simply: Science determines existing experience because experience is reducible to calculable social forces, processes of production and distribution. These processes determine social relations which, in turn, determine experience. Education, therefore, must teach students to "master and direct" social forces in order to create better and more useful experience.

The only way that "a better social order can be brought into existence" (1997, 81), which is the real goal of learning, is to apply scientific and pragmatic methods not just to problems of social engineering, but to the project of education, itself. That is, the "intellectual organization" generated in the population via programs of scientific, pragmatic, and experiential learning "is not an end in itself but is the means by which social relations, distinctively human ties and binds, may be understood and more intelligently ordered" (83). The purpose and meaning of learning, for Dewey, is the creation of stewards of social progress who will serve the society by controlling and improving those objects of experience most valued by the society.

The "better social order" Dewey imagines is one in which greater control over objects of practical experience and "everyday life" (1997, 80) is valued throughout the educational system. The Deweyan attitude toward experience may become second nature in students if educators apply consistent training in science and its pragmatic value-orientation so as to develop "intense emotional allegiance to the method" (1997, 81). And the task of the educator can be measured (only) by "what it accomplishes, or fails to accomplish, for a future whose objects are linked with those of the present" (76). That is, a Deweyan education is valuable not for what changes it may affect in students, but for what improvements in social conditions are forged on behalf of the objects and experiences of the future.

Since Dewey offers no usable guideline to define what is "better" or "worse" other than "the enriched growth of further experience" (1997, 73), we run into a paradox of pragmatic moral philosophy: that what is "good" is what "works," and what "works" is "good" because it "works." Pragmatic orientations, then, while seeming progressive in spirit, often tend both toward instrumentalism and conservatism, for accepting the equation of "the good" with "what works" requires a high degree of adaptation to existing political, social, and economic conditions. One strives, that is, to improve experiences *within* existing frameworks and infrastructures. The Deweyan student does not question science, itself, but uses the scientific method to enhance experience. He does not question the need for 'economic progress' but applies his experience in producing it. The depth of the critique offered by experience-oriented education is limited by the conception of experience itself. If one has not directly experienced a world without science or capitalism, one has no data, no prior experience from which to draw in order to learn about it, and one is relegated to what Dewey dismisses as reflection upon "emotional and fantastic ideals" (1929, xvi).

That a "better social order" is the true aim of a Deweyan education is made evident by his account of the power of external conditions to determine our internal states:

> Every genuine experience has an active side which changes in some degree the objective conditions under which experiences are had. The difference between civilization and savagery, to take an example on a large scale, is found in the degree in which previous experiences have changed the objective conditions under which subsequent experiences take place. The existence of roads, of means of rapid movement and transportation, tools, implements, furniture, electric light and power, are illustrations. Destroy the external conditions of present civilized experience, and for a time our experience would relapse into that of barbaric peoples.
>
> *(1997, 38–39)*

If changes in external conditions would lead directly to changes in our experience, then the "interactive" quality of experience would seem asymmetrically interactive, heavily weighted toward the external. That is, one might imagine an alternative case in which external conditions changed dramatically, and yet selves were capable of withstanding such changes, continuing to forge experiences in line with self-directed goals and expectations. Such selves would have to possess within them a strong sense of place and purpose, and would have to be capable of creatively acting upon, rather than merely reacting to, a changing environment.

One would think that the goal of education might be to create such sturdy selves, a goal in keeping with our contemporary imagination of ourselves as living in a world of rapid change and even recurrent crisis. That it is not suggests that our vision of the control and power produced by education, like Dewey's, resembles the capitalist ideology in which the worker is imagined to master the machine, manipulating its numerous handles and levers to produce on command, when, in fact, it is the machine, its designer, and its owner who have, in effect, mastered the worker, who have trained the worker to move when the machine requires it, and who have therefore facilitated the mechanization of the human being.

In the following related excerpt from Dewey's essay "The Need for a Recovery of Philosophy" (1917), we see what begins as an attempt to balance naïve philosophies of absolute subjectivity transform itself into a confusing account of human action and reaction, control and adaptation:

> Experiencing means living; and ... living goes on in and because of an environing medium, not in a vacuum. ... The successful activities of the organism ... react upon the environment to bring about modifications favorable to their own future. The human being has upon his hands the problem of responding to what is going on around him so that these changes will take one turn rather than another, namely, that required by its own further functioning. While backed in part by the environment, its life is anything but a peaceful exhalation of environment. It is obliged to struggle – that is to say, to employ the direct support given by the environment in order indirectly to effect changes that would not otherwise occur. In this sense, life goes on by means of controlling the environment.
>
> *(1960, 48)*

We may notice here how Dewey lumps together precisely what ought to be distinguished. His phrase *"reacting upon* the environment" is an interesting combination – or perhaps *parapraxis* – merging the phrases "reacting to" and "acting upon." While, of course, there is likely no pure action and no pure reaction without admixture, Dewey's conflation of the two leads him to equate our task of "responding to what is going on around" us with living, and living with "controlling the environment." It leads him to equate self-preservation with self-realization, and to claim that our self-realization depends, paradoxically, upon "independent changes in the surroundings" (1960, 48).

Once again, we see that Dewey grants more autonomy to the environment than to the human being. So, far from a philosophy of naïve individualism, his philosophy borders on naïve determinism, in which the human being's role is, by and large, to "react upon" changes that occur around her to preserve her life, which, unfortunately for Dewey's philosophy, is the same as preserving her self.

If "all human experience is ultimately social," if freedom is equated with self-control, and if adaptation requires self-control that is confused with self-determination and controlling the environment, then there is really no refuge for the self, no place or moment of separation, no point where the self's experience might escape or transcend the social environment and the objects in it. If it is true that our experience would "relapse" to that of barbaric peoples simply because our external conditions changed, then "the individual factor that enters into making an experience" seem not even to belong to the individual, but to the external world. Dewey is not wrong that human actions affect the world in which future human actions occur, nor is he wrong that human experience is largely dependent upon external conditions. Yet he seems to imagine the idea of "interaction" in such a way that it always privileges the objects of experiences to such a degree that the self disappears in an 'educative' program of adaptation.

Dewey advocates a model of teaching and learning by experience that, like theories of the state of nature discussed in Chapter 8, confuses submission to experience with self-realization, self-control with self-development. It is from an examination of his theory of education, and a reflection upon how highly esteemed his pedagogy remains, that we see how deeply entrenched are our commitments to self-failure, deprivation, and even trauma: the trauma that includes the erosion of the capacity to be a solitary self. So deeply held are our commitments to the experiential value of learning that we hasten to apply them even to children and young adults, ultimately to serve the needs of social groups and community institutions that depend upon the absence of selves to build a social order of merely experienced and experiencing beings.

Notes

1 It may be worth mentioning that Dewey's educational philosophy was not targeted specifically at university students, although he did not exclude them from his theories. While his work remains influential throughout the educational system, some of the ideals now appropriated for use in colleges and universities were originally aimed at secondary-school- and even primary-school-aged children.

2 This proposal, of course, is reminiscent of Rousseau's educational ideal in *Émile* (1979), where the objective is to persuade Émile that his limits are natural, and not the result of the superior force of others' wills.

3 According to the National Survey of Student Engagement (NSSE), such efforts have succeeded in encouraging college students to invest time and energy in their communities. In 2011, over fifty-seven percent of American Baccalaureate students reported

that they had "performed community service as part of a class," while over eighty-seven percent indicated that they had performed "volunteer work" in the past year (Pryor et al. 2011). Although the NSSE disclaims its validity as a generalizable or comparable measure of student trends, the effect of such surveys has been broad acceptance of the belief that community-engagement is what students, faculty, administrators, community organizations, employers, and public officials desire.

4 Although in some sense natural to the process of narcissistic object-relating, it is nevertheless surprising when communities that rely on narcissistic defenses wield accusations of narcissism at those who defy their demands. One may readily see how common and how dangerous such dynamics can be in broader political culture. For instance, in Jeffery Toobin's (2013) *The New Yorker* essay on Edward Snowden, Snowden is described as a "grandiose narcissist" for leaking classified NSA information related to telephonic surveillance. Here, the attribution of narcissism serves to frame Snowden's act, and to re-frame the political import of the leaked information itself. If Snowden is merely a "narcissist," then his act is not political. It becomes, instead, Snowden's effort to aggrandize himself at the expense of a government agency and a nation whose interests he was supposed to serve. At issue when considering whether Snowden and others like him deserve to be considered heroes, criminals, or whistleblowers is really the way we interpret individual behaviors that defy the demands of organizations and the society of which they are a part. The attribution of narcissism, here, strips the individual and his actions of meaning, such that he and they appear to be the result of a lack of control and a disregard for the stability of the social order, a social order which is, in fact, built upon a narcissistic relationship in which the individual obtains value *only* by serving agreed-upon ideals or objects of social utility. The narcissistic attribution given to dissenters, protestors, and whistleblowers may be seen as part of the social punishment for, and, therefore, part of the coercive deterrent against, violating the rules of an already narcissistic exchange, which is, itself, part of the bond that unites the group.

References

Barack, L., S. Mintz, and C. Emba 2014. "Higher Education in the 21st Century: Meeting Real-World Demands." *The Economist*. Sponsored by: Academic Partnerships. www.economistinsights.com/sites/default/files/EIU_AcademicPartns_WEBr1.pdf. Accessed December 30, 2015.

Berlin, I. 1969. *Four Essays on Liberty*. Oxford: Oxford University Press.

Berrett, D. 2012. "Can Colleges Manufacture Motivation?" *Chronicle of Higher Education*. April 15. http://chronicle.com/article/Can-Colleges-Manufacture/131564. Accessed December 30, 2015.

Bowker, M.H. 2012. "Defending the Ivory Tower: Toward Critical Community-Engagement." *Thought and Action: The NEA Higher Education Journal* 28(1): 106–117.

Bowker, M.H. 2015. "Narcissism, Experience, and Compliance in American Higher Education." *Clio's Psyche: Psycho-History Forum* 21: 452–457.

Browning, C. 1998. *Ordinary Men: Reserve Police Battalion 101 and the Final Solution in Poland*. Reprint Edition. New York: Harper Perennial.

Courtney, N. 2009. *Academic Library Outreach: Beyond the Campus Walls*. Westport, CT: Libraries Unlimited.

Curtis, D. 2001. "Project-Based Learning: Real-World Issues Motivate Students." *Edutopia: What Works in Education*. George Lucas Educational Foundation. www.edutopia.org/project-based-learning-student-motivation. Accessed December 30, 2015.

Dartmouth College. 2015. "Collaborative Learning/Learning with Peers." *Institute for Writing and Rhetoric Webpage.* https://writing-speech.dartmouth.edu/teaching/first-year-writing-pedagogies-methods-design/collaborative-learninglearning-peers. Accessed December 30, 2015.

Deci, E., and R. Ryan 1985. *Intrinsic Motivation and Self-Determination in Human Behavior.* New York: Plenum.

Dewey, J. 1929. *Experience and Nature.* Second Edition. La Salle, IL: Open Court Publishing Co.

Dewey, J. 1960. "The Need for a Recovery of Philosophy." In *John Dewey on Experience, Nature, and Freedom,* edited by R. Bernstein, 19–69. Indianapolis, IN: Bobbs-Merrill.

Dewey, J. 1997. *Experience and Education.* New York: Touchstone.

Duckworth, A., C. Peterson, M. Matthews, and D. Kelly 2007. "Grit: Perseverance and Passion for Long-Term Goals." *Journal of Personality and Social Psychology* 92(6): 1087–1101.

D'Youville College 2015. http://voices.dyc.edu/students/files/2012/10/dyc_tag_line.png. Accessed December 30, 2015.

Earls, C. 2012. "Bloom's Lament for American Higher Education: A Deweyan Critique." *Journal of Thought* (Spring): 38–56.

Foucault, M. 1975. *Discipline and Punish: The Birth of the Prison.* Second Vintage Books Edition. Translated by A. Sheridan. New York: Vintage.

Foucault, M. 1980. *Power/Knowledge: Selected Interviews and Other Writings (1972–77),* edited by C. Gordon. New York: Pantheon Press.

Georgia College. 2015. "Collaborative Learning: We're All in This Together." www.gcsu.edu/make-difference/collaborative. Accessed December 28, 2015.

Godsey, M. 2015. "When Schools Overlook Introverts." *The Atlantic.* September 25. www.theatlantic.com/education/archive/2015/09/introverts-at-school-overlook/407467/. Accessed December 30, 2015.

Gonzalez, H., and J. Kuenzi 2012. *Science, Technology, Engineering, and Mathematics (STEM) Education: A Primer.* Washington, DC: Congressional Research Service.

Gray, P. 2015. "Declining Student Resilience: A Serious Problem for Colleges." *Psychology Today.* www.psychologytoday.com/blog/freedom-learn/201509/declining-student-resilience-serious-problem-colleges. Accessed December 30, 2015.

Haney, C., W. Banks, and P. Zimbardo 1973. "Interpersonal Dynamics in a Simulated Prison." *International Journal of Criminology and Penology* 1: 69–97.

Haynes, J. 2015. "Cooperative Learning Strategies and Engaging Social Intelligence." *Top Hat.* (Pedagogy Weblog.) August 10, 2015. http://blog.tophat.com/cooperative-learning-strategies/. Accessed September 10, 2015.

Hurley, R. 2013. "Learning to Serve, Serving to Learn." *The Huffington Post.* December 6. www.huffingtonpost.com/richard-v-hurley/learning-to-serve-serving_b_4393948.html. Accessed December 30, 2015.

Kihlstrom, J., and N. Cantor 2000. "Social Intelligence." In *The Handbook of Intelligence,* Second Edition, edited by R. Sternberg, 359–379. Cambridge: Cambridge University Press.

Kolb, A., and D. Kolb 2009. "Experiential Learning Theory: A Dynamic, Holistic Approach to Management Learning, Education and Development." In *The Sage Handbook of Management Learning, Education and Development,* edited by S. Armstrong and C. Fukami, 42–68. London: Sage.

Kolb, D., and R. Fry 1975. "Towards an Applied Theory of Experiential Learning." In *Theories of Group Processes,* edited by C. Cooper, 33–58. New York: Wiley.

Levine, D.P. 2011. *The Capacity for Civic Engagement: Public and Private Worlds of the Self.* New York: Palgrave Macmillan.

Milgram, S. 1974. *Obedience to Authority: An Experimental View.* New York: HarperCollins.

Mooney, L., and B. Edwards 2001. "Experiential Learning in Sociology: Service Learning and Other Community-Based Learning Initiatives." *Teaching Sociology* 29(2): 181–194.

Moore, V. 2015. "Beyond the Campus Walls and Into the Community." *Furman University News and Events Webpage.* http://newspress.furman.edu/2015/03/beyond-the-campus-walls-and-into-the-community/. Accessed December 30, 2015.

Pryor, J., L. DeAngelo, L. Palucki Blake, S. Hurtado, and S. Tran 2011. *The American Freshman: National Norms, Fall 2011.* Los Angeles, CA: Higher Education Research Institute, University of California, Los Angeles.

Rousseau, J.-J. 1979. *Émile, or on Education.* Translated by A. Bloom. New York: Basic Books.

Rousseau, J.-J. 1987. *The Basic Political Writings,* edited and translated by D. Cress. Indianapolis, IN: Hackett.

Ruben, B. 1999. "Simulations, Games, and Experience-Based Learning: The Quest for a New Paradigm for Teaching and Learning." *Simulation and Gaming* 30: 498–505.

Sartre, J.-P. 1989. *No Exit and Three Other Plays.* Vintage International Edition. Translated by S. Gilbert. New York: Vintage.

Steinhart, R. 2015. "Learning to Serve and Serving to Learn." *GW Today Webpage.* May 6. http://gwtoday.gwUniversityedu/learning-serve-and-serving-learn. Accessed December 30, 2015.

Svetlik, D. 2007. "When the Academic World and the Real World Meet." *Thought and Action: The NEA Higher Education Journal* 23(1): 47–55.

Toobin, J. 2013. "Edward Snowden Is No Hero." *The New Yorker.* June 10. www.newyorker.com/news/daily-comment/edward-snowden-is-no-hero. Accessed December 30, 2015.

Twenge, J. 2006. *Generation Me: Why Today's Young Americans are More Confident, Assertive, Entitled – and More Miserable than Ever Before.* New York: Free Press.

Twenge, J., and W. Campbell 2009. *The Narcissism Epidemic: Living in the Age of Entitlement.* New York: Simon and Schuster.

Wolf, P. 2015. "The Growing Trend for Active Learning Classrooms." George Mason University. *School of Business Webpage.* http://business.gmu.edu/news/980-the-growing-trend-for-active-learning-classrooms/. Accessed December 31, 2015

6

ALONENESS AND ITS OPPOSITES

The previous chapters have explored ways in which ideologies of experience set themselves against authentic aims of the self. We have devoted some attention to what might be termed the pro-social tendency within ideologies of experience: the tendency to over-value social objects of experience at the expense of the development of the self. In Chapter 2, we noted how thinking may be perceived as a threat to the group, and to the necessary transformation of the 'bad' to the 'good.' In Chapter 3, we considered how valorizations of self-failure and trauma recommended the incorporation and re-transmission of unthinkable, traumatizing experience for the sake of advancing collective goals and the preservation of shared experience. In Chapter 4, we remarked how Jan's fantasy of re-enacting and re-engaging an experience of self-loss lead him to mistake reunion with his family for a creative activity that might help him find his "place" or come "alive again." And in Chapter 5, we studied the example of experience in higher education to demonstrate the lamentable situation in which students may be sacrificed to venerated objects of social experience in the name of higher learning. There, we explored the confusion between self-determination and self-control, the latter being, for Dewey and others, a means of social control.

This latter confusion I take up again in the following two chapters, but from the other side, as it were. Just as some ideologies of experience encourage forms of self-control that are little more than self-repressive efforts aimed at forging connections with experience's social objects, there are equally recognizable ideologies of experience that recommend social isolation and withdrawal under the aegis of self-protection and self-mastery. In an important sense, however, the differences between these strategies of obscuring the self are merely apparent, for the student immersed in a group project and the individual in extreme isolation may be equally wedded to internal objects of experience and their representatives in collective life. Indeed, by confusing isolation with aloneness, by confusing hiding and mystification with the capacity for interior solitude appropriate to the development of self, the attitudes and behaviors described in this chapter leave individuals even *more* deeply fused to experience's objects, for their inner and outer worlds become so empty that there is little else left. As will be discussed more thoroughly in Chapter 7, what those who hide are hiding from is, in many cases, their selves, or the need, desire, or potential to make contact with and express their selves. In these cases, however, the erroneous solution advanced is not identification with or immersion in a group, but the secession from relatedness with others.

Because the literatures upon which I draw use both the terms 'solitude' and 'aloneness' frequently and interchangeably, so shall I. Both may be taken to refer to the capacity of *being alone* I describe here. This capacity, it shall be made clear, refers not primarily to the physical presence or absence of others, just as it differs substantially from self-imposed isolation or other-imposed exclusion.

Being alone

In this chapter, I attend to the matter of the self's capacity to be alone in the context of the demands of the family, group, or community. I wish to argue that it is from the capacity to be alone – which is not identical with hiding, isolation, or withdrawal, and which depends, in part, upon the capacities to feel real and to think and act autonomously – that both vital selfhood and authentic relationships with others may arise. Thomas Merton summarizes this view rather succinctly:

> When men are merely submerged in a mass of impersonal human beings pushed around by automatic forces, they lose their true humanity, their integrity, their ability to love, their capacity for self-determination. When society is made up of men who know no interior solitude it can no longer be held together by love: and consequently it is held together by a violent and abusive authority. But when men are violently deprived of the solitude and freedom which are their due, the society in which they live becomes putrid, it festers with servility, resentment and hate.
>
> *(1958, 13)*

Merton wisely notes that to be incapable of "interior solitude," or to deprive the self or others of such solitude, is to thwart the self's capacity for healthy and loving contact with itself and, therefore, for healthy and loving relationships with others. What is more, the absence of solitude is an absence of a form of freedom, without which love is replaced by hate, and creative and ethical activity is replaced by either compliant or defiant resentful reactivity to others.

Well-known methods of punishment and torture, such as extended solitary confinement, are designed to force isolation upon an individual in a way that deprives her of the solitude needed to psychically survive it. There is an identifiable category of abuse and maltreatment in which neglect, abandonment, or punishing isolation undermines the ability to maintain contact with the self, such that these experiences are tantamount to psychic annihilation. In such cases, isolation means self-disintegration, to which even violent or abusive contact with another may seem preferable.

There is all the difference in the world between imposed confinement and an experience of aloneness or "interior solitude" because the experience of aloneness or solitude depends upon the relationship between an individual's inner (or psychic) experience and the external world. The most important factor in this relationship is the factor of control: whether the isolated or solitary individual in question possesses the capacity to "limit access" to the inner world (Levine 2003, 60–61), and, at the same time, possesses the ability to "control ... the initiation, maintenance, termination, and avoidance of social contact" (Stern 1985, 21–22). Without such controls, the individual is constantly at risk of being intruded upon, emptied, or abandoned. Such control entails the capacity to generate valuable experiences in the internal world, for if one wishes to *be* when alone, and not merely to physically survive, one must be able to generate and possess some of the vital stuff of being.

If experiences of aloneness or solitude are created by the self and undertaken with the expectation that there are good things to be found 'inside' the solitary experience, experiences of isolation – whether self- or other-imposed – are intended to deprive the individual of good things which are thought to exist only on the 'outside.' We may even say that isolation – again, whether applied by others or by the individual – strives to inflict a type of deprivation by which the isolated individual's dependence on the punishing (internal or external) object is re-affirmed. This, we shall see, forms a large part of the condition known as *hikikomori*, a self-imposed period of incarceration, often lasting for several years, in which the individual both seems to seek an absolute severance of contact with family and the social world, and yet, at the same time, behaves in such a way as to re-affirm and even revive a dependent and indulgent relationship with others.

Montaigne observes that "there are ways to fail in solitude as well as in company," for "it is not enough to have gotten away from the crowd ... we must get away from the gregarious instincts that are inside us." "Ambition, avarice, irresolution, fear, and lust," he continues:

> often follow us even into the cloisters and the schools of philosophy. Neither deserts, nor rocky caves, nor hair shirts, nor fastings will free us of them. ... We take our chains along with us; our freedom is not complete; we still turn our eyes to what we have left behind, our fancy is full of it.
>
> *(1965, 176, 182–183)*

It is strange, to say the least, that a thinker like Montaigne would celebrate solitary experience as the individual's emancipation from "the crowd" and from our "gregarious instincts," while claiming, as we have seen in Chapter 3, that the vanity of thought and imagination are the ruin of both individual and society. Indeed, Montaigne is not alone among modern champions of experience in endorsing an ideal of solitude while rejecting the grounds upon which the capacity for such solitude could develop and thrive.

Contemporary social theorists follow in Montaigne's confusion, inveighing against pervasive social powers while at the same time insisting that solitary individuals cannot and *must not* exist, lest they threaten the community. Several theorists already discussed, including Georges Bataille, Michel Foucault, Jacques Lacan, and others, would agree that modern and postmodern individuals are 'always already' mediated by symbolic environments, normalized by custom, disciplined by power/knowledge, and implicated in the work of overlapping cultural, economic, and political institutions. The factual claim of the impossibility of aloneness and the normative claim that none ought to be alone are not terribly different in nature, as both reflect the desire to make solitary experience impossible, to ensure that no one ever be alone. As we shall see at the end of this chapter and in the next, the inability or unwillingness to be alone implies, in almost every case, an inability or unwillingness to recognize and support others' being alone, which is to say, others' being. This means that the capacity to be alone is, in an important and often overlooked sense, central to the capacity to relate ethically to others.

For Winnicott, the capacity to be alone is effectively "synonymous with emotional maturity" (1965, 31), for it entails readiness for true, authentic experience not marked by reactivity or defense and "relatively free from the property we call withdrawal." Of course, "the basis of the capacity to be alone is a paradox" because the experience of being alone as an infant or child occurs "in the presence of mother" (30–31). Nevertheless, from this initial paradox, an adult self with the capacity to be alone may eventually develop around the internalization of a safe, bounded, and benign environment provided by the parent (32).

Consider how vastly this benign internal environment differs from Nietzsche's famous discussion of the independent "free spirit" in *Beyond Good and Evil*:

> Independence is for the very few; it is a privilege of the strong. And whoever attempts it even with the best right but without inner constraint proves that he is probably not only strong, but also daring to the point of recklessness. He enters into a labyrinth, he multiplies a thousandfold the dangers which life brings with it in any case, not the least of which is that no one can see how and where he loses his way, becomes lonely, and is torn piecemeal by some minotaur of conscience. Supposing one like that comes to grief, this happens so far from the comprehension of men that they neither feel it nor sympathize. And he cannot go back any longer. Nor can he go back to the pity of men.
>
> *(1989, 41–42)*

For Nietzsche, himself one of the great solitaries of recent memory, the solitary individual is lost, endangered, imperiled. Most terrifying is her secession from the "comprehension" (*Verständnis*) of the group. To be uncomprehended, to be incomprehensible, means that the group can no longer 'hold' or 'grasp' her, that she is permanently exiled from the care, recognition, and understanding of others.

Because Nietzsche here describes independence without the capacity to be alone – not unlike the *hikikomori*'s isolation without aloneness – the way for such an individual to survive is to call up an "inner constraint" to substitute for the lost dependence upon the group or community. This "inner constraint" is not the same as a "strong" or secure self, and may be more restrictive than the moral code of the group that has been quit, for it may signify the incorporation of the self-occluding values encoded in experience's grandest objects, as we have discussed in Chapters 2 and 3.

The idea of an "inner constraint" is helpful in distinguishing between false independence or defensive withdrawal and the genuine experiences of being alone with which they are so often confused. Specifically, what is confused is the matter of self-control and control over the boundary between internal and external experience that allows for the protection of the inner world. An appropriate facilitating environment does not control the child but protects the inner world of the child, such that if the child is not at risk of being intruded upon, emptied, or displaced by others or events, then the emerging adult may one day enjoy a sense of inner security and interior solitude.

The governing feature of the facilitating environment is not "constraint" or control but creativity, such that meaningful and valuable experiences may be generated and contained within the inner world. Without these, being alone could not be fulfilling. That is, if one is wholly dependent upon control over the self to bring it in line with the needs of others, upon the reinforcement of "inner constraint," then experiences of solitude can be little more than experiences of fear or psychic starvation.

For those unable to *be* when alone, the condition of physical or psychological distance from others or from representatives of others may be experienced as a threat of annihilation. Such individuals cease to *be*, in a psychological sense, as soon as they are disconnected from others or from their environmental substitutes. They exist – or feel they exist – only when plugged into a circuit of connectedness. Break the circuit, and *being* ends. In such a vulnerable condition, avoiding the disintegrative experience of non-being depends upon assuring reliable connection with others, such that rigid and compulsive behaviors may be undertaken to ensure that connectivity is retained in all circumstances and that the threat of aloneness is minimized at all times.

Put another way, if being a self entails being alone, and if an individual's sense of survival depends on *not being alone*, then surviving, paradoxically, depends on *not being*, while *being* means death. The idea of selfhood, in such a condition, becomes meaningless. What is more, the experience that best resembles or simulates *being* depends upon constant contact and group-belonging, such that, although one finds the means therein to secure survival and a facsimile of aliveness, one survives under constant threat of annihilation by separation. Survival is precarious, reliant upon satisfying internal and external conditions that assure one's place in the group.

In this case, self-control takes on a repressive meaning, since it amounts to the need to withdraw, repress, or even extinguish aspects of self that threaten to disrupt identification with or membership in the group or its ideals. Self-development, self-protection, and self-determination, on the other hand, are necessary and healthy aspects of mature selfhood. Too often, these self-affirming ideals are reduced to self-control, as in Nietzsche's quotation above. As we shall see, self-control is often invoked as a value designed to assist in the project of self-suppression, to avoid and deter genuine experiences of aloneness, both in the self and in others.

Controlled but not alone

At this point, we may remind ourselves that to *be alone*, in the sense I have described above, it is not necessary that the self be literally or physically alone. Indeed, the presence of the other, at certain times and in certain forms, is required in order for the self to be alone. Thus, in considering the following, we must keep in mind the idea that being alone is coincidental with, and not contradictory to, being oneself among others and relating to others as a separate self.

Many celebrants of experience, modern and postmodern, upon close examination, defend positions of false aloneness: superficial rebellion against society that actually reinforces identifications with objects of experience embodied in the will of the majority, a community, a nation, or a privileged or sacred group. Advocacies of experience as a vehicle for independence may actually express the opposite wish: the wish to be fused with the object of social or political experience with which one may identify at the expense of separate selfhood. Ironically, the grandiose experience found in fusion becomes more important than the genuine experience of selfhood that is found in being alone, which also contains the potential for an ethical relatedness we may call public being.

The Stoic

The Cyprus-born slave turned Stoic philosopher Epictetus is perhaps best known for his insistence upon the difference between that which is in our power or "up to us" (ἐφ' ἡμῖν) and that which is "not up to us." "Our bodies are not up to us," states the *Enchiridion*, often to the surprise of today's readers, "nor are our possessions, our reputations, or our public offices." By contrast, only "our opinions ... our impulses, desires, aversions" are within our control (1983, 11). While not excluding periods of literal sequestration, the Stoics emphasized a metaphorical, moral solitude in which the mind or soul was severed from the external world, removing desire from any object of which one was not truly the master.

Based upon a rather complicated theory of knowledge and natural determinism (see Saunders 1994), the Stoic goal was to 'comprehend' (*katalepsis*) the laws of Nature such that we would be untroubled by events that might otherwise be distressing. If we truly comprehended Nature's Law and the natural inevitability of death, for example, we would appreciate that living and dying are not "up to us." Thus, we would not suffer even at a loved one's loss. "If you kiss your child or your wife," instructs Epictetus, "say that you are kissing a human being; for when it dies you will not be upset" (1983, 12).

The Stoic's apparent liberty is won by a profound identification with the will of Nature, such that desire is never at odds with actual events, which are both inevitable and well ordered, that is, 'as they should be.' Indeed, to achieve the Stoic's false solitude, one converts oneself into an object of Nature's will: "Do not seek to have events happen as you want them to, but instead want them to happen as they do happen, and your life will go well" (1983, 13). That is, suppress, control, and change your authentic impulses, desires, and emotions such that they accord with whatever occurs, and you will live in harmony with Nature.

For Seneca, a soul so aligned "is independent in its own fortress; and every weapon that is hurled falls short of the mark" (quoted in Foucault 1988, 65). The Stoic's psychological distance from social life and its vicissitudes represents not an effort to be alone in a robust sense but, rather, a defensive withdrawal. His effort is not to be alone with his self, but the opposite: to sever contact with his self and to replace his authentic needs and desires with those that accord with the object of experience *par excellence*: Nature. "Remember," advises Epictetus, "that you are an actor in a play, which is as the playwright [Nature] wants it to be" (1983, 16).

The American

Alexis de Tocqueville's prodigious *Democracy in America* (2000), first published in 1840, still influences political theorists concerned with the deterioration of civil society. More recent studies like David Riesman's *The Lonely Crowd* (1950), Robert Putnam's *Bowling Alone* (2000), and Robert Bellah and his co-authors' *Habits of the Heart* (1996), to name but a few, echo Tocqueville's major concerns. Tocqueville worried that the American democratic revolution had created a lamentable creature known as an "individual."

Individualism, for Tocqueville, was not something of which Americans should be proud. Individuals in a democratic society, rather, are minimal, withdrawn, and alienated from others and from themselves. American society "make[s] each man forget his ancestors ... hides his descendants from him and separates him from his contemporaries; it constantly leads him back toward himself alone and threatens finally to confine him wholly in the solitude of his own heart" (2000, 484). Tocqueville's claim was that individualism in a mass democracy convinced citizens not of their autonomy but of their inevitable dependence upon the greater power of the majority.

It may seem paradoxical to argue that Americans' mental energies are regularly turned back toward 'private' concerns, while at the same time, Americans are enthralled to the will of the majority. It is a condition in which individualism and democratic liberty reinforce majority rule, popular opinion, and even the force of 'common sense.' For Tocqueville, American society resembled nothing more than a royal court in which citizens sang the praises of 'the people' in lieu of the king, and in which value was located only in deeds that accorded with ideals that were 'popular' (i.e., related to or in service of 'the people').

The philosophical underpinnings of democratic practice partly explain this apparent paradox. In a democratic society, the will of the majority is the majority of individual wills, each of which, according to the democratic premise of moral equality, is as worthy as any other. Under the assumption of moral equality, two heads are better than one, and a majority of heads is better than a minority. But there is more than mathematics involved in the American worship of both 'the people' and 'the individual.' American devotion to practical experience, conceived as a form of democratic education available to all, endowed experience with a nearly divine authority in American philosophies and literatures of the nineteenth and twentieth centuries (see Lundin 2005, 163–165). Thus, 'good' acts and 'good' individuals are those that are aligned with the will and opinion of the people, not because the majority forces them to be so, but because men of experience are:

> like travelers dispersed in a great forest in which all the paths end at the same point. If all perceive the central point at once and direct their steps in this direction, they are insensibly brought nearer to one another without seeking each other, without perceiving and without knowing each other, and they will finally be surprised to see themselves gathered in the same place.
>
> *(Tocqueville 2000, 588)*

The dangerous consequence of democratic, majoritarian thinking, for Tocqueville, could not be overstated. Whereas a king:

> has only a material power that acts on actions and cannot reach wills, the majority is vested with a force ... that acts on the will as much as on actions, and which at the same time prevents the deed and the desire to do it. I do not know any country where, in general, less independence of mind and genuine freedom of discussion reign than in America.
>
> *(2000, 243–244)*

In such a society:

> the public therefore has a singular power ... the very idea of which aristocratic nations could not conceive. It does not persuade of its beliefs, it

imposes them and makes them penetrate souls by a sort of immense pressure of the minds of all on the intellect of each.

(409)

The power of the majority, vested in part in the American ideology of experience, condemned most Americans to unwitting conformism, agitation, and pursuit of social status and material wealth: busy yet trivial existences in which selfhood, solitude, and creativity could find no place. As American culture lost its capacity to facilitate being alone, Americans increasingly reverted to the kinds of activities that express *not being* a self, what Winnicott calls "the doing that arises out of [not] being ... a whole life ... built on the pattern of reacting to stimuli" (1986, 39):

> [T]here is nothing less fit for meditation than the interior of a democratic society. ... Everyone is agitated: some want to attain power, others to take possession of wealth. In the midst of this universal tumult, the repeated collision of contrary interests, the continual advance of men toward fortune, where does one find the calm necessary to the profound combinations of the intellect? How does each man bring his thought to a stop at such and such a point, when everything moves around him and he himself is carried along and tossed about every day in the impetuous current that swirls all things along?
>
> *(Tocqueville 2000, 434)*

In Tocqueville, then, we find a critique of democratic individualism on the grounds that, while it seems to isolate citizens, it also rivets them to revered objects of shared experience – the majority and 'the people' – in a way not at all dissimilar to the Stoic's submission to the will of Nature.

Perhaps the most frightening thing about Tocqueville's thesis is that he does not suggest that Americans, nor citizens of other modern democracies, would outwardly recognize much less advocate conformism. Quite the opposite: Tocqueville saw that Americans held to their illusory independence religiously. That democratic individuals, as well as those inhabiting what we now refer to as 'mass cultures,' unknowingly propitiate the will of the mass while espousing their own unlimited independence reminds us that attempts at achieving solitude and selfhood may fail because they are thwarted by unconscious desires for their opposites.

The vampire

In American popular culture, perhaps no figure conveys the ideological confusion of false independence, "inner constraint," and self-control with genuine solitary experience and the possibility of self-determination more effectively than the vampire. Like the vampire of old, today's vampire suffers from an intense craving for blood. Being immortal, the vampire would not die without blood, but would experience eternal weakness and hunger. In this sense, the vampire drinks blood not precisely to survive but to feel alive, to find the feeling of existing, or "to come alive" (Levine 2003, 104).

Typically, vampire protagonists or 'good' vampires stoically control their desire to consume fresh human blood, settling instead for animal blood, synthetic blood-substitutes, and the like. This resistance to the vampire's most fundamental desire is apparently no mean feat, since the experience of being surrounded by humans, particularly young and attractive ones, is depicted as an excruciating torment.

In the *Twilight* series, the 'good' vampires of the Cullen coven, with whom (the human) Bella Swan associates, demonstrate their superhuman power not only in displays of physical speed and strength but in holding themselves to their strict dietary regimen. They have committed themselves to an eternal life of repressing their most basic desire, and of contending with the anxiety of being overtaken by desire, either in the form of an irresistible impulse to kill or in the (externalized) form of rivaling, murderous, 'bad' vampire gangs.

In the penultimate chapter of the series, Bella is impregnated by her vampire lover, Edward, and faces a grim prognosis due to the destructive half-human, half-vampire fetus she carries. The story of Bella's labor is a story of anxious self-control and its relationship to the demands of the group. To nourish her baby, Bella must submit to being consumed from the inside out, until she is on the very brink of death. Indeed, the fetus is so destructive to Bella's body that, for her to survive the birth physically, she must become a vampire, herself, and risk being overtaken by her own vampire-related destructiveness.

That is, in order for Bella to survive the birth physically, she will have to become non-human. But in order for her to survive the birth *psychically*, in order for her to remain 'herself' after her metamorphosis, she will have to commit to the eternal suppression of her desire for human blood, and to the eternal suppression of her child's identical desire. The child Bella carries thereby represents the dilemma of the parent who must facilitate the development of a child (and a potential self), while suspecting that the child's desires are dangerous and destructive, likely to overwhelm the parent with an all-too-familiar temptation. If the parent fears the desire of the child to become himself, then the parent will not lay the groundwork for the child's separate selfhood, but will insist that the child become a 'good' child – in this case, a 'good' vampire – by learning to suppress his fundamental desires in order to retain contact with his parent, his family, or his community.

In the world of the vampire, moral behavior is understood to be a matter of depriving the self. To be moral means to be a member of a 'good' group, which requires the control of one's basic desire, which is not exactly to eat and kill but what these activities represent to the vampire: to feel alive. To be moral, then, means *not* to feel alive. What is more, to be moral means *not* to be alone, for, as we were told in the popular television show *True Blood*, when vampires spend too much time apart from human beings, when they retreat into solitary hunting or 'nest' with other vampires, they countenance their true desires and rationalize their blood-thirst. Constant contact with human beings – or with 'Humanity,' as a more abstract object of experience – is necessary for the vampire to remain in control of herself, which is the same as being good, which is confused with the vampire remaining 'herself.'

Being good, if we approach the life of the self and the group in this way, comes to mean controlling and repressing the self in service of others, and identifying with others' needs more than with our own, ironically ensuring our continued goodness by reminding ourselves of our essential badness. If our attempts to act upon desire and feel alive will destroy others, then we must learn to scorn our desire as a shameful or monstrous transgression. The vampire, therefore, is stuck in a position of shameful compliance, in which she must eternally enforce the repression of her desires – and others' desires – on the grounds that they are repugnant and destructive.

The repression of the vampire's vitality is rewarded not only by immortality and certain supernatural abilities, but by the good favor of the human community, by the vampire's ability to identify with and even live alongside humans in spite of her inhuman condition. Once again, we find an identification in place of an identity, and it should be remarked here that what the vampire identifies with is not merely the human community but the capacity to sacrifice, control, and discipline the self for the sake of others, held up in such narratives as a quintessential 'human' virtue. Here, we are reminded of contemporary efforts in political theory to outline the moral value of shame, discussed in Chapter 1, and taken up again below.

If the good vampire's humanity, like the good Stoic's identification with Nature, may be considered a kind of internal object set in the service of controlling and constraining desire while ensuring that the vampire is never alone – never *alone with its desire* – then contemporary vampire sagas present us a picture of the good life as a life of belonging and moral virtue, but also a life of independence without aloneness, of supernatural power without aliveness.

Rejecting others' solitude

Taken together, Freud's *Civilization and Its Discontents* (1961), *Group Psychology and the Analysis of the Ego* (1959), and "Totem and Taboo" (1938) make a convincing case that fundamental ambivalences between the assertion of and the atonement for independence lie at the heart of psychic life. In Gabriel García Márquez's *One Hundred Years of Solitude* (2006), this fine Freudian line between totem and taboo is tested as the Buendía family isolates itself from the rest of the world in a surreal, collective solitude. As this small community is necessarily incestuous, anxieties about its separation are expressed in the terror of a child born with a dreaded defect: a pig's tail.

The incest taboo has particular relevance for us because it symbolizes the autarchy of the primal father and his pre-societal coercive power, which must be overturned to establish a society ruled by equal subjection to the law. Thus, fears about withdrawal from society may be thought of as fears about the *incestuous* nature of solitude, which invite guilt and dread of punishment for risking the survival of the social group. To the extent that we misconstrue aloneness as withdrawal from or rejection of the social group, we will link aloneness with immorality, since morality is the code of conduct endorsed by the group.

Whether we consider the capacity for aloneness and its realization healthy or unhealthy, ethically necessary or morally threatening, is in some ways *the* crucial political question. As in Jan's family in *Le Malentendu*, the specter of separation raises tremendous anxieties about the survival of groups that depends upon the belonging and co-presence of their members. The notion of a solitary self threatens the group with doubt, doubt cast upon the immediacy and needfulness of the objects of experience that unite the group, adverse, injurious, or traumatic though they may be.

An alternative approach to solitude and collective life, such as that advanced by Merton, would suggest that groups need not fear the solitary capacities of members, and that selves' capacities to be solitary depend upon healthy and functioning groups. A self with the capacity to be alone not only possesses that degree of "ontological security" needed to "live out into the world and meet others" (Laing 1969, 39), but retains the capacity to retreat from or oppose others should a situation arise in which the vitality of any self – not just his own – is unduly endangered.

That is, the achievement of a self with the capacity to be alone is the foundation for ethical respect of others' selves, since, if a self finds itself to be "real, alive, whole, and ... continuous," it reaches out toward "a world and others experienced as equally real, alive, whole, and continuous" (Laing 1969, 39). A fair number of contemporary social and psychological theories would agree that individuals who experience themselves as selves or subjects are likely to recognize others as selves or subjects deserving of respect (see, e.g., Benjamin 1998; Buber 2004, Fraser 2000; Kohlberg 1973; Lasch 1984). On the other hand, individuals who may only behave or misbehave according to the rules of a group in which they are thoroughly embedded are relegated to *re*acting (positively or negatively) to others' demands. The experience of such individuals consists only of coercion, compliance, or opposition.

Both the self and the mature group ought to desire the continued development of selves, for, in so doing, the individual may become more than just an individual, and the group may become more than just a group. Without a dedication to developing the self's capacity to be alone, in the sense defined above, individuals are likely to enter into what Harry Guntrip refers to as "schizoid compromise" (1992), in which the self is split into two or more parts. Typically, one is withdrawn, hidden from others and even from itself, while another is fused with the group or the objects and experiences cherished by the group. In such cases, individuals fail both at being alone and at being related to others because "the split self is not enough for either the self or the group. Each is impoverished, and each impoverishes the other" (Alford 1994, 52–53).

Such a situation is apparent in Jonathan Franzen's well-known essay on the erosion of the public sphere, "The Imperial Bedroom," where he claims that reading the Starr Report on the Clinton–Lewinsky scandal, while sitting alone in a Manhattan apartment, marked a personal violation, a feeling of "being intruded upon" (2003, 41). When Franzen writes that "what's threatened isn't the private sphere. It's the public sphere" (48), he seems to mean that details of personal lives have come to pervade public spaces, that there is no more room for public discourse, only for the exchange of intimate yet trivial 'dirty laundry.' Thus, reading the Starr Report over breakfast becomes an instance of "private life brutally invading the most public of public spaces" (51), a "flood of dirty suds from the Office of the Independent Counsel, oozing forth through official and commercial channels to saturate national consciousness" (40).

In his opposition to casual Fridays, modern décor, gossip columns, internet chatrooms, and personalized voicemail, Franzen is not alone in extolling the virtue of shame and the dream of escaping the "tangled sheets" and "in-your-face consumerism" of private life, where "flashers and sexual harassers and fellators on the pier and self-explainers on the crosstown bus all similarly assault our sense of the 'public' by exposing themselves" (49). Instead, he envisions a public sphere, exemplified, oddly, by an art museum, where someone may "promenade" in a "place to go when you want to announce to the world … that you have a new suit, or that you're in love, or that you suddenly realize you stand a full inch taller when you don't hunch your shoulders" (50).

Franzen is right that it is possible, and possibly dangerous, for the private to invade the public in a way that prevents meaningful communication. When political discourse is infused with narratives of sex and desire, and when details about intimate encounters "ooze" into public space – we may note Franzen's preoccupation with his experience of boundary invasion – it may seem more difficult to interact with others as selves and to be treated as a self. But it would seem that Franzen has made an error in designating as 'public' the promenading of one's private possessions, one's latest romance, or one's taller stature, while condemning as 'private' not only the details of the Starr Report but all those who "assault" us by "exposing themselves."

Of course, we may imagine that there are some differences between revealing one's new suit and discussing unsavory personal matters within earshot of others, or between "dress[ing] to the nines" for a party and "flashing" one's naked body on the subway (54). The difference Franzen alludes to here is not merely a difference between controlling exposure and being forced to see what one does not wish to see. Rather, his account suggests that all (others) should be dominated by self-repression and shame. It is, after all, the "delicious ... enforced decorum" in the corporate offices of the "upper echelons of business" where "codes of dress and behavior are routinely enforced, personal disclosures are penalized, and formality is still the rule" that Franzen lauds, and with which he appears to identify (50–51). He defends a concrete standard that determines who may display what, where, and when. People who fail to adhere to the standard 'should be ashamed,' for "without shame there can be no distinction between public and private" (49).

Thus, Franzen strives to define and defend a public sphere, a sphere traditionally associated with the government, the law, and the abstract citizen, ostensibly to protect us from intrusion. And he is right that a public sphere should protect us, for there is no outlawed idea or 'thought-crime' in a public sphere, just as a public sphere must be governed by the rule of law, not the rule of particular interests or privileged groups. But Franzen surprises us by imagining a public sphere where we give private performances, rather than enter into reasoned reflection or undertake action as public citizens. As a true public sphere would safeguard and even underwrite the importance of a private sphere, one would imagine that such performances could be conducted in private without losing any of their significance, plurality, or visibility (see Arendt 1998; Kohn 2000).

Émile Durkheim's understanding of the State as the instantiation of the public realm in political life may be helpful to better understand the relationship between the citizen and the public realm that Franzen seems to be after:

> Far from its tyrannizing over the individual, it is the State that redeems the individual from society. ... It is not this or that individual the State seeks to develop, it is the individual in genere [in the abstract], who is not to be confused with any single one of us.
>
> *(1958, 69)*

For Durkheim, the State protects the individuality of each citizen equally, thus in following the law, each is freed from merely complying with or rebelling against the forces of the majority, the market, or the people. Instead, the laws of the State make what Durkheim calls individuality, but what we might call subjectivity or selfhood, politically possible, so "whilst we give the State our cooperation ... we do not become the agents of a purpose alien to us" (69). A genuine public realm, civil society, or, in Durkheim's language, "State," would be one in which each citizen finds *not* a demand to repress herself for the sake of others, but an environment that protects her from the coercive push and pull of the group, such that the anxieties about attempts at separation are made manageable.

As for Durkheim, for Hannah Arendt the public or political sphere represents an emancipation from the coercion of "the social" realm (1998, 22–49), which Hanna Pitkin (2000) famously caricatured as "the blob." Like Franzen's "dirty suds," the social "blob" swallows up all in its path, destroying both public and private lives in an embroilment of private interests, intimate exchanges, and banal pursuits. Indeed, for Arendt, the social realm of consumption, labor, money, and the like turns what could be a nation into little more than a vast, multiplied family which, by eliminating the boundaries that separate individual citizens, reduces all to "only one opinion and one interest" (1998, 39). This coerced conformity:

> excludes the possibility of action. ... Instead, society expects from each of its members a certain kind of behavior, imposing innumerable and various rules, all of which tend to "normalize" its members, to make them behave, to exclude spontaneous action or outstanding achievement.
>
> *(40)*

Arendt's vision of a despotic social realm, then, echoes Tocqueville's concern about the "omnipotence" and "tyranny of the majority" over both action and thought (2000, 235–249).

Although a public sphere is necessary to protect the individual from undue coercion by powerful groups, it is possible to abuse distinctions between public and private to enforce repression by demanding that some be held to standards of 'public' behavior while others retain the right to behave 'privately.' This abuse is prevalent in Franzen's essay, in which some must refrain from certain forms of self-exposure while others may go to the art museum to show off their new clothing or lovers. Some individuals' self-expressions, that is, enjoy the label of 'public' since they accord with the norms of powerful groups, while others' self-expressions are an unwelcome invasion of "privacy" and should be "shame[d]" out of consciousness.

Such defenses of a false public sphere typically deploy the words 'public' and 'private' as cudgels, defining both in ultimately 'private' terms. What is public, for Franzen, is merely conformity with the norms and codes of the privileged or 'good' group. While it is not Franzen's argument, it would not be inconsistent with his logic to argue that certain displays of affection (for instance, those between two men, or between people of different ethnicities) are not appropriate for 'public' spaces. This logic defines a false public sphere because the fundamental criterion of publicity, that each citizen be treated as an abstract (separate) and equal entity, has been violated.

It is surely not uncommon for thwarted desires related to self-expression to find a modicum of fulfillment in aggression directed at others, such that "the energy of desire gets channeled into the sadistic impulse to repress others" (Levine 2004, 106–107). If desire must be repressed, then it may also be translated into a demand that others repress themselves, in which case I may "convince myself that desire and duty are one and the same, or that I am forced to act on self-interest to protect myself from the immoral and threatening conduct of others" (Levine 2004, 107).

As mentioned above and as discussed in Chapter 1, advocacies of the political value of shame are not at all unpopular in political theory (see, e.g., Deonna, Rodogno, and Teroni 2012; Nussbaum 2004; Saxonhouse 2006; Tarnopolsky 2010). These accounts often rely on fears of social degeneration that seem to reflect unconscious anxieties about the devaluation of the inner world, anxieties addressed by affirming the importance of controlling and repressing the self, not only for the self but for others. Just as the vampire's moral status demanded self-repression, being a 'public' citizen here demands shame, such that, once again, moral behavior comes to be equated with the rejection of the self, particularly in its separateness from the norms of the 'good' group.

If mature selfhood is perceived as a threat to the social group, then we arrive at the curious situation in which agents of the social group take it to be their responsibility to shame would-be selves into non-existence. Too often, defenses of the public sphere disguise attacks on selfhood in which the demands, standards, or codes of a powerful group are enforced with shame. Rather than protecting the boundaries of abstract individuality and the possibility that selves be conceived of as separate beings, such projects subject all individuals to the will of a majority or group that believes its interests represent the interests of all.

As alluded to above, a world in which the self is never alone, and, therefore, where others also ought never be alone, is precisely what many contemporary political theorists have prescribed. Some who have followed in the tradition of Emmanuel Levinas have defined moral being as the destruction of the ability *to be alone* that we have associated with selfhood, where the other must always overwhelm the self and where ethical action requires "the putting into question of my spontaneity by the presence of the other" (Levinas 1969, 43) as well as the suspension "of my spontaneity, of my jouissance, of my freedom" (Critchley 1996, 30).

Levinas claims that it is my ethical obligation even to give up my right to exist: "The ethical I is a being who asks if he has a right to be!," for, contra Spinoza:

> my duty to respond to the other suspends my natural right to self-survival, *le droit vitale*. ... To expose myself to the vulnerability of the face [of the other] is to put my ontological right to existence into question. In ethics, the other's right to exist has primacy over my own.
>
> *(Levinas and Kearney 1986, 23–24)*

We have already noted how this line of thought has been picked up by several contemporary theorists, most notably by Judith Butler, who claims that loss and grief are valuable because these emotional states display "the thrall in which our relations with others hold us ... in ways that often interrupt the self-conscious account of ourselves as autonomous and in control" (2004, 23). What is to be *gained* from this enthrallment and from "remaining exposed to its unbearability" is precisely the *loss* of the capacity to be alone. Instead, we are assured, if we develop "a point of identification with suffering itself" (30), we may possess the other in ourselves, alienating ourselves from our selves, and protecting others from our innate destructiveness: "My own foreignness to myself," Butler writes, "is, paradoxically, the source of my ethical connection with others" (46).

Here, a loss of self-contact and a loss of the ability to *be* when alone becomes "the tie" that binds the group together (Butler 2004, 22). The postmodern call for moral self-sacrifice appears more and more like a demand that each be enthralled by experiences of other-intrusion. Instead of supporting public institutions and public spaces that, in turn, support the development of separate selves, we are urged to share in the experience of losing our selves, our autonomy, and our aloneness, which losses make "a tenuous 'we' of us all" (20).

References

Alford, C.F. 1994. *Group Psychology and Political Theory*. New Haven, CT: Yale University Press.

Arendt, H. 1998. *The Human Condition*. Second Edition. Chicago, IL: University of Chicago Press.

Bellah, R., R. Madsen, W. Sullivan, A. Swidler, and S. Tipton 1996. *Habits of the Heart: Individualism and Commitment in American Life*. Berkeley: University of California Press.

Benjamin, J. 1998. *Shadow of the Other: Intersubjectivity and Gender in Psychoanalysis*. New York: Routledge.

Buber, M. 2004. *I and Thou*. Revised Edition. Translated by R. Smith. New York: Continuum.

Butler, J. 2004. *Precarious Life: The Powers of Mourning and Violence*. London: Verso.

Critchley, S. 1996. "Prolegomena to any Post-Deconstructive Subjectivity." In *Deconstructive Subjectivities*, edited by S. Critchley and P. Dews, 13–45. Albany, NY: State University of New York Press.

Deonna, J., R. Rodogno, and F. Teroni 2012. *In Defense of Shame: The Faces of an Emotion*. Oxford: Oxford University Press.

Durkheim, É. 1958. *Professional Ethics and Civic Morals*. Translated by C. Brookfield. Glencoe, IL: Free Press.

Epictetus 1983. *The Handbook (Enchiridion)*. Translated by N. White. Indianapolis, IN: Hackett.

Foucault, M. 1988. *The History of Sexuality, Volume III: The Care of the Self*. First Vintage Books Edition. Translated by R. Hurley. New York: Vintage Books.

Franzen, J. 2003. *How to be Alone*. New York: Picador.

Fraser, N. 2000. "Rethinking Recognition." *New Left Review* 3: 107–120.

Freud, S. 1938. "Totem and Taboo: Resemblances Between the Mental Lives of Savages and Neurotics." In *The Basic Writings of Sigmund Freud*. Translated and edited by A.A. Brill, 807–930. New York: Random House.

Freud, S. 1959. *Group Psychology and the Analysis of the Ego*, edited and translated by J. Strachey. New York: W.W. Norton.

Freud, S. 1961. *Civilization and Its Discontents*. Translated by J. Strachey. New York: W.W. Norton.

García Márquez, G. 2006. *One Hundred Years of Solitude*. Reprint Edition. New York: Harper Perennial Modern Classics.

Guntrip, H. 1992. *Schizoid Phenomena, Object Relations, and the Self.* Madison, CT: International Universities Press.

Kohlberg, L. 1973. "The Claim to Moral Adequacy of a Highest Stage of Moral Judgment." *The Journal of Philosophy* 70(18): 630–646.

Kohn, J. 2000. "Freedom: The Priority of the Political." In *The Cambridge Companion to Hannah Arendt*, edited by D. Villa, 113–129. Cambridge: Cambridge University Press.

Laing, R.D. 1969. *The Divided Self: An Existential Study in Sanity and Madness.* London: Penguin Books.

Lasch, C. 1984. *The Minimal Self: Psychic Survival in Troubled Times.* New York: W.W. Norton.

Levinas, E. 1969. *Totality and Infinity: An Essay on Exteriority.* Translated by A. Lingis. Pittsburg, PA: Duquesne University Press.

Levinas, E., and R. Kearney 1986. "Dialogue with Emmanuel Levinas" In *Face to Face with Levinas*, edited by R. Cohen, 13–33. Albany, NY: State University of New York Press.

Levine, D.P. 2003. *The Living Dead and the End of Hope: An Essay on the Pursuit of Unhappiness.* Denver, CO: Broken Tree Press.

Levine, D.P. 2004. *Attack on Government: Fear, Distrust, and Hatred in Public Life.* Charlottesville, VA: Pitchstone.

Lundin, R. 2005. *From Nature to Experience: The Search for Cultural Authority.* Lanham, MD: Rowman and Littlefield.

Merton, T. 1958. *Thoughts in Solitude.* New York: Farrar, Straus and Giroux.

Montaigne, M. de 1965. *The Complete Essays of Montaigne.* Translated by D. Frame. Stanford, CA: Stanford University Press.

Nietzsche, F. 1989. *Beyond Good and Evil: Prelude to a Philosophy of the Future.* Translated by W. Kaufmann. New York: Vintage.

Nussbaum, M. 2004. *Hiding from Humanity: Disgust, Shame and the Law.* Princeton, NJ: Princeton University Press.

Pitkin, H. 2000. *The Attack of the Blob: Hannah Arendt's Concept of the Social.* Chicago, IL: University of Chicago Press.

Putnam, R. 2000. *Bowling Alone: The Collapse and Revival of American Community.* New York: Simon and Schuster.

Riesman, D., with R. Denney, and N. Glazer 1950. *The Lonely Crowd: A Study of the Changing American Character.* New Haven, CT: Yale University Press.

Saunders, J., ed. 1994. *Greek and Roman Philosophy After Aristotle.* New York: Free Press.

Saxonhouse, A. 2006. *Free Speech and Democracy in Ancient Athens.* New York: Cambridge University Press.

Stern, D.N. 1985. *The Interpersonal World of the Infant: A View from Psychoanalysis and Developmental Psychology.* New York: Basic Books.

Tarnopolsky, C. 2010. *Prudes, Perverts, and Tyrants: Plato's Gorgias and the Politics of Shame.* Princeton, NJ: Princeton University Press.

Tocqueville, A. de 2000. *Democracy in America.* Translated by H. Mansfield. Chicago, IL: University of Chicago Press.

Winnicott, D.W. 1965. *The Maturational Processes and the Facilitating Environment: Studies in the Theory of Emotional Development*, edited by M. Khan. London: Hogarth and the Institute of Psycho-Analysis.

Winnicott, D.W. 1986. *Home Is Where We Start from: Essays by a Psychoanalyst*, edited by C. Winnicott, R. Shepard, and M. Davis. New York: W.W. Norton.

7

HIKIKOMORI

Deprived, isolated, and disfigured selves

In this chapter, I carry further the line of thought developed in the previous chapter by interpreting the behavior of individuals in *hikikomori*, as well as the attitudes of those who study and treat them, as an attempt to isolate the individual while abandoning the self in a way that is the opposite of being alone. Specifically, *hikikomori* represents an isolation from and deprivation of familial and social experience which, paradoxically, expresses the desire to return to lost experiences of dependence and indulgence. The extreme self-incarceration of *hikikomori*, along with apparent difficulties in understanding *hikikomori* in the psychiatric and medical communities, derive from denials and mystifications of the desire to be alone in the sense outlined in Chapter 6. The current scholarly and clinical practice of treating *hikikomori* as a "culture-bound" Japanese phenomenon, for instance, obscures more than it clarifies and may be interpreted as an attempt to hide it away, rather than to acknowledge the inner crisis of desire and deprivation that it represents, one that is not unique to Japanese individuals.

Amae (甘え), the Japanese term for loving indulgence – typically parental or familial – is both sought after and refused in *hikikomori*, for the desire for *amae* has come to be experienced by the individual as monstrous and intolerable. *Amae* coincides in several respects with Winnicott's notion of a facilitating environment, a condition that facilitates aloneness but is not identical with actually being alone, a condition in which a potential self may develop the capacities to become a self. While current applications of the construct of *amae* to the phenomenon of *hikikomori* find *amae* to be a *cause* of the disorder, *amae* need not be read as culturally unique nor pathogenic. On the contrary, it is the deprivation of emotional indulgence that ultimately leads individuals to the shame, self-incarceration, and self- and family-victimization that defines *hikikomori*. What is unfortunate about the *hikikomori* population and the academic and popular communities concerned with the phenomenon is that, within both, we find the self's desire to be loved, to be indulged, and to be capable of being itself represented as something monstrous and shameful.

This disfigurement of desire, I propose, reflects not only a misunderstanding of the dependency involved in facilitating aloneness and selfhood, but an ideological orientation toward maturation, in which the impingement of others' needs is regarded as natural and normal, something to which the individual must learn to adapt. *Hikikomori*, then, appears to be an attempt to retroactively shut out impingement and to be alone, but, as we noted in the previous chapter, and as we will see, the attempt is not only too late, but is undertaken without the inner resources needed to be alone in a meaningful sense.

What is *hikikomori?*

Hikikomori (ひきこもり) derives from the Japanese words *hiku*, or pulling in, and *komoru*, or retiring. It means, literally, "pulling away and being confined" (Hairston 2010, 311; Wong 2009, 128), or "to be confined to the inside" (Ohashi 2008, iii). It is used to refer to the state of isolation ('to be *in hikikomori*') as well as to an affected individual ('a *hikikomori*'). The construct, which describes a period of severe social isolation often lasting for several years, has gained notoriety in Japan and worldwide since the year 2000. It was first introduced to the Japanese lexicon with the publication of Tamaki Saitō's *Hikikomori: Adolescence without End* (2013). With new estimates that over one million Japanese citizens, roughly twenty-five percent of Japan's young population, will suffer from *hikikomori* in their lifetimes, the phenomenon is regarded as a dangerous national crisis, "a disease that can bring the nation to collapse" (Shimoyachi 2003).

Hikikomori is not classified in any version of the *DSM* (*Diagnostic and Statistical Manual of Mental Disorders*) or *ICD* (*International Classification of Diseases*). Surveys of mental health professionals and pediatricians in Japan and around the world reveal familiarity with the phenomenon but equally extensive disagreement about its diagnosis. *Hikikomori* is most commonly treated as a symptom of an alternative underlying condition, although differential diagnoses range from schizophrenia to depression to autism to unspecified stress-related disorders (Tateno et al. 2012). The phenomenon affects both sexes, with males in the slight majority, usually in their teens, twenties, and thirties, hailing from middle- to upper-middle-class families (Tateno et al. 2012). The average duration of *hikikomori* is thought to be approximately four years (Koyama et al. 2010; Ohashi 2008; Saitō 2002), although some studies suggest average durations of up to nine years (Sakai et al. 2010). In some cases, individuals have been known to remain in *hikikomori* for over thirty years.

The Japanese Ministry of Health, Labor, and Welfare defines *hikikomori* simply as the "state of confining oneself to one's house for more than six months and strictly limiting communication with others" (Ministry of Health, Labor, and Welfare 2003; Umeda and Kawakami 2012, 121). Alan Teo and his colleagues recently set out slightly more detailed diagnostic criteria which include: a period of at least six months characterized by "spending most of the day and nearly every day confined to home," "marked and persistent avoidance of social relationships," "marked distress in the individual or impairment in occupation … academic … , or interpersonal functioning," and "the lack of a better differential diagnosis such as social phobia, major depressive disorder, schizophrenia, etc." (Teo, Stufflebaum, and Kato 2014, 447).

Both the *hikikomori* construct and the *hikikomori* population overlap substantially with psycho-social categories of *futoko* (school-refusal) and *NEET* (an acronym derived from the UK meaning those 'Not in Education, Employment, or Training'), as well as the slang category *freeter*, meaning the willingly unemployed or underemployed. Although *hikikomori* are often casually referred to as "parasites" (see Furlong 2008), the population does *not* coincide with the newly defined social group maligned as *parasaito shinguru*, or "parasite singles": employed, unmarried females without children often living with their parents into young adulthood (Watts 2002; Yamada 1999; Yamada 2006).

Case analyses have suggested that some, but not all, individuals in *hikikomori* have suffered negative precipitating events in their social lives. But such events are hardly unique to those in *hikikomori*, and it is not clear that they interact uniquely with aggravating conditions within the individual's family or personal history. Most researchers have found no significant correlations between *hikikomori* and extraordinary precipitating events, "general parenting style," parental mental illness, physical or sexual abuse, or poverty (Umeda and Kawakami 2012, 126). And while it is not uncommon to find single studies that report correlations between *hikikomori* and other psycho-social variables, such as anxiety and insecure parental attachment (e.g., Hattori 2005; Krieg and Dickie 2011; Nagata et al. 2011), such findings are not consistently confirmed and, more importantly, have not been employed to develop a robust theory of the phenomenon.

As attention to *hikikomori* has increased over the past two decades, so, too, have public funds for research and treatment increased. In fact, Japanese law now requires every prefecture to establish at least one *hikikomori* treatment center. No available evidence, however, suggests that such efforts have contributed to the prevention or treatment of *hikikomori* on a measurable scale. An important obstacle to effective treatment remains the professional and scholarly disagreement about whether *hikikomori* is a definable disorder with medical and/or psychological causes. In spite of numerous attempts to define and classify the phenomenon, one finds at every turn "conflicting results and lack of empirical findings on risk factors" (Umeda and Kawakami 2012, 121), such that even the most fundamental elements of the condition remain in question. Communities and family members also play their part in hiding *hikikomori* and making detailed information about the phenomenon hard to come by, for "in order to avoid criticism and even ostracism, the parents of those with *hikikomori* hide their shut-in children from their relatives, neighbors, and their communities" (Hattori 2005, 198).

But the foremost difficulty arises from the nature of the phenomenon itself. That is, the *hikikomori* population is, by definition, *incommunicado*, and, as such, extremely averse to clinical and social contact. The Yokayoka treatment center in Fukuoka, a "one-room support center" ironically "linked to a youth employment facility," mainly fields phone calls from "worried parents" of *hikikomori*, while "only a small number of *hikikomori* actually show up at the center. Of those, a minority are treated successfully" (Wang 2015). If a rare individual in *hikikomori* does present herself for treatment, she may offer little or no insight into her experience. One of the more typical responses when asked what caused a period of *hikikomori*, or what the experience was like is, simply: "I don't know" (Kato et al. 2012, 1063; see also Jones 2006).

To the extent that *hikikomori* is or is not distinctly Japanese – a question to be taken up momentarily – it can be difficult to distinguish between its academic, clinical, and popular understandings. Terms like *hikikomori* occupy a unique lexical space in Japan, reserved for psycho-social phenomena attributed to changes in Japanese society and often associated with globalization and the clash between foreign and 'traditional' values. For instance, in the early 1990s, a highpoint of economic growth, "there was a sudden rush of concern about *karoshi* (death by overwork) that suggested the country was labouring itself to an early grave" (Watts 2002, 1131). Today, in the virtual age, the term *otaku* denotes a growing segment of the youth population seen as "'oddballs,' 'geeks' or 'nerds' … avid readers of *manga* comics and heavy internet users" who are thought to be "somewhat socially inept" (Furlong 2008, 321–322; see also Tateno et al. 2012, 169).

Although there are variations in theories concerning the cause of *hikikomori*, Jonathan Watts remains correct that "there is broad agreement that this illness is a product of the affluence, technology, and convenience of modern Japanese life" (2002, 1131). That is, while not ignoring "wider sociological trends," such as "the breakdown of communication and collapse of the family and human relations" in Japan (Allison 2013, 74), scholars and pundits return to what might be seen as parallel phenomena at national and familial levels: *Hikikomori* is understood to be a disease born of excess, permissiveness, and indulgence (Kato et al. 2011, 67; Murakami 2000; Zielenziger 2006).

These trends help explain why Japanese individuals in *hikikomori* have received such negative treatment in the Japanese media and public (Hattori 2005, Kitayama et al. 2001). The broader Japanese public remains quite:

> hostile to *Hikikomori* and assumes that it is a moral weakness, rather than a legitimate psychological disorder. … [T]he man or woman on the street regards people with *Hikikomori* as spoiled, lazy young people who willfully disregard their parents' wishes and arbitrarily avoid social obligations.
>
> *(Hattori 2005, 198)*

Although recent depictions of *hikikomori* in youth-directed media are sometimes sympathetic, more frightening portrayals, as in films such as *Hikikomori: Tokyo*

Plastic (2004), which depicts a cruel *hikikomori* corrupting innocent young women from his solitary lair, are not uncommon.

Hikikomori's pejorative connotations are also inseparable from its introduction to Japanese consciousness via two widely publicized crimes committed by individuals with a history of the disorder, one involving the hijacking of a bus and the killing of a passenger, the other involving the kidnapping and extended captivity of a child (Rees 2002). Accounts of *hikikomori* physically assaulting their parents are also well known and have been confirmed by multiple studies. In the 2003 study sponsored by the Japanese government, forty percent of *hikikomori* cases involved domestic "violence." Although "violence" here included "both verbal and physical abuse," "nearly a third of domestic violence cases perpetrated by the *hikikomori* warrant[ed] the evacuation of family members" (Ohashi 2008, 14).

Thus, in the early days of moral panic regarding the condition, *hikikomori* were regarded as over-indulged yet violent and unpredictable criminals. Unofficial "boot-camp facilities" were established in which "parents coerce[d] youth with *Hikikomori* into military-like training programs," where they were "forced to perform manual labor for disciplinary purposes" (Hattori 2005, 198). One 'recovery' organization was recently sued for having run "an 'abduction and confinement' regime" in which a detainee died after being "chained to a pillar for four days." Although condemned for their actions, such organizations apparently "received an enormous amount of sympathy from a public who regard *hikikomori* as free-riding parasites and feel that parents are not providing the discipline necessary to reform this anti-social behaviour" (Furlong 2008, 317).[1] Such responses suggest fear, hatred, and perhaps even envy of *hikikomori* and what it represents.

'Bound' by culture

Hikikomori is widely, although unofficially, recognized by mental health practitioners and researchers around the world as a "culture-bound syndrome." While acknowledging the flaws of the term, and even while recognizing the existence of similar phenomena in other countries, Teo, Stufflebaum, and Kato argue that *hikikomori* must be considered 'culture-bound' because:

> (i) it is a discrete, well-defined syndrome; (ii) it has been argued as a specific illness; (iii) it is expected, recognized and to some degree sanctioned as a response to certain cultural precipitants; and (iv) it has a higher incidence of prevalence [in Japan] compared to other cultures.
>
> *(2014, 449)*

This designation affects not just theory but practice. Numerous cross-national studies have found, for instance, that Japanese care-providers tend "to be more passive in providing medical intervention in *hikikomori* cases" (Tateno et al. 2012, 4), a reluctance to act that may reflect the belief in the inevitability of *hikikomori* in Japan or in the futility (or even undesirability) of treating Japanese sufferers.

What is certain is that if *hikikomori* is to be defined as a Japanese phenomenon, then it is comprehensible only within the context of Japanese cultural life. And while scholars continue to debate the details of the disorder, few have recognized the consequences of approaching *hikikomori* as a "culture-bound syndrome," itself (see Sakamoto et al. 2005). To define *hikikomori* as a syndrome that "thrives in one particular country during a particular moment in its history" (Jones 2006) is to insist upon a very specific relationship between it and contemporary Japanese culture. This means that individuals in *hikikomori*, their experiences, and all they represent are sequestered from theories and constructs that are not specific to Japan (e.g., agoraphobia or social withdrawal) and that are not similarly culture-bound (e.g., intrapsychic dynamics, attachment patterns, or early childhood experiences).

It is unfortunately beyond the scope of this chapter to review the extensive literature that contests the viability of the concept of 'culture' (see, e.g., Eagleton 2000; Finkielkraut 1987). It is undeniable, however, that, in the realm of the social and behavioral sciences, 'culture' has often served a less-than-noble function, tending to promote stereotyping, chauvinism, and orientalism (see Said 1979) as much as or more than meaningful understanding. In the domain of psychology, Ethan Watters justly quips that the so-called "culture-bound syndromes" treated so delicately in the final pages of the *DSM*, such as *koro* and *amok*, end up being for the reader little more than "carnival sideshows" that "might as well be labeled 'Psychiatric Exotica: Two Bits a Gander'" (2010, 5).

Defining *hikikomori* as a culture-bound syndrome also permits *hikikomori* to function as a weapon in mounting attacks on Japanese society, whether those critiques run for or against 'traditional' values. Michael Zielenziger, for instance, has argued that young people in Japan "want to be different than their parents and different from their peers, but Japan is so collectively engineered that it's very difficult, if not impossible, for them to really express themselves" (2006). Similarly, in her article entitled "Hikikomania," Kathleen Todd argues that Japanese society has created a situation in which a young person's "original personality" is effaced, "while the [false] front personality compulsively conforms to perceived expectations" (2011, 137–138). While such critiques could be applied to practically any youth population on the planet, the high rates of *hikikomori* in Japan seem to serve as anecdotal evidence in support of such claims. The literature on *hikikomori* uses the self-punishment and self-deprivation of those suffering from the syndrome to direct criticism at the relatively easy targets of "Japanese society" and "Japanese culture" (Todd 2011, 136).

If, as discussed in Chapter 3, "every instance of severe traumatic psychological injury is a standing challenge to the rightness of the social order" (Herman quoted in Shay 1995, 3), it is this belief that has made the concept of trauma so fascinating to social theorists in Europe and North America for the past three and a half decades. This same link – the link between the victims of a psychological syndrome and their potential use as evidence to ground social critique – is part of what has made *hikikomori* such an attractive concept for the clinical, academic, and popular imagination both within Japan and beyond.

It remains unclear to what extent broader social critiques reflect individuals' understandings of the causes of their own *hikikomori*. It may be, for instance, that blaming the growing Japanese economy or rapid changes in Japanese society for the psychic pain associated with *hikikomori* is in some sense 'necessary' for the individual to 'recover' in Youth (*Hikikomori*) Support Centers and, more generally, in a society that comprehends *hikikomori* symptoms solely along such lines. Thus, it may be that, even in 'recovery,' the individual's authentic feelings and self-understandings are supplanted by accommodation to others' needs to frame and interpret the *hikikomori* experience in a particular way. To use *hikikomori* as a sign that something is amiss in Japanese society, the meaning of *hikikomori* must be discussed but never pinned down, experienced but never understood. Defining *hikikomori* as a culture-bound syndrome effectively isolates the disorder from thought and understanding, echoing, in a metaphorical sense, *hikikomori*'s primary symptom. These reflections shed light on another salient aspect of the literature and phenomenon of *hikikomori* taken up below: the relationship between victimization and mystification.

The distortion of *amae*

A careful reading of the scholarly and popular literatures makes it difficult to avoid the conclusion that those who treat and study *hikikomori* have (ambivalently) psychologically identified with their subjects, such that comprehending the behavior of *hikikomori* comes to represent a betrayal of *hikikomori* and their experience. Like those who, as we noted in Chapter 2, feel that there is an "absolute obscenity in the project of understanding the holocaust" (Lanzmann 1995, 204), those who forge identifications with individuals in *hikikomori* see themselves as privileged witnesses to an experience of suffering which it is their obligation to protect and defend. Without trivializing the horrors of the Nazi camps, the self-incarceration of the individual in *hikikomori* is in some ways akin to a private concentration camp, one whose secret sufferings are carefully guarded against outsiders' understandings (see also Bowker 2014).

An excellent example of this protective dynamic may be found in the acclaimed Japanese film *Tobira no Muko* (literally: *The Other Side of the Door*) (2008), which borders on documentary, and which stars Kenta Nigishi, himself a recovering *hikikomori*. The film depicts the struggle of the Okada family and their son Hiroshi, a teenaged boy who, one day, enters his room and is hardly seen or heard by the audience again. The film illustrates the effects of Hiroshi's *hikikomori* on his mother, father, and younger brother, while introducing audiences to Sadatsugo Kudo, who plays himself, as the director of a local Youth (*Hikikomori*) Support Center.

The film's depiction of all characters is sympathetic, and yet Hiroshi's *hikikomori* is inscrutable to audiences, who must guess what has precipitated his isolation, what his experience of it is like, and when or how he might emerge from it. In many ways, it is really the audience who is left on 'the other side of the door,' restricted from seeing and understanding Hiroshi in a way that suggests the film's real intent: to *transmit*, rather than to communicate, the frustration and confusion experienced by those confronting *hikikomori*. To see the film is to wonder why it is necessary that nothing about Hiroshi, and *hikikomori*, be clearly understood.

Indeed, one is left with the impression that the denial of understanding *is* Hiroshi's goal, the goal of the film, the goal of many individuals in *hikikomori*, and, perhaps, the goal of scholarly and popular treatments of *hikikomori* as well. If the individual in *hikikomori* refuses to communicate and to be understood, as do the researchers working in the cottage industry of *hikikomori* scholarship, then what exactly must be hidden in *hikikomori* and what is the psychic meaning of this hiding? The answer to these questions lies in a closer examination of the concept of *amae* and, strangely enough, in its consistent misapplication by researchers on *hikikomori*.

The Japanese term *amae* and the verb *amaeru* are quite close to the English noun 'indulgence' and the verb-forms 'to indulge oneself' and 'to presume indulgence.' In English, 'indulgence' has a rather complex range of meanings, since, for instance, one may indulge oneself, one may indulge one's baser instincts, one may indulge another person, and one may indulge in the indulgences offered by another. In all cases, indulging involves yielding or acceding, either to one's own desires, or to the desires or demands of another.

In Japan, and one might argue in many cultures, it is expected that an infant or child will *amaeru* to his parents: that he will indulge in their indulgence of him. That is, the child is expected to permit himself to become dependent upon his parents, to expect some adaptation to his needs and desires, and to enjoy this experience – at first unknowingly, but in time with some recognition of his state. It is also expected that the child's parents will not refuse or reject his demands and dependence, and that a good many indulgences will be offered to the child. And the parents, of course, come to depend upon the child's dependence, and may be said to indulge themselves in the child's indulgent use of them.

Takeo Doi must be credited with bringing the idea of *amae* into clear focus and applying it to a wide range of psycho-social phenomena, both in Japan and elsewhere, in his two best-known books, *The Anatomy of Dependence* (1973) and *The Anatomy of the Self* (1986). In one's immediate family, argues Doi, even as an adult, it is permissible to *amaeru* and thus to be self-indulgent, since one may depend upon the indulgence of family members. One need not restrain oneself nor follow the (sometimes stringent) norms of courtesy, as one might in less intimate social relationships. One need not worry about imposing upon others, nor apologize for one's inevitable impositions. In the ideal Japanese family, Doi claims, one exists in a state of secure interdependence: One is assured that one's requests will be met, and, more importantly, one is assured that the desire for indulgence will not lead to rejection or the loss of the good will of loved ones.[2]

Here, it is important to associate indulgence and dependence not with merely physical needs, but with the emotional needs that compose the infant's and the child's primary relationships. The concept of *amae*, then, may describe not only the orientation of the child toward primary attachment-figures but the broader web of relatedness (and separateness) in which both indulgence and dependence occur. *Amae* is more robust than what attachment theorists would describe as a "secure base" (Bowlby 1988), more complex than what Freud would call "the child's primary object-choice" (Freud 1964, 180). It accords best with what Winnicott would refer to as an adaptive and nurturing facilitating environment (1965). Indeed, the widely held Japanese belief, cited by Doi (1973, 20), that a healthy *jibun* (self) grows from "the soil" of *amae* in early relationships is quite similar to the Winnicottian notion that the infant's and the child's capacities for creativity and autonomy are facilitated through satisfactory early experiences of facilitation and attunement.

An adequately 'indulgent' environment permits dependence to be experienced as omnipotence and predictability as creativity, which affords opportunities for the infant and child to explore her own authentic desires, emotions, and needs. The child who is able to indulge herself in all that is offered is able to establish the feeling that not just her external world but her internal world is safe, benign, and good.

A child whose need for indulgence has been unmet inhabits a world quite different from that of the "ontologically secure" individual, for whom "relatedness with others is potentially gratifying," as is being alone. The ontologically insecure person must be "preoccupied with preserving rather than gratifying himself: the ordinary circumstances of living threaten his *low threshold* of security" (Laing 1969, 42, emphasis in original). An individual suffering from losses or deprivations of *amae*, then, contends with a world whose "everyday happenings … come to have a different hierarchy of significance from that of the ordinary person." The ontologically insecure individual begins to "'*live in a world of his own*' or has already come to do so" (43, emphasis added).

Frustration in the desire for *amae* is a complex phenomenon, and is too often blamed squarely on some essential attribute of the child (e.g., his 'temperament') or on some obvious failing of the parent. Doi describes a conversation with the mother of an anxious, non-*hikikomori* patient who characterized her child as someone who "did not *amaeru* much … kept to herself, never 'made up to' her parents, never behaved childishly in the confident assumption that her parents would indulge her" (1973, 18). Such children in Western countries might be described as 'independent,' when, in fact, underlying their apparent self-sufficiency may be profound anxiety that their desires for care and attention cannot or will not be met.

A relational approach, on the contrary, would suggest that frustration in *amae* arises from a set of unfortunate experiences, fantasies, and fears developed within the parent–child relationship. Specifically, the child who does not *amaeru* may not only fear the experience of frustration of her immediate needs or desires, but, more fundamentally, may fear the negative psychic consequences of becoming aware of, expressing, or fulfilling, such desires. These consequences may include the shameful perception of herself as needy, greedy, unworthy, or ridiculous, as well as the feared rejection or loss of love of the parent.

What is striking about the literature on *hikikomori* is that, in almost every case, *amae*, seen as a Japanese cultural norm, is *also* understood to be a cause of *hikikomori*. Although *amae* is not a new construct, believed instead to have been a part of Japanese culture for centuries (Doi 1973), it is, ostensibly, this same Japanese dynamic that has rather suddenly struck down millions of otherwise healthy individuals who are now unable to leave their rooms. *Amae*, then, is understood to be both an impinging parenting practice that cripples the child's capacity for social functioning and a proud cultural tradition that is, in spite of all, still "considered adaptive by Japanese standards" (Teo, Stufflebaum, and Kato 2014, 449).

We may wonder why so many studies on *hikikomori* that discuss *amae*, even those that cite Doi's well-known work (see, e.g., Hein 2009; Horiguchi 2012), view the notion in this confused way, as both a healthy tradition and an unhealthy parental dependence. Although dependence surely accompanies an indulgent early childhood environment, a less conflicted notion of *amae* would be one in which the child's receipt of loving indulgence were imagined to contribute to a secure attachment and a stable self-relationship. It is tempting, on this point, to speculate that the ambivalence expressed in research on *amae* expresses a conflict at its core, a denial of dependence and a denial of desire for *amae*, achieved by pathologizing a desirable aspect of the child's environment. The concomitants of such denials, which include repressed rage and envy, are discussed in further detail below.

As Heinz Kohut notes, and as has been alluded to in relation to education and narcissism in Chapter 5, difficulties in school or work, specifically difficulties in mobilizing energy or 'intrinsic motivation' to achieve goals, are rarely the result of indulgent love or excessive self-esteem, but the opposite: "Many of the most severe and chronic work disturbances," Kohut argues, are "due to the fact that the self is poorly cathected with narcissistic libido and in chronic danger of fragmentation." Since "a relationship to an empathetically approving and accepting parent is one of the preconditions for the original establishment of a firm cathexis of the self" (1971, 120), the individual who has been indulged in *amae* is *less* likely to refuse school, to refuse work, or to withdraw into *hikikomori*.

It is true, of course, that the demands of school and work can be experienced, in any society, as impinging and oppressive. Nonetheless, to understand *hikikomori* as the result of experiencing school or work in this way would be to see only the surface, for individuals who have been afforded appropriate facilitating environments are more likely to develop the capacities needed not only to withstand occasional impingement but to create and transform their experiences in ways aligned with the self's authentic needs and desires. That is, to the child who has been 'indulged,' courses of study and, later, periods of work represent opportunities to realize the self in the world, rather than cruel, foreign impositions that demand passive compliance or refusal. The difference between these two types of experience is, obviously, considerable: If there is "a living self in depth [that] has become the organizing center of the ego's activities," then the individual's work is "undertaken on his own initiative rather than as if by a passively obedient automaton ... [with] some originality rather than being humdrum and routine" (Kohut 1971, 120).

The misconstrual of *amae* as an overly indulgent attitude, instilled in the child via a unique parenting style and exacerbated by recent decades of affluence, suggests exactly the wrong solutions: the imposition of increased "grit" and toughness and the deprivation of indulgence and care in the home, in school, and in the workplace. At a practical level, this line of thinking has led to the popular belief that "*hikikomori* can be cured with tough love and being kicked out of their nest" (Hairston 2010, 319), and to the development of organizations like the aforementioned 'recovery' camps where individuals in *hikikomori* were mistreated and, in some cases, tortured and killed (Furlong 2008, 317). This line of thinking threatens the (already-threatened) individual in *hikikomori*, and what he represents, with renewed deprivations of indulgence and care. In maligning *amae* as a dangerous desire, and in threatening those who do desire *amae*, current theory and practice surrounding *hikikomori* may be read as a rejection of, even a hatred of, individuals in *hikikomori*, who are imagined to greedily presume upon their families for food, clothing, shelter, and more. Individuals in *hikikomori*, then, symbolize a powerful desire for *amae* that must be repressed as a defense against the pain of its articulation and its potential frustration.

The disfigurement of desire

Interpreting scholarly, clinical, and popular discourses on *hikikomori* with an eye to defensive resistance proves to be a helpful method of approaching the phenomenon of *hikikomori* itself. Of course, understanding psycho-social phenomena like *hikikomori* in their socio-political and cultural contexts is often valuable, but in this case, a sort of intellectual protectionism of *hikikomori* has mystified rather than illuminated the condition. At the same time, in spite of insistences that researchers focus on culturally unique interpretive keys, the most relevant of Japanese socio-cultural norms, *amae*, has been consistently mistaken and misapplied.

If we focus on the individual's desire for *amae*, we see that this desire is not in itself unreasonable, just as the desire to be loved and cared for is a healthy and fundamental desire of every child. But individuals with frustrated desire for *amae*, having internalized a prohibition against experiencing this desire in order to avoid the pain of failing to fulfill it – along with the pain of being aware of a desire that is unfulfilled and, perhaps, unfulfillable – come to believe it to be shameful and inappropriate, deny that they experience it, and recruit others to agree with these beliefs. By making it appear as if parental love is equivalent to damaging over-indulgence, it is implied that the desire, itself, is imposed, that it is not the individual's own. That is, the individual in *hikikomori* would never have developed his symptoms had not his parents and his culture foolishly over-indulged him. By construing *amae* as a form of culturally sanctioned parental abuse that causes life-long mental anguish, and by implicitly threatening those in *hikikomori* with the 'solution' of further withdrawing support and care, those concerned with *hikikomori* translate frustrated desires for *amae* into critical and sadistic attitudes toward those who seem to demand the indulgences they envy. What may be really feared about *hikikomori* is not that someone in *hikikomori* may commit a violent act, but that the truth about *hikikomori* will be revealed, the truth of a desire that cannot be recognized without shame.

This state of affairs can only be sustained via a sort of ideology of *hikikomori* and a systematic effort at mystification, a Marxist term popularized in psychoanalytic theory by R.D. Laing (1961, 1985; see also Laing and Esterson 1964), meaning to prevent understanding or to insist upon a false reality. Like ideology, mystification often involves both subtle and overt forms of aggression to prevent recognition of that which might threaten the holder of power, or, what amounts to the same thing, to protect a cherished belief or fantasy that would be lost if subjected to conscious scrutiny. Laing notes that mystification primarily involves the abuse of others to shore up internal repressive efforts, since "if the one person does not want to know something or to remember something, it is not enough to repress it (or otherwise 'successfully' defend himself against it 'in' himself); he must not be reminded of it by the other" (1985, 348).

A host of fearsome consequences awaits the one who attempts to break through the veil of mystification. The skeptic, the whistle-blower, or the psychoanalyst who questions the false reality protected by mystification may be cast as irresponsible, cruel, heretical, insane, or worse. In most cases, the resistance to penetrating what has been mystified is grounded not primarily in reasonable fears about likely negative consequences, but in unconscious associations and ancient terrors of bad objects that mis-represented and mis-figured themselves (i.e., mystified themselves) as good.

In light of this connection between the frustration of *amae* in the family, its misconstrual in the literature, and the isolation and non-communication which are the defining features of *hikikomori*, it is difficult not to recall Franz Kafka's famous story, *Die Verwandlung* (*The Metamorphosis*), wherein traveling salesman Gregor Samsa awakens one morning to find that he has been 'mysteriously' transformed into an *ungeheuren Ungeziefer*, a "monstrous vermin."[3] What presses most heavily on Gregor's mind at the outset is that, in his newly transformed state, he is quite *unable to leave his room* to go to work.

Particularly interesting about Kafka's story is the way Gregor's transformation transforms and even reverses the relationships of dependence and indulgence between him and his family. Since the collapse of his father's business, Gregor's "sole desire was to do his utmost to help the family ... so he had set to work with unusual ardor" (Kafka 1971, 110). While his tireless work for an abusive chief clerk meant that he was "able to meet the expenses of the whole household" (111), Gregor's family had become accustomed to depending upon his extraordinary self-sacrifice: "They had simply got used to it, both the family and Gregor; the money was gratefully accepted and gladly given, but there was no special uprush of warm feeling" (111).

In one sense, Gregor's transformation sets him free from his toil. In fact, the German word *Verwandlung* can mean not only 'metamorphosis' or 'transformation' but 'commutation,' as in the commutation of a prison sentence. But in another sense, Gregor's 'freedom' now depends upon the indulgence of his family. He must be taken care of; he must be fed and his room must be cleaned. To the extent that the family continues to regard the vermin as Gregor, his physical survival requires that they nourish and protect him. Gregor is therefore both free and dependent. In this way he returns to a child-like condition, perhaps one he never knew as a child. But Gregor is also *ungeheuren*, monstrous and hideous. His disfigurement, which might be interpreted as the consequence of trying to return to a child-like condition that never was, means that, unlike an adored and indulged child, he must lock himself away in his room lest he upset his family, must bar himself from meaningful contact, and must deprive himself of all but the most basic of necessities.

Japanese therapist Yuichi Hattori, who stands somewhat apart from his contemporaries in defining *hikikomori* as a "trauma-based disorder" that is nonetheless lacking most defining characteristics and symptoms of PTSD (2005, 184), studied thirty-five clients at a suburban Tokyo clinic, some of whom revealed similar family dynamics.[4] While the dependencies and indulgences of the Samsa family, and then Gregor, are cast in terms of physical need and accommodation, so are the behaviors of *hikikomori*, whose self-incarceration may be highly symbolic. In an illustrative case, a twenty-eight-year-old woman recovering from *hikikomori* explained that, in her childhood:

> My mother depended on me for comforting. My mother treated me like her personal teddy bear and used me to satisfy her own emotional needs. She wasn't interested in knowing my feelings and thoughts. I don't think my mother regarded me as a human with free will. She sometimes looked like a zombie to me. I felt emotionally suffocated, as I couldn't communicate with her. I secretly feared my mother, but I tried always to please her. I wanted freedom. I felt emotionally abandoned as a child.
>
> *(2005, 197)*

So, if we read Kafka's story in one way, we find a set of dynamics quite similar to those of the individual in *hikikomori*, who returns to a child-like state, but one distorted by the realities of the individual's deprived childhood. Like the young woman described in Hattori's study, Gregor had been used to indulge his parents' needs, rather than the other way around. Certainly, the Samsa family does not seem "interested in knowing [Gregor's] feelings and thoughts," nor do they regard him, either before or after his transformation, "as a human with free will." Gregor's demand for care and attention, therefore, can be expressed only through hideous self-transformation and isolation.

Gregor's physical death is caused by starvation, but his existence, his self or his psychic existence, is terminated the moment his sister Grete convinces the family that they "must just try to get rid of the idea that this is Gregor" (Kafka 1971, 134), a notion that she defends by arguing that the *real* Gregor would be too considerate to presume upon his family's indulgence for so long. That is, the *real* Gregor would have killed himself or exiled himself from the home for their sakes long ago and would be ashamed to hang around requiring care and sacrifice on their parts.

If we imagine, for a moment, that Gregor has not physically changed at all, that his 'transformation' has been a transformation of emotion or attitude, then we may read his metamorphosis as a metaphor for his desire to indulge himself and to be indulged by others. Of course, Gregor's discovered desire 'monstrously' disfigures him with respect to his own self-concept and his family's impression of him. In a sense, Grete is right that, if all the family knows of Gregor is his will-ingness to repress and exploit his needs in their service, he no longer exists, and the "idea" of Gregor, which mistakes him for his self-occluding role in the family, has already been lost. Tragically, in the moment of his death, Gregor comes to agree with the family that, in his new "monstrous" form, he is *not* himself, is not lovable, and therefore must be eliminated:

> [Gregor] thought of his family with tenderness and love. The decision that he must disappear was one that he held to even more strongly than his sister. ... In this state of vacant and peaceful meditation he remained until ... his head sank to the floor of its own accord and from his nostrils came the last faint flicker of his breath.
>
> *(1971, 135)*

Gregor's 'mysterious' transformation, then, may be read as a claim to indulgence, a self-incarceration, an escape from a painful condition, and a disfigurement of his self's most basic desire, one that makes his desire unrecognizable. What is com-pelling and tragic about the story, of course, is that it should not be necessary that Gregor be disfigured, or that he conceive of himself as disfigured, in order to discover his own desire for love and care. That is, Gregor's transformation may be read as a botched attempt to rediscover his capacity to *amaeru*. This attempt ulti-mately fails because he is unable to experience or act upon his desire for *amae* without becoming overwhelmed by shame and self-loathing, disfiguring his desire into something hideous. Gregor both strives to fulfill and sabotages his own struggle for *amae* by becoming "monstrous" to himself and to those from whom he most deeply desires love and indulgence.

If it is the internal conflict between Gregor's shame and his desire to *amaeru* that causes his disfigurement, then his metamorphosis appears very much like the metamorphoses of scores of young men and women who enter *hikikomori*, who feel that their desire for *amae*, expressed in an isolation that demands a half-measure of indulgence, also makes them monstrous and unworthy of *amae*. It would seem that the metamorphosis of the socially functioning individual to the individual in *hikikomori* is characterized by both profound shame and impossible hope, or, to be more precise, hope made impossible by an equally powerful sense of shame.

Since the individual in *hikikomori* experiences his desire to *amaeru* as childish, shameful, or monstrous, consciously seeking to distance himself from it as much as possible, his silent self-incarceration might also be understood as a desperate attempt to enter a protective 'cocoon' from which he may one day emerge not as a disfigured vermin full of monstrous desires but as a person worthy of certain indulgences. As Winnicott might say, such an individual and his "antisocial tendenc[ies]" reflect an effort to "get back behind the deprivation moment or condition" (1986, 92), to return to a state of freedom, security, and indulgence, perhaps lost long ago. But the ambivalence about this desire, owing to the shame the individual has internalized as a defense against its frustration, suggests to him that returning to this state is neither possible nor desirable. The impossibility of his hope, then, turns the individual in *hikikomori* to rage and anger, as he repeats rather than redeems his moment of deprivation while seeking to impose his deprivation onto others. To understand these final characteristics of *hikikomori*, we must turn briefly to Winnicott's work on deprivation and delinquency.

Deprivation and victimization

In his short paper entitled "Delinquency as a Sign of Hope," Winnicott is concerned with children who have experienced deprivation: the loss or withdrawal of care, dependability, and indulgence in their worlds. Deprivation may be painful in terms of the frustration of momentary needs or desires, but, more importantly, it occasions a tremendous change in the entire psycho-social experience or "the whole life of the child" (1986, 91). That is, deprivation is *not* experienced by the child as a trivial or temporary environmental failure. The child, possessed at first by "unthinkable anxiety" about his new condition, quickly strives to comply with the new order of things, fundamentally because "there is nothing else that the child is strong enough to do" (92). But adaptation to a depriving and impoverished environment means the loss of the spontaneity, safe expressions of aggression, and creativity appropriate to facilitating environments. Although she had little choice, the child who identifies with the framework of control and deprivation inflicts a greater loss upon herself. She compounds her initial loss – we might even say she unwittingly colludes with her depriving objects – to produce a state of profound self-deprivation.

Winnicott posits that it is common for children who can still recall an earlier state of indulgence to seize upon an occasion for hope, and to strive to "get back behind the moment of deprivation" by "reach[ing] out" and, perhaps, compulsively stealing or breaking something (1986, 92–93). This initial impulsive act represents, for Winnicott, creative object-seeking more than anti-social or criminal delinquency. That is, such acts of theft or destructiveness are really attempts to rediscover and safely express authentic and aggressive impulses (94–95). Ultimately, what is hoped for in apparently 'delinquent' behavior is the return to the state – composed of both reality and fantasy, of conditions in both the inner and outer world – in which spontaneous gestures and authentic desires may be experienced safely, indulged by the parent, enacted freely, and tolerated by the environment.

The same may be said of individuals in *hikikomori*: that they have suffered deprivation, that they are behaving in a way that appears, if not delinquent, then at least anti-social, but that ultimately they seek not rebellion but the return to a condition of connection with their own desires and impulses, perhaps especially the infantile and childish ones. They seek, for lack of a better term, the 'indulgent self-experience' facilitated by a nurturing environment that, since it belongs properly to childhood, has to a large degree already been lost, and can only be mourned, never fully restored in adolescence or adulthood. But, of course, internal conflict about this desire makes behavior of *hikikomori* a curious mixture of self-defense and self-sabotage, ultimately ill suited to achieving this aim.

In the minority of cases in which *hikikomori* verbally or physically attack family members, it is possible to see attempts to reverse early emotional deprivation, attempts which are, given the circumstances, almost certain to fail. Hattori relates the case of a twenty-one-year-old man who "pinned his unresponsive mother to the wall, squeezed her neck with his hands, and said, 'Tell me how you feel about me.' The mother said repeatedly, 'I'm sorry. I am to blame.'" Hattori concludes that the mother's irrelevant and tangential response "disappointed" the young man "overwhelmingly," although we must imagine that such disappointment had very likely already been experienced by the young man in *hikikomori* and that its effects had already overwhelmed him (2005, 189–190).

If several of Hattori's clients "withdrew even more after domestic violence ceased," it would seem that such individuals in *hikikomori*, having failed to create an indulgent environment for themselves in self-incarceration, and having subsequently failed even in last-ditch attempts to re-ignite loving or indulgent relationships with their parents, simply give up. At this stage of hopelessness, the individual in *hikikomori* can only compulsively re-enact his deprivation, attaching a more regressive aim to his expressions of despair: to share his agony with others by visiting it upon them.

It is important not to overlook how the self-deprivation imposed by the individual in *hikikomori* also denies family members the freedom and autonomy due to subjects as separate individuals. Family members caring for an individual in *hikikomori* provide meals, clothing, shelter, and other basic needs, often making tremendous sacrifices in their own lives. But it would be a mistake to imagine that an individual's state of *hikikomori* forces family members to return to 'care' in a rich sense, or to *amae*. At least, such an interpretation would seem to offer a very shallow understanding of what *amae* signifies and what is ultimately hoped for, since family members are prevented from emotionally interacting with the individual and are relegated to the status of servants.

The refusal, on the part of the individual in *hikikomori*, to help the family understand its sudden servitude and the trying situation (self-)imposed upon the individual leaves family members unsure whether the *hikikomori* is a punishment for some misdeed, or whether it will lead to greater physical or mental sickness, suicide, or violence. Parents and family members of individuals in *hikikomori* frequently report feelings of guilt and shame concerning their *hikikomori* family member. By denying communication, by shutting family members out, and by abandoning family members in their shame, worry, and fear, the individual in *hikikomori* victimizes her caretakers while similarly occupying the position of a victim. Part of the deprivation involved in *hikikomori*, then, is that the individual who is shut away in her room manages to deprive others of psychological well-being, comfort, self-esteem, participation in normal activities and relationships, and the ability to indulge themselves or to enjoy the indulgences of others. The individual in *hikikomori* makes others responsible for her survival and, by implication, for her *hikikomori* state as well.

Gary Paul's very short story "Hikikomori" shares something of its effect on a sibling with painful simplicity (2012, 69–70, emphasis added). In the story, Satoshi writes a note to his sister to accompany her nightly meal, left outside her door. Satoshi has not seen her in five years:

> I hope you're still alive and well. I mean, someone eats the plates of food I leave outside your door. ... I'm just writing this letter because I wanted to talk to you in some way or another. ... Oh, don't think I'm pressuring you to come out or something. Just want to talk. ... As for me, I had a girlfriend last year! You may have heard us talking and laughing loudly late at night. She made me laugh. She wanted to meet you, you know, but ... we're not together any more. *I couldn't leave the house for too long*, not with you left all alone here. I don't mean to sound bitter, I like looking after you. Think I'm a little bit hikikomori myself, haha. I don't do much these days. I don't know why ... I just feel sort of numb. The world has gotten harder in the last few years. I'm not sure I want to be a part of it any more. Honestly, caring for you is the only thing I think I'm good at, and, even then, I don't know if I'm succeeding ...
>
> I love you.
>
> Happy Birthday.
>
> *—Satoshi*

To consider *hikikomori* a means of punishing others by punishing the self, and, as such, as a form of victimization via self-victimization, is to interpret *hikikomori* along the lines of Theodor Reik's understanding of masochistic behavior as symbolic aggression that announces: "That's how I would like to treat you" (see Uebel 2013, 480–481). Indeed, it would not be out of order to speculate that a goal of the individual in *hikikomori* is to transmit to family members and others her own isolation, shame, and fear, just as Satoshi's sister forces him to become something of a *hikikomori* just to tend to her *hikikomori* state. Doing so may permit the individual in *hikikomori* to experience her own deprivation, perhaps for the first time, and to contend with her confusion and anger by projectively identifying with the family's suffering.

Developmentally speaking, we may say that the deprivation of indulgence, dependence, or *amae* is the original act of victimization. To be deprived of *amae* is a form of victimization that leads many individuals to carry with them, throughout life, a sense of having been profoundly harmed. In adulthood, individuals and groups continue to make use of the mechanism of projective identification to re-create this early victimization, to experience their own feelings through others' reactions to being victimized, and to impose upon others the responsibility for their own acts of victimization. In the final chapter, I discuss the state of nature as a fantasized original, natural condition in which what is most obviously lacking is not political authority but something like *amae*. It may be read, I will argue, as a fantasy about re-experiencing the original act of victimization in a way that is not entirely dissimilar to the phenomenon of *hikikomori*.

Indeed, in politics, the dynamic by which victimizers hold onto and strive to re-experience victimization may be frequently seen, as in the Zenkyōtō movements in Japan in the 1960s, discussed by Doi, who noticed that both *amae* and *higaisha-ishiki* (the sense of grievance and of being a victim) were at work, and that the two constructs were closely connected. Doi remarked how the students of the Zenkyōtō movements were able to operate aggressively while, at the same time, framing their actions in ways that succeeded in "putting themselves in the position of victims" (1973, 25–26).

More recently, in the United States, the killings of black males by police officers in Ferguson, Missouri, New York City, Baltimore, Maryland, and elsewhere, and the unfortunate police responses to public protest and outrage, have shown that police, government, and diverse civilian groups are all capable of casting themselves as victims and, as such, of acting with the objective of transmitting and re-transmitting their own experiences of suffering, imposing upon others the agony, confusion, and incomprehension of the victim.

These protests have struggled with conflicting desires related to the experience of victimization. On one hand, protestors have seemed to wish to know and to make known to others exactly what has happened to victims such as Freddie Gray, Michael Brown, Eric Garner, and many others. On the other hand, protestors seek to transmit to fellow protestors, to the police, to the media, and to the public the message that it is impossible to understand what being a victim is like unless one is or has been a victim. That is, protests such as these, and the media discussion and intellectual discourses that surround them, are concerned with both sharing and hiding the experience of being a victim, an experience that, itself, seems to include both confusion and certainty, fear and rage, frustration and gratification.

That individuals in *hikikomori* remain shut away in their rooms and refuse, for years and even decades, gestures of understanding and care from family members and social workers implies that the behavior involves a powerful compulsion to repeat an early failure in the relationship between child and parent, a compulsion that cannot be resolved because the individual in *hikikomori* is unable to accept his own desire but is also unable to abandon it. The resistance to accepting a belated form of *amae* by the individual in *hikikomori* may be, as suggested above, related to the shame felt by such individuals: the disfiguring of their desire as something monstrous, which only deepens their sense of unworthiness. At the same time, the inability to abandon the desire for *amae* may be related to unyielding feelings of rage and resentment at having lost the indulgence and care due a child and the subsequent losses suffered by the adolescent or adult.

By focusing on the 'mysteriousness' of *hikikomori*, and by preserving its mystery, individuals in *hikikomori* and those who study and treat them condemn them to repeating and re-experiencing their losses. We may even say that the individual in *hikikomori* is stuck in a paradox out of which he might think, but this thinking has so far been elusive to most. He wishes to be alone, as he should have been once, but finds that all he can do is lock himself in isolation. He needed others in order to be alone, and now he rejects others to try to undo his need. He is unaware of his desire to be meaningfully related to others, which is also a psychic potential that seems impossible to him. Finding no words or thoughts to communicate these feelings to himself or others, the complexities of these apparent contradictions overwhelm him, just as they seem to overwhelm scholars and theorists who study and treat the phenomenon.

Notes

1 According to some, the idea that *hikikomori* are over-indulged corresponds to their typically middle-to-high socio-economic status. Other explanations, not unique to *hikikomori* or Japanese culture, may be equally relevant, such as the well-known tendency of poverty to both exacerbate and obscure mental illness. Poverty leaves many undiagnosed and untreated, owing to unemployment, inadequate housing, physical illness, lack of access to psychiatric resources, and related socio-economic problems (see, e.g., Saxena et al. 2007; Thompson 2007; World Health Organization 2009). Concomitantly, as recently collected data on the high prevalence of *hikikomori* in Lagos, Nigeria, suggests (Bowker, Ojo, and Bowker 2015), *hikikomori* may be simply impossible under conditions of subsistence-level family economies, where non-employment and dependence upon family-based home-care are inconceivable.

2 Doi writes that in Japanese society, a useful distinction may be drawn between the inner and outer circles of relationship. According to Doi, when in the inner circle, both the

child and the adult are "protected and permitted to *amaeru*" (1973, 107), while, within the outer circle, the individual is asked to restrain (*kigane*) herself, to refrain from expressing willfulness or personal desires, and to strive primarily for the harmony of the group. To *amaeru* where one ought not is to presume upon the indulgence of those who do not owe one indulgence, and is a criticism that has been levied against insufficiently sober individuals and student protest movements alike (see Doi 1973, 1986). Today, to the extent that *hikikomori* is considered a "national" problem with consequences for the entire Japanese society, this criticism is applied to individuals in *hikikomori* and their families.

3 The term, *ungeheuren Ungeziefer*, literally means "monstrous vermin," and is translated into English either as such, or as "gigantic insect," based upon details given later in the story that suggest Gregor's form to resemble that of a beetle or roach.

4 There are some limitations to Hattori's study. First, although his qualitative case studies are not statistically significant or representative with respect to the Japanese *hikikomori* population, he sometimes draws broad conclusions based upon his quantitative results. Second, one must regard with a certain degree of suspicion the fact that no qualitative or quantitative study, conducted either before or after Hattori's, has replicated such significant correlations between *hikikomori* and trauma or dissociative personality systems, the latter being Hattori's area of personal expertise.

References

Allison, A. 2013. *Precarious Japan*. Durham, NC: Duke University Press.

Bowker, J.C., A. Ojo, and M.H. Bowker 2015. "Brief Report: Perceptions of Social Withdrawal during Emerging Adulthood in Lagos, Nigeria." *Journal of Adolescence* 47(1): 1–4.

Bowker, M.H. 2014. *Rethinking the Politics of Absurdity: Albert Camus, Postmodernity, and the Survival of Innocence*. Series: Routledge Innovations in Political Theory. New York: Routledge.

Bowlby, J. 1988. *A Secure Base: Parent–Child Attachment and Healthy Human Development*. New York: Basic Books.

Doi, T. 1973. *The Anatomy of Dependence*. Translated by J. Bester. Tokyo: Kodansha International.

Doi, T. 1986. *The Anatomy of the Self: The Individual Versus Society*. Translated by M. Harbison. Tokyo: Kodansha International.

Eagleton, T. 2000. *The Idea of Culture*. Oxford: Wiley-Blackwell.

Finkielkraut, A. 1987. *La défaite de la pensée*. Paris: Gallimard.

Freud, S. 1964. "On the Universal Tendency to Debasement in the Sphere of Love." In *The Standard Edition of the Complete Psychological Works of Sigmund Freud, Volume XI*, edited and translated by J. Strachey, 179–190. London: Hogarth.

Furlong, A. 2008. "The Japanese Hikikomori Phenomenon: Acute Social Withdrawal Among Young People." *The Sociological Review* 56: 309–325.

Hairston, M. 2010. "A Cocoon with a View: Hikikomori, Otaku, and Welcome to the NHK." *Mechademia* 5: 311–323.

Hattori, Y. 2005. "Social Withdrawal in Japanese Youth: A Case Study of Thirty-Five Hikikomori Clients." *Journal of Trauma Practice* 4: 181–201.

Hein, P. 2009. *How the Japanese Became Foreign to Themselves: The Impact of Globalization on the Private and Public Spheres in Japan*. New Brunswick, NJ: Transaction Publishers.

Hikikomori: Tokyo Plastic. 2004. Film. Dir. Adario Strange. BAHX Films.

Horiguchi, S. 2012. "Hikikomori: How Private Isolation Caught the Public Eye." In *A Sociology of Japanese Youth: From Returnees to NEETs*, edited by R. Goodman, Y. Imoto, and T. Toivonen, 122–138. London and New York: Routledge.

Jones, M. 2006. "Shutting Themselves In." *The New York Times Magazine*. January 15. www.nytimes.com/2006/01/15/magazine/15japanese.html?pagewanted=all&_r=0. Accessed December 30, 2015.

Kafka, F. 1971. "The Metamorphosis." In *The Complete Stories*, edited by N. Glatzer, 89–139. Translated by W. Muir and E. Muir. New York: Schocken Books.

Kato, T.A., N. Shinfuku, D. Fujisawa, M. Tateno, T. Ishida, T. Akiyama, N. Sartorius, A. Teo, T. Choi, A. Wand, Y. Balhara, J. Chang, R. Chang, B. Shadloo, H. Ahmed, T. Lerthattasilp, W. Umene-Nakano, H. Horikawa, R. Matsumoto, H. Kuga, M. Tanaka, and S. Kanba 2011. "Introducing the Concept of Modern Depression in Japan: An International Case Vignette Survey." *Journal of Affective Disorders* 135: 66–76.

Kato, T.A., N. Shinfuku, D. Fujisawa, M. Tateno, T. Ishida, T. Akiyama, N. Sartorius, A. Teo, T. Choi, A. Wand, Y. Balhara, J. Chang, R. Chang, B. Shadloo, H. Ahmed, T. Lerthattasilp, W. Umene-Nakano, H. Horikawa, R. Matsumoto, H. Kuga, M. Tanaka, and S. Kanba 2012. "Does the 'Hikikomori' Syndrome of Social Withdrawal Exist Outside Japan? A Preliminary International Investigation." *Social Psychiatry and Psychiatric Epidemiology* 47: 1061–1075.

Kitayama, O., T. Saitō, T. Watanabe, and S. Muto 2001. *"Zadankai Hikikomori Ni Tsuite [Round Table: About Hikikomori]."* In *Hikikomori [Gendai No Esprit: 403]*, edited by T. Watanabe and S. Muto, 5–34. Tokyo: Shibundo.

Kohut, H. 1971. *The Analysis of the Self: A Systematic Approach to the Psychoanalytic Treatment of Narcissistic Personality Disorders*. Chicago, IL: University of Chicago Press.

Koyama, A., Y. Miyake, N. Kawakami, M. Tsuchiya, H. Tachimori, and T. Takeshima 2010. "Lifetime Prevalence, Psychiatric Comorbidity and Demographic Correlates of 'Hikikomori' in a Community Population in Japan." *Psychiatry Research* 176: 69–74.

Krieg, A., and J. Dickie 2011. "Attachment and Hikikomori: A Psychosocial Developmental Model." *International Journal of Social Psychiatry* 59: 61–72.

Laing, R.D. 1961. *Self and Others*. New York: Pantheon.

Laing, R.D. 1969. *The Divided Self: An Existential Study in Sanity and Madness*. London: Penguin Books.

Laing, R.D. 1985. "Mystification, Confusion, and Conflict." In *Intensive Family Therapy: Theoretical and Practical Aspects*, edited by I. Boszormenyi-Nagy and J. Framo, 343–364. New York: Harper and Row.

Laing, R.D., and A. Esterson 1964. *Sanity, Madness and the Family*. New York: Basic Books.

Lanzmann, C. 1995. "The Obscenity of Understanding: An Evening with Claude Lanzmann." In *Trauma: Explorations in Memory*, edited by C. Caruth, 200–220. Baltimore, MD: Johns Hopkins University Press.

Ministry of Health, Labor, and Welfare. 2003. *Community Mental Health Intervention Guidelines Aimed at Socially Withdrawn Teenagers and Young Adults*. Tokyo: Ministry of Health, Labor, and Welfare.

Murakami, R. 2000. "Japan's Lost Generation: In a World Filled with Virtual Reality, the Country's Youth Can't Deal with the Real Thing." *Time Asia*. November 8. www.cnn.com/ASIANOW/time/magazine/2000/0501/japan.essaymurakami.html. Accessed December 30, 2015.

Nagata, T., H. Yamada, A. Teo, C. Yoshimura, T. Nakajima, and I. van Vliet 2011. "Comorbid Social Withdrawal (Hikikomori) in Outpatients with Social Anxiety

Disorder: Clinical Characteristics and Treatment Response in a Case Series." *International Journal of Social Psychiatry* 59: 73–78.

Ohashi, N. 2008. *Exploring the Psychic Roots of Hikikomori in Japan*. Doctoral Dissertation. Pacifica Graduate Institute. Ann Arbor, MI: UMI/ProQuest.

Paul, G. 2012. *I Don't Think the Moon Is Real: Collected Flash Fiction from the Wordsmith Challenge*. Raleigh, NC: Lulu.

Rees, P. 2002. "Hikikomori Violence." *BBC News*. http://news.bbc.co.uk/2/hi/programm es/correspondent/2336883.stm. Accessed December 30, 2015.

Said, E. 1979. *Orientalism*. New York: Vintage Books.

Saitō, T. 2002. *Hikikomori Kyusyutsu Manual: How to Rescue Your Child from 'Hikikomori.'* Japan: PHP Research.

Saitō, T. 2013. *Hikikomori: Adolescence without End*. Translated by J. Angles. Minneapolis, MN: University of Minnesota Press.

Sakai, I., S. Nonaka, A. Oono, and National Hikikomori KHJ Parental Group. 2010. *Research on the Reality of Hikikomori*. Tokyo: Ministry of Health, Labour, and Welfare.

Sakamoto, N., R. Martin, H. Kumano, T. Kuboki, S. Al-Adawi 2005. "Hikikomori, Is it a Culture-reactive or Culture-bound Syndrome? Nidotherapy and a Clinical Vignette from Oman." *International Journal of Psychiatry in Medicine* 35: 191–198.

Saxena, S., G. Thornicroft, M. Knapp, and H. Whitford 2007. "Resources for Mental Health: Scarcity, Inequity, and Inefficiency." *Lancet* 370: 878–889.

Shay, J. 1995. *Achilles in Vietnam: Combat Trauma and the Undoing of Character*. New York: Simon and Schuster.

Shimoyachi, N. 2003. "Group Seeks Care for Socially Withdrawn." *Japan Times*. April 22. www.japantimes.co.jp/news/2003/04/22/national/group-seeks-care-for-socially-with drawn/#.VKy3xyvF-8A. Accessed December 30, 2015.

Tateno, M., T. Park, T. Kato, W. Umene-Nakano, and T. Saitō 2012. "Hikikomori as a Possible Clinical Term in Psychiatry: A Questionnaire Survey." *BMC Psychiatry* 12: 169–176.

Teo, A., K. Stufflebaum, and T. Kato 2014. "The Intersection of Culture and Solitude: The Hikikomori Phenomenon in Japan." In *The Handbook of Solitude: Psychological Perspectives on Social Isolation, Social Withdrawal, and Being Alone*, edited by R. Coplan and J. Bowker, 445–457. Oxford: Wiley-Blackwell.

Thompson, M.L. 2007. *Mental Illness*. Westport, CT: Greenwood Press.

Tobira no Muko. 2008. Film. Dir. Laurence Thrush. Size and Growth Films.

Todd, K. 2011. "Hikikomania: Existential Horror or National Malaise?" *Southeast Review of Asian Studies* 33: 135–147.

Uebel, M. 2013. "Psychoanalysis and the Question of Violence: From Masochism to Shame." *American Imago* 69: 473–505.

Umeda, M., and N. Kawakami 2012. "Association of Childhood Family Environments with the Risk of Social Withdrawal ('Hikikomori') in the Community Population in Japan." *Psychiatry and Clinical Neurosciences* 66: 121–129.

Wang, S. 2015. "The Fight to Save Japan's Young Shut-ins." *Wall Street Journal*. January 26. www.wsj.com/articles/the-fight-to-save-japans-young-shut-ins-1422292138. Accessed December 30, 2015.

Watters, E. 2010. *Crazy Like Us: The Globalization of the American Psyche*. New York: Free Press.

Watts, J. 2002. "Public Health Experts Concerned about 'Hikikomori.'" *Lancet* 359: 1131.

Winnicott, D.W. 1965. *The Maturational Processes and the Facilitating Environment: Studies in the Theory of Emotional Development*, edited by M. Khan. London: Hogarth and the Institute of Psycho-Analysis.

Winnicott, D.W. 1986. *Home Is Where We Start from: Essays by a Psychoanalyst*, edited by C. Winnicott, R. Shepard, and M. Davis. New York: W.W. Norton.

Wong, V.C., ed. 2009. "Working with Youth in Social Withdrawal." In *Initiatives with Youth-at-risk in Hong Kong* , edited by F. Lee,127–146. Caring for Youth Series. Hong Kong: City University of Hong Kong Press.

World Health Organization. 2009. "Mental Health, Poverty and Development." In *ECOSOC Meeting: Addressing Noncommunicable Diseases and Mental Health: Major Challenges to Sustainable Development in the 21st Century* (July), 1–32. www.who.int/nmh/p ublications/discussion_paper_en.pdf. Accessed December 30, 2015.

Yamada, M. 1999. *The Time of Parasite Singles [Parasaito Shinguro no Jidai]*. Tokyo: Chikuma Shobō.

Zielenziger, M. 2006. "Retreating Youth Become Japan's 'Lost Generation.' Interview with Michelle Norris." November 24. *National Public Radio*. www.npr.org/templates /story/story.php?storyId=6535284. Accessed December 30, 2015.

8

'NATURAL' EXPERIENCE AND THE STATE OF NATURE

The idea of a state of nature, a human condition preceding organized society and government, may be found in the texts of Judaic, Dharmic, Islamic, and Christian religions, in the classical thought of Plato and Hesiod, in contemporary theories of justice advanced by John Rawls and David Gauthier, in the psycho-historical imagination of Sigmund Freud, in the apocalyptic visions of dozens of postmoderns, including many of those mentioned in previous chapters, along with Maurice Blanchot, Jean Baudrillard, and others (see also Jay 1993), and in popular representations of catastrophic events that eliminate law and political order, leaving survivors to contend with warring groups and assorted monsters. But its purest expression, and its distinctively modern presumption of a natural right or freedom as the basis for legitimate civil government, is found in the works of Hugo Grotius, Thomas Hobbes, Samuel von Pufendorf, John Locke, and Jean-Jacques Rousseau.

Its critics, who object to the terms of the social contract as well as to the characterization of the state of nature, have grown in number over the past several decades, from Carole Pateman's influential critique with respect to the status of women (1988), to Charles Mills' similar critique with respect to race (1997), to psychologically attuned and care-ethical approaches that question the internal logic and validity of the assumptions of the social contract as a primary foundation for liberal individualist thought.

The best-known critique of the state of nature is that it presents a picture of the subject as asocial, disembedded, independent, and abstract, that the realities of human dependence and interdependence seem to have no bearing upon contractarians' view of "humans as originally isolated and self-enclosed" (Gerson 2004, 777). This argument has been advanced by a number of contemporary theorists such as Annette Baier (1994), Seyla Benhabib (1987), Christine

DiStefano (1983, 1991), Virginia Held (1993), and Martha Nussbaum (2000), as well as earlier critics like Mary Astell (1704) and Mary Wollstonecraft ([1792] 2004), all of whom have correctly pointed out the denials of dependence and intimate human relationships in the state of nature.[1]

This critique, however, is in one important respect inaccurate, for it is not precisely subjects or selves that are portrayed in the state of nature. Rather, the state of nature presents us with a picture not just of an ungoverned, unrelated human being, but a being without a self. The difference amounts to more than hair-splitting, not only for contract theory but for its consequences in contemporary political discourse. Consider, for instance, the longstanding liberal–communitarian debate, represented in part by figures like John Rawls, Michael Sandel, Charles Taylor, and Alasdair MacIntyre. A prominent – perhaps *the* prominent – point of contention is how to regard the political subject or self, whether it is possible to abstract the self from her commitments and community, and whether it is desirable, even in theory, to do so.

While it is not the focus of this chapter, this debate could be clarified to a great degree if distinctions could be preserved between human beings, individuals, and selves. Human beings cannot develop the capacities of selfhood without the interventions of civil society and its institutions, especially the family. At the same time, the human being does *not* become a self in a non-problematic alignment with the traditions and commitments of family or community. Selves do not develop in isolation, but neither do group identities and traditions encourage the development of selves. Human beings live and have always lived in groups. But this fact does not mean that group contexts are at the center of what it means to be a self. Rather, the self depends upon families, groups, and even states that facilitate its capacities both to resist their pull and to meaningfully participate in them. To become a self requires having been afforded, by others, the ability to escape, return, and re-negotiate contact with those same others on the self's own terms.

In this chapter I do not delve into this particular debate, nor do I defend the construct of the state of nature against a flawed aspect of its critique. Rather, I wish to show that the state of nature's representation of a natural, originary experience – again, *not* of free and independent selfhood but of a selfless freedom and innocence – reinforces a primitive orientation to selves and groups that could otherwise help facilitate their mutual development. That is, the fantasy of the state of nature both contributes to and helps us understand the preoccupation with preserving experiences of 'natural' psychic devastation in our private and civil lives.

Holding onto experiences of psychic devastation, which may have occurred in reality, in fantasy, or both, and deeming them 'natural,' 'original,' or 'inevitable' means unconsciously reinforcing paranoid-schizoid orientations toward the self, others, and civil institutions. These orientations and dynamics have been discussed throughout this book, perhaps most memorably in Chapters 2 and 3, where Bill Holm asked us to imagine that civil institutions seek to "rob us" of our experience and then "kill" us. Instead, we must quickly "kill" them "inside us" and "damage" them in the external world (Holm 2010, 15–16). That is, contrary to the stated purpose of the state of nature thought-experiment, the fantasy of the state of nature impedes the development of sane, healthy attitudes toward civil institutions that might otherwise support selves.

Heuristical or historical?

As is well known, the states of nature commonly imagined in the seventeenth and eighteenth centuries, as well as their contemporary variations, such as Rawls' famous "original position" (1971), are presented as heuristic devices to assess the legitimacy of government. Fictions, thought-experiments, tests by which to assess the justice of laws and restrictions imposed by a civil state, states of nature are essentially narratives of abstract moral criteria. State-of-nature theorists tell stories about pre-social individuals who never existed, in order to make claims about the limits of governments and institutions that do exist.

It would be nothing new to say that the defense of a social contract based on a hypothesized – or hypostatized – state of nature contains logical fallacies, including the unwarranted assumption fallacy, where conclusions are drawn from premises that are unlikely or untrue. More problematic is that, although most serious state-of-nature theorists (except Locke) explicitly deny the historical reality of the state of nature – as they should, given all available anthropological evidence (see e.g., Gamble 1999; Leakey and Lewin 1978) – somehow this fact is elided in both elaborations of and critiques of the construct. Even Carole Pateman (1988), vociferous critic of the social contract and the patriarchal domination carried over from the state of nature, treats these scenarios as both male fantasy and historical reality.

Hobbes frankly admits that "there was never such a time, nor condition of warre" as his state of nature suggests, only then to remind the reader that "there are many places, where [people] live so now," such as "the savage people in many places of America ... [who] have no government at all" (1985, 187).[2] Similarly, Rousseau famously opens his second *Discourse* by "putting aside all the facts, for they have no bearing on the question. The investigations that may be undertaken concerning this subject should not be taken for historical truths, but only for hypothetical and conditional reasonings" (1987, 18). The state of nature is a state "which no longer exists, which perhaps never existed, which probably never will exist, and yet about which it is necessary to have accurate notions in order to judge properly our own present state" (1987, 34). Nonetheless, Rousseau simultaneously proclaims:

> O man, whatever country you may be from ... listen: here is your history, as I have thought to read it, not in the books of your fellow men, who are liars, but in nature, who never lies. Everything that comes from nature will be true; there will be nothing false except what I have unintentionally added.

The times about which I am going to speak are quite remote: how much you have changed from what you were!

(1987, 19)

Locke is something of a special case, for he obscures the unreality of the state of nature right from the beginning. The chapter in the *Second Treatise* devoted to it opens with the assertion that "to understand political power right ... we must consider what state men are naturally in" (1980, 8). Locke soon cites one of his favorite authorities, the "judicious [Richard] Hooker," in affirming the historical reality of the transition from "living single and solely by ourselves" to a civil state:

> To those that say, there were never any men in the state of nature, I will ... oppose the authority of the judicious Hooker ... where he says ... "forasmuch as we are not by ourselves sufficient to furnish ourselves with competent store of things, needful for such a life as our nature doth desire ... as living single and solely by ourselves, we are naturally induced to seek communion and fellowship with others: this was the cause of men's uniting themselves at first in politic societies."
>
> *(1980, 13)*

When addressing the "mighty objection" that men cannot be found in the state of nature anywhere in the world, Locke replies, "since all princes and rulers ... all through the world, are in a state of nature, it is plain the world never was, nor ever will be, without numbers of men in that state" (13). Locke's point is that the state of nature may have been real in the past, and, more importantly, remains real as a psycho-political potentiality, given up but not extinguished upon entry into civil society: "All men are naturally in that state, and remain so, till by their own consents they make themselves members of some politic society" (13–14). This notion is not original to Locke, for Hobbes notes as well that "in all times, Kings, and Persons of Soveraigne authority, because of their Independency, are in continuall jealousies, and in the state and posture of Gladiators," which is to say, in a condition of liberty like the state of nature, but "because they uphold thereby the Industry of their Subjects," their 'natural' liberty leads not to the same misery as the ungoverned individual (1980, 187–188).

It will come as no surprise to students of political theory that state-of-nature theorists, while perhaps ambivalently denying the historical component of the fantasy, nevertheless use the state of nature to define human nature, such that the construct of the state of nature becomes a descriptor not only of external conditions governing states and sovereigns but of internal conditions governing states of mind. For Locke, as C.B. Macpherson notes, "natural is not the opposite of social or civil. The natural condition of mankind is within man now, not set apart in some distant time or place" (1971, 74). The same may be said of Hobbes, who argues that if one doubts the veracity of the picture of the state of nature he has drawn, then one may have it "confirmed by Experience." That is, the incredulous person should recall that:

> when taking a journey, he armes himselfe … when going to sleep, he locks his dores; when even in his house he locks his chests … what opinion he has of his fellow subjects. … Does he not there accuse mankind by his actions, as I do by my words?
>
> *(1985, 186–187)*

Whether the hypothetical status of the state of nature is muddled with a historical one, or whether its relatively aggressive and paranoid orientation is carried over into civil society partly or fully, it is clear that there remains a powerful connection between imaginative accounts of 'natural' humanity and contemporary human experience. That is, the imagination of the state of nature demands analytic interpretation, interpretation as an unconscious driver of contemporary ideologies of experience. As I demonstrate below, the state of nature may be considered a fantasy, for it contains powerful elements of wishful and even magical thinking: the wish that wishing could change reality. That the hypothetical is often confused with the historical, and that the principles of the natural condition are carried over, explicitly or implicitly, into the civil state, suggest not merely conceptual inexactitude but the influence of disavowed elements of fantasy upon the individuals and institutions that have, directly and indirectly, arisen from contractarian formulations.

Born free?

"Man is born free, and everywhere he is in chains." These words open Rousseau's *Social Contract*. "How did this change take place?," Rousseau asks. And he answers: "I have no idea." What concerns Rousseau is "what can render [this change] legitimate" (1987, 141). And, of course, what legitimizes humanity's passage from a natural to a civil state is the total alienation of the individual from himself to the political community, as well as "the remarkable change in man" produced by it, as set out by Rousseau in the well-known formulae of the general will.[3]

But if, as Rousseau and others admit, the state of nature is an ahistorical contrivance, then in what sense are humans "born free"? Are we "born free" to Rousseau because, in this moment of his writing, he is affirming the historical reality of the state of nature, the "original state of man" which "differ[s] so greatly" from civilized man (1987, 80)? Or, are we "born free" only in the fictional scenario of the state of nature but not in our actual (pre)history? Does the phrase "born free" merely refer to the premise of natural liberty derived from the *imagination* of the state of nature? And if so, are we "born free" simply because it is possible for us to imagine ourselves having been "born free" in this natural state? *Can* we, in fact, imagine ourselves "born free" in such a state? If our freedom depends upon our capacity to imagine ourselves as possessing freedom, then is our freedom magically derived, such that we become free simply by wishing we were born free?

Perhaps we may understand the claim that we are "born free" ontogenetically, as individuals. It is true that many infants enjoy an experience we ought not object to call 'natural' and 'free.' This experience of "primary narcissism," as Freud described it, includes the experience of omnipotence: an illusion of perfect control over the infant, others, and the world, which are not yet differentiated. Primary narcissism, which is the "libidinal complement to the egoism of the instinct of self-preservation" (1914, 74), is related to but not equivalent with the "secondary" or pathological narcissism that presents itself in adult personality disorders and in grandiose and persecutory delusions.

Primary narcissism, we might say, is the psychic state of the human being in the state of nature, particularly Rousseau's state of nature in which we are "born free." Rousseau presents us with a child-like creature in the body of an adult, a being who lives "in himself" (1987, 81), who lives to preserve himself, and who happily gratifies his own desires:

> Wandering in the forests, without industry, without speech, without dwelling, without war, without relationships, with no need for his fellow men, and correspondingly with no desire to do them harm ... savage man ... had only the sentiments and enlightenment appropriate to that state. ... If by chance he made some discovery, he was all the less able to communicate it to others because he did not even know his own children. Art perished with its inventor. There was neither education nor progress; generations were multiplied to no purpose. Since each one always began from the same point, centuries went by with all the crudeness of the first ages; the species was already old, and man remained ever a child.
>
> *(1987, 57)*

Consider, by comparison, Rousseau's intellectual ancestor Michel de Montaigne, who informed Europeans about the life of the Brazilian "cannibals" and their infantile yet Edenic state. Montaigne invokes Plato in his famous essay in order to allude to the differences between the "cannibals" and the utopian *Republic*. Where the *Republic* calls for decades of education and generations of 'civilizing' to achieve its aims, Montaigne wishes to show that the 'children' of Nature are 'born free' of constraint, corruption, servitude, and imperfection:

> This is a nation, I should say to Plato, in which there is no kind of commerce, no knowledge of letters, no science of numbers, no title of magistrate or of political superior, no habit of service, riches or poverty, no contracts, no inheritances, no divisions of property, only leisurely occupations, no respect for any kinship but the common ties, no clothes, no agriculture, no

metals, no use of corn or wine. The very words denoting lying, treason, deceit, greed, envy, slander, and forgiveness have never been heard. How far from such perfection would he find the republic that he imagined: "men fresh from the hands of the gods."

(1993, 110)

Of course, the primarily narcissistic infant who experiences something of a natural freedom is not aware that it has been provided for her by a perceptive and generous parent. As far as she knows, others and the environment do not impinge upon her because she *is* the environment, or, rather, she controls the environment and others, who seem to bend readily to her wishes.

As ideology, the state of nature may deny not only a reality confirmed by anthropological evidence, but a reality of individual human development. Freud rightly links the state of primary narcissism to the propensity for magical thinking and to the "omnipotence of thought" (1938, 873–4): the belief that wishing can alter reality, that wishing makes things so. And Winnicott was more correct than not when he famously claimed in his 1952 paper on "Anxiety Associated with Insecurity" that "there is no such thing as a baby" because there is always "someone caring for the baby," always "a 'nursing couple'" (1992, 99). In only slightly different language, in a 1959 paper on "The Fate of the Transitional Object," he argues that "there is no such thing as an infant," only the same "'nursing couple'" because "when we see an infant … we know we will find infant-care with the infant as part of that infant-care" (1989, 54). "It is not logical," therefore, "to think in terms of an individual because there is not yet an individual self there" (Winnicott 1988, 131; see also Bowlby 1988). Even in Rousseau's language, far from being "born free," a human infant seen objectively, and not from *within* the infant's fantasy, would be necessarily "enslaved," since the infant's needs make him utterly "incapable of doing without another" (1987, 59).[4]

So, although the infantile illusion of magical power may ground later, more mature experiences of autonomy and creativity, what belongs to the state of nature is the *fantasy* of omnipotence, not the reality of the psychological or political origins of civility and maturity. Put more simply: What is wrong with the state of nature is not that it depicts isolated and independent selves but that it depicts magical and narcissistic infants. This means that the denial of dependence in the state of nature may *not* be the most misleading aspect of the fantasy. More confounding, rather, is how the primary narcissistic component of the state-of-nature fantasy is carried over into the psychic experiences of individuals living in civil society.

The 'bad' self, the 'natural' self, and the not-self

Several years ago, I interviewed a young woman named Maria who told me about her gruesome experience of having been kidnapped and held in captivity, by herself, for four days in a small room, until she was eventually rescued by the police (see Bowker 2014).[5] A fourteen-year-old girl at the time, Maria's experience of captivity was traumatic and terrifying.

"I screamed so much I forgot my talking voice," she recalled. And "by the third or fourth day, I really didn't know who I was. I was afraid of how I behaved. I was full of rage," she said, holding up her forearms to demonstrate how she injured herself by continually pounding against the locked door. In the years following her abduction, Maria experienced uncertainty, anxiety, paranoia, difficulty performing in school, and a feeling that she was involved in a constant struggle to "figure out what was going on." "I'm not normally a person who yells and screams," she explained, "but I behaved in the most odd manner and, for months after, [I] behaved strangely."

In spite of all this, Maria referred to her experience of captivity as her "natural state," presumably because she was alone in a bare room, with no one explicitly interfering with or physically abusing her. Of course, as has been discussed in Chapter 6, her involuntary confinement was an explicit form of interference and abuse, but she did not experience it in precisely this way. In fact, the link between her confinement and what she called her "natural state" was what troubled her the most. Maria wondered why she was so afraid to confront her "natural state." "Why didn't I feel safe there?," she asked. "Should I have really been afraid of myself that much?," she wondered. Of course, there is nothing "natural" about a child held in captivity, just as one would imagine that Maria had many things to fear during those four days other than "herself."

Maria's attempt to comprehend her experience as "natural," like her expressed wish to "thank" her captors and to "buy them dinner," seemed intended to transform a horrific experience into a learning experience. Maria reported that, in time, she came to recognize that her captors were her most valuable teachers, because they showed her "the most crucial purpose and thing in my life," which is "to understand me."

The 'bad' self

Maria's story, then, returns us to Lichtenberg's cruel joke about experience, with which Chapter 2 began: "Experience means experiencing what one does not wish to experience." Maria had turned her involuntary, injurious experience into something 'good,' or at least she had tried to. She had relied on the concept of a "natural state" to do so, lending an aura of benevolent and even divine purpose to what others might regard as a violent experience inflicted upon her by the cruelest of criminals.

While some will be tempted to see in Maria's eventual attitude toward her captors a mere identification with them, her attempt to find something good in her experience did not strike me as such. Maria's attempt to 'take' something from her experience was not merely a defense against it, nor a denial of her need to mourn her pain and what she had lost. Her error lay in the much more basic assumption that her "natural" self was to be found inside a screaming, panicked, helpless child, forcibly locked away in a room. This error lies at the foundation of an apocalyptic fantasy, derived from the state-of-nature fantasy, that in experiences of *psychic* annihilation of the self, one becomes 'free' to return to the natural state in which one was 'born,' that in self-death one's naturalness and freedom are restored.

In *Rethinking the Politics of Absurdity* (2014), I argued that desubjectifying conditions and apocalyptic, disaster-oriented, survivalist fantasies served the psychic interests of individuals seeking regressive experiences of illusory freedom and innocence. I might have done more there to explain the relationship between freedom and innocence, which is not difficult to understand. To use Kleinian language, what weighs on the psyche is guilt and fear, guilt and fear concerning one's own rage, hate, and destructiveness: For Klein, "the central conflict in human experience ... is between love and hate, between the caring preservation and the malicious destruction of others" (Greenberg and Mitchell 1983, 142).

But if external conditions are disastrous enough, one need no longer feel guilt or fear about destructive rage, for one finds oneself in a world where there are no good objects left to harm. Put another way, the external world mirrors the paranoid-schizoid outlook, where good and bad objects are radically split and clearly distinguishable, such that one hardly risks mistaking one for the other. A form of innocence, then, is imagined to belong to the one who has no need for guilt or reparation. This situation would also seem to afford a kind of primitive freedom: the freedom to act upon any impulse, even the most violent, without internal consequence. While we may harm or be harmed, kill or be killed, in such a condition "nothing can be Unjust. The notions of Right and Wrong, Justice and Unjust have there no place" (Hobbes 1985, 188). To become accommodated to a state of nature, one has to learn how to survive physically, and doing so would seem to rely, in many apocalyptic fantasies and narratives, on accepting, psychically, one's unlimited "right to every thing: even to one another's body" (190).

Maria was "full of rage," and it was, above all, her own uncontrollable rage that frightened her, as she became aware of her own destructive potential, awakened by the violence she was suffering. But, having no one before her toward whom to direct her rage, having been blindfolded so that she could not even call up the face of one of her tormentors, she was stuck. The only object available for her to hate was the self she had become in her captivity. Maria attributed her rage and hate to this 'bad' self, and attempted to conquer this 'bad' self by embracing her captivity as a learning experience. Her 'natural state,' along this reasoning, must be one that is not afraid of capricious violence or confinement, one in which there is no reason to struggle against abuse.

Maria's experience of being "blindfolded" serves as a horrific yet apt metaphor for those who experience captivity, abuse, and unfreedom in less literal forms, but who are quite uncertain of whom to blame, not least because they have been 'blinded' by ideologies that convince them that their experiences are 'natural,' 'normal,' or 'good.' In Chapter 3, I suggested that something like a 'straw self' was constituted in trauma to be destroyed, and that this self would inevitably be characterized as 'bad' in its expulsion from the psyche and its replacement with traumata or traumatizing objects. The logic here is the same: If painful, depriving, or terrifying experiences of life inspire hatred, fear, or rage, but such experiences are conceived to be 'natural,' then it is our feelings that must be out of touch with 'nature.' 'Nature,' then, must recommend a selfless state, or at least a state where the self is unguarded, where it has no expectation of *not* being impinged upon, violated, overtaken, or possessed by trauma.

The 'natural' self

What is the experience of the human being in its 'natural state'? Does this human being have a 'natural' self? If so, we must be cautious not to confuse that fantasy with the notion of the "true self" as elaborated in Winnicott's well-known sense of the term (1965), although it may well be that this very confusion between a Winnicottian "true self" and a 'natural' self born of self-destruction, a confusion sponsored by a particularly violent ideology of experience, lies at the heart of the matter. In order for the 'natural' self not to be afraid, it must detach itself from the former 'bad' self, which contains authentic emotions, attachments to others, and expectations of physical and psychic integrity and safety.

While differing accounts of the state of nature describe widely differing degrees of desperation, chaos, and violence, what they hold in common is that the natural state is by and large a state of loneliness. Even if there are some forms of relationship between human beings, as in Locke's account, there remains what Frieda Fromm-Reichmann would call "a want of intimacy" (1959). If the state of nature is not primarily a fantasy of independent adults but of magical infants, it is also, perhaps paradoxically, a fantasy of deprived children. That is, the state-of-nature fantasy features a selfless, relationless homeostasis that is *also* clearly marked by deprivation, abandonment, and loneliness. This, we ought to remember, is the condition that is regarded as 'natural.'

As I have argued, the self is an ideal, a potential and complex human achievement. This means that, if by 'natural' we mean 'that which has not known human interference,' there is some truth to the claim that *not* becoming a self is 'natural.' Winnicott admits as much when he argues, citing Foucault, that:

> before a certain date it is possible that there was only very exceptionally a man or woman who achieved unit [self] status in personal development. Before a certain date the vast millions of the world of human beings quite possibly never found or certainly soon lost at the end of infancy or childhood their sense of being individuals. … We cannot so easily identify ourselves with [these] men and women.

(1971, 70)

While Winnicott at least does not pretend that mature adults spring up from the ground "like mushrooms" (Hobbes 1972, 205), he does overlook the potential for psychic *identification* with the selfless. It is this identification, via the construct of Nature and the conditions of deprivation and abandonment, that I wish to argue is served by the fantasy of the state of nature.

As has been discussed more thoroughly in Chapter 7, individuals such as those in *hikikomori* may re-create forms of deprivation and isolation in misguided attempts to "get back behind the moment[s] of deprivation" in their familial, social, and civil lives (Winnicott 1986, 92). What is agonizing is "the neutral state," a phrase by which Winnicott means a condition of self-loss in the face of deprivation, a state governed largely by annihilation anxiety and terror (92). From within this neutral state, however, there may be some occasion to find "hope." This hope, which is not unrelated to wish or fantasy, is for Winnicott the hope of rediscovering the capacity for creative experiencing.

But at the stage of development in which holding and creative finding are most closely tied together, there is not only "no such thing as a baby" (1992, 99), but there is no such thing as an object-relationship (Winnicott 1965, 37–55).[6] That is, the state or condition that the hopeful yet deprived individual is after is not, as Winnicott puts it, a hope to "rediscover himself" exactly (1986, 95), but, rather, a hope to return to the impulsivity and aggressiveness that may arise in the holding relationship between infant and parent and its "indestructible" environmental features that safely contain expressions of aggression and destructiveness.

To be abandoned is different from playing hide-and seek, and yet the child who plays hide-and-seek a great deal, or who plays hide-and-seek compulsively, may have a special purpose driving his behavior, one that, unfortunately, removes it from the category of play and locates it much closer to reactivity to deprivation or repetition of trauma. In this way, the individuals in *hikikomori* discussed in Chapter 7 may be understood as attempting to find, in reality, a fantasy inspired by the state of nature. Isolating, depriving, and abandoning their selves, these individuals rediscover powerfully aggressive (and passively aggressive) impulses as they attempt (tragically) to revive a magical, selfless, and relationless experience that has been lost. That they fail to find in their *hikikomori* experience the more mature capacities of selves, such as creativity, authenticity, or genuine aloneness, is no great surprise.

In speaking of the discovery, in reality, of a 'natural' fantasy of self- and other-abandonment, it is difficult not to recall Peter Shaffer's extraordinary 1973 play *Equus*. In it, Alan Strang becomes passionately, religiously, and erotically identified with horses and with the god "Equus" that lives in all of them. He creates an elaborate religious ritual where, every three weeks, he rides alone at night, naked on a horse, praying to Equus that He "make us one person" (Shaffer 2007, 58).

Alan declares that no one understands the nakedness and naturalness of horses as he does. While others don bowler hats and "'[dress] for the horse'," Alan sneers, "the horse isn't dressed. It's the most naked thing you ever saw! More than a dog or a cat or anything" (2007, 33). Only Alan understands how "filthy" and corrupt it is to "indulg[e]," as his mother's family did, in "equitation" of this sort (33). Rather, Alan and cowboys understand. Of cowboys, Alan cries:

> They're free! They just swing up and then it's miles of grass. I bet all cowboys are orphans! I bet they are! No one ever says to cowboys, "Receive my meaning"! They wouldn't dare. Or "God" all the time, "God sees you, Alan. God's got eyes everywhere."
>
> *(2007, 33)*

Here, the fairly common childhood fantasy of being abandoned or orphaned is used to great effect, illustrating what Alan detests about the oppressiveness of his home and social life: a father who bosses him around, a mother who subjects him to an omnipresent, watchful God, and a social condition that similarly affords him no privacy, no aloneness, no freedom to be himself, nowhere to be 'naked.' Orphaning or abandonment by such parents, such a society, even such a god, might be welcomed as a chance at self-liberation. Alan's retreat, however, into his seemingly more 'naked' and 'natural' religion, unfortunately, does not liberate his self so much as it binds him fast to a new yet equally self-occluding experience of worship, awe, and dread.

We might understand Alan's behavior in terms of aggression if Winnicott, and Freud before him, were correct in asserting that a common "method for dealing with aggression in the inner reality is the masochistic one by which the individual finds suffering, and by one stroke expresses aggression, gets punished and so relieved of guilt feelings, and enjoys sexual excitement and gratification" (Winnicott 1984, 90). Alan's efforts at freeing his 'natural' self by turning to a highly esoteric and ecstatic suffering not only release aggression but direct it at the very capacities of the self he might have wished to liberate. Alan is nearly destroyed by his all-consuming passion for Equus: He is not free, nor is he himself. And Equus, who becomes to Alan the same jealous, all-seeing, all-knowing god he abandoned in Christ, exerts a terrible 'inner constraint' upon him, preventing him both from being alone and from being with others, as demonstrated so memorably in the most famous scene of the play, in which his inability to make love with Jill Mason, owing to intrusive thoughts of Equus, leads him to rise up and blind six horses in their stable.

The not-self

Perhaps we may now consider a different aggressive and masochistic fantasy: that proposed by John Rawls in his conception of the original position, the most influential contemporary version of the state of nature. Critiqued most famously by Michael Sandel, Rawls' original position is a thought-experiment that consists of a rational, choosing subject dislodged from its community, family, language, personal qualities, values, interests, and commitments. This so-called 'subject,' whether it be 'abstract,' 'metaphysical' or simply 'utterly deprived,' seems difficult to imagine, and, even if it were imaginable, would appear quite distinct from a self. "Even if it could be imagined," writes Fred Alford, "a self shorn of its interests, ends, talents, goals, and relationships with others … is a self that seems hardly worth protecting" (1991, 9). Now, Rawls does not claim that such a subject should persist or that we should strive to remain in the original position, but it is not difficult to find others who do.

Popular spiritualist Eckhart Tolle, for one, claims in his best-selling book *The Power of Now* (2004, 34) that "the secret of life is to 'die before you die' – and find that there is no death." Tolle is not referring to near-death experiences but to the premise that:

> the most common ego identifications have to do with possessions, the work you do, social status and recognition, knowledge and education, physical appearance, special abilities, relationships, personal and family history, belief systems, and often also political, nationalistic, racial, religious, and other collective identifications. None of these is you.

Death is "a stripping away of all that is not you," which means that "death," for Tolle, can happen at any moment in life, or, perhaps, throughout life (34).

If these aspects of what Tolle calls "ego" – including work, knowledge, abilities, relationships, family, beliefs, and identifications – are "not you," then, what are "you"? Furthermore, why should we associate "death" with the stripping away of what is *not* 'us'? Is Tolle not using the word "death" to describe a fantasy in which all that might be construed as socially determined or potentially 'unnatural' about the self is purged from the 'natural' self underneath? What is this 'natural' self, and why does it seem to require the experience of death-in-life?

Algerian philosopher and mentor of Albert Camus Jean Grenier would understand the relationship between the ideal of Nature and the impulse toward self-deprivation and self-destruction as the very nexus of primitive desire, even the *fundamental* desire repressed in modern society. Grenier asserts that a common if not universal wish, not entirely distinct from *Thanatos*, is "to go from the state of being a man to being a brute, to go from the state of being an organism to being an element" (1967, 92). To suffer a thoroughgoing "*dépossession*" (deprivation), writes Grenier, while agonizing, also "makes all psychological constraints disappear" (53), and "frees us of everything … first of all from ourselves" (93).

The fantasy of a state of nature, even in a figure as sober as Rawls, may contain traces of the apocalyptic fantasy of death-in-life and life after death. It is no coincidence that scholars have used the phrase "death in life" frequently to refer to experiences of surviving devastating trauma and atrocity (see, e.g., Lifton 1991), which, of course, bear heavily upon the ideologies of experience discussed throughout this book. Of course, if one discovers one's 'natural' self only by experiencing death-in-life, a destruction of all that might constitute a self, then we may say that the 'natural' self is really the not-self.

The 'not-self' can only be attained when self-identity is obliterated in ecstatic – from *ek-stasis*, meaning displacement, departure from the self – identification with the objects of experience available in a condition governed by impulse and not thought, the body and not the mind, the survival of the organism and not attention to the needs of the self. It is more difficult, although perhaps less painful, to achieve this state of not-self in meditation or spiritual reflection than in overwhelming experiences that short-circuit, as it were, the self's nervous system. This might make experiences of deprivation, failure, and trauma, even vicarious experiences of the same, appealing as a quick fix for the unfulfilled individual.

If the death of the self is natural, then the self is unnatural, perhaps even a 'crime against nature,' a notion that resonates throughout Eastern and Western thought, from the Buddhist principle of *anātman* or non-self, to Attic tragedy, to Christian dogma, to modern and postmodern discourses of anti-subjectivity. By suffering deprivation and abandonment, the self collapses into its 'natural' state of failure, and so is reunited with the reality of the human being. This reality includes a paradoxical account of a human being who is not a self but is nevertheless free.

To be sure, the deprivations that individuals suffer, whether inflicted by families, by social groups, or even by individuals upon themselves, are regularly blamed on powerful institutions and governments. As Bill Holm suggests, to "kill" the organizations that "rob" us of our experience we must "put [our] arms around everything that has ever happened to [us], and give it an affectionate squeeze." We must "accept [our] experience" as our new "teacher, mother, state, church" (2010, 15–16), which is to say: Civil institutions must be reshaped in our own image, an image that finds its form in the fantasized, narcissistic experiences of a 'natural,' selfless, and childish state.

Although we may consciously acknowledge the fiction of the state of nature, semi-consciously or unconsciously the fiction has come to be accepted as reality. This 'reality' has been used to frame and comprehend countless modern and contemporary moral and political projects: the constitutions of liberal states; ideas and ideologies concerning the legitimate scope and function of governments (see also Curtis 2010); and the tenets of contemporary moral philosophies.[7] Of course, efforts to shape civil institutions according to an infantile fantasy of a not-self are unlikely to be conducive to the development of mature selves and institutions that respect selves' needs and capacities. Instead, efforts to ensure that natural experiences are preserved in our private and civil lives may come to mean "kill[ing]" our selves and killing others' selves by turning and returning to experiences of trauma, failure, and deprivation in the name of upholding nature, reality, and freedom.

Paranoid-schizoid politics

Ultimately, the state of nature suggests a regressive and dangerous ideology, for at least two reasons. First, the achievements of robust selfhood that would best suit a liberal vision of democratic citizenship actually rely upon the kinds of care, dependence, and facilitating environments that are denied in much of social contract theory. Second, and what may be worse, instead of "design[ing] their accounts so as to help men and women become more autonomous and free," state-of-nature theorists and their intellectual progeny merely set out about "convincing them that they already are" (Alford 1994, 7). Indeed, one might argue that when even a philosopher as astute as Richard Rorty suggests that "words" are the only tools available to the contemporary individual to "get out from under inherited contingencies and make his own contingencies ... by redescribing [the past] in his terms, thereby becoming able to say, 'Thus I willed it'" (Rorty 1989, 97), we encounter a similar fantasy, a return to the magical powers of the narcissistic infant who believes he can reshape objective reality in his own image. In civil life, of course, redescriptions of past contingencies are almost indistinguishable from ideologies, used to cover over errors and injustices that might otherwise be met square-on.

Foucault's remarks on Marx come close to accurately assessing the situation, in which imagined experiences of natural freedom are not presumed to be either historically or factually accurate but fictional, yet nevertheless possessing considerable psychic meaning for those in conversation with them. "Experience is neither true nor false," writes Foucault. "It is always a fiction, something constructed, which exists only after it has been made, not before; it isn't something that is 'true,' but it has been a reality" (1991, 36).

To understand the idea of an experience that is not true but has, nevertheless, been a reality, we have turned to the notion of psychic experience and psychic reality, fantasies lived or even remembered, although never realized. On this account, our original, natal, natural freedom is not true or false but is a "reality" because it coincides with something in our psychic "experience." I propose that what it coincides with is not merely, as others have held, a desire to be an adult free of dependence, but a fantasy of an infant free of both self and relatedness. Assertions of natural freedoms derived from the state of nature are therefore quite unlikely to support the development of robust selves in civil society because, at bottom, such assertions suggest that the self is unnatural and undesirable, if not impossible.

If state-of-nature theorists imagine an original freedom and independence from others, those who seek to confirm this premise in their experience must identify with and internalize the demands of superior forces of Nature and of others as their own in order to retain the illusion of omnipotence. At the same time, they must enforce the will of Nature, however it may be construed, and the will of the majority or group with which they identify, upon others, assuring that no separate self be permitted to arise, since – because freedom has become equated with a fantasy of omnipotence – the separate self now represents an attack on the experience of original freedom. Put another way, as we have discussed above, particularly in Chapters 5 and 6, adaptation and compliance may be masked as self-determination, if the more one adapts to the needs of others or the environment, the better one is able to predict, manage, and master internal and external reactions. When this pattern of behavior is applied in political settings, then groups and institutions tend to direct their energies toward the suppression of the self in the name of the preservation of collective fantasies of control and power.

In Melanie Klein's 'paranoid-schizoid' position (1975), the good and the bad must remain dis-integrated, such that sources or symbols of vitality must be kept separate from sources or symbols of pain and frustration. Of course, a degree of 'splitting' – separating good from bad, self from other – is normal and even healthy; it becomes unhealthy primarily when the severity of the split exaggerates the qualities of goodness and badness or exaggerates the difference between self and others, when it prevents individuals from *integrating* good and bad aspects of themselves and others into wholes that can be tolerated and related to in healthy ways.

If a 'bad' part of the self – and every other – is construed as dangerous to the group, then an all-good, salvific object must eventually arise in order to suppress this bad element. This object, itself, is created from the putatively 'natural' parts of individuals, which we have identified with material related to infantile, undifferentiated, and omnipotent fantasies. Perhaps this explains, to some degree, the properties with which we invest "a God who would assist in the perpetration of every sort of atrocity" (Klein 1975, 203n).

Or, perhaps the famous frontispiece to the *Leviathan*, created by Abraham Bosse, in which the body of the Sovereign king is literally composed of members of the commonwealth, better illustrates this dynamic. The biblical epigraph atop the image, like the name Leviathan, appears in the Book of Job: "*Non est potestas Super Terram quae Comparetur ei*" [No power on Earth may be compared with him]. The King James version reads: "Upon earth there is not his like, who is made without fear" (Job 41:33, AV). Like the Leviathan, made without fear, Hobbes' Sovereign both contains the fears of all those who constitute his power and embodies a fearsomeness before which citizens tremble in reverence and awe. But as this "Mortall God" is made in the citizens' image (1985, 227), citizens may identify themselves with it to soothe the pains of having surrendered themselves to it. It is important to note that, in Bosse's frontispiece, the citizens are all turned to face not the audience, nor each other, but the Leviathan, suggesting that so long as their attention is directed primarily toward a shared, collective object to which they all owe allegiance, they can suffer – although likely not relate with, support, or nurture – their own and each other's existence.

In Locke, where some have seen a moderate, liberal balance of individual and collective rights, a more careful analysis reveals an idealized mode of domination – the acquisition of property – in response to the threat of domination. Locke's assertions of ongoing, 'natural' independence seem to lead him to use the acquisition of property as a sublimation for the aggressive and destructive desires that remain "within man now" in society. Locke's civil individualism, argues Macpherson, "can only be realized fully in accumulating property, and therefore, realized only by some at the expense of the individuality of others" (1971, 82–83). Thus, what seem to be lawful and innocent actions of civil beings, for Locke, actually express "greedy, acquisitive, domineering" impulses (Alford 1991, 121). Here, selves do not really contend with the dilemma of retaining contact with the self or others' selves, but, rather, equate selfhood with the pursuit of acquisitions and public esteem that symbolize the connection to a fantasized experience of freedom and power.

For Rousseau, the legitimate subjugation of a free individual requires that the individual identify with the sovereign will, which is the general will, the will of the community as a community (1987, 151–154). Rousseau's idea is that if an individual identifies himself with the authority he obeys, and if he accepts the authority's will as what he ought to have willed, then subjection to authority is not humiliating or alienating but a form of self-government. Like Hobbes, Rousseau asks citizens to establish an idealized object and to identify with this object as the most important part of themselves. Thus, for Rousseau, the way to avoid the experiences of alienation and domination associated with subjugation to others is to demand "the total alienation of each associate, together with all of his rights" to the idealized object that is the general will. In so "giving himself to all," Rousseau claims, "each person gives himself to no one" (148), because, once fully identified with the community, in obeying the community one only obeys oneself, and "obedience to the law one has prescribed for oneself is liberty" (151).

According to contract theorists, to learn from our imaginary experience of the state of nature is to learn that we must split ourselves and identify with the will of a superior power, even if that power is merely, as in Rawls, an abstract imaginary power that temporarily decouples us from our identities, causing us to see the world from what might be imagined as a 'traumatic' vantage point, from behind "the veil of ignorance," which is the point of the annihilation of the self (Rawls 1971). The result of this process is to turn away from the self and others as sources of danger, and to look, as in Bosse's frontispiece, to an idealized object of experience to save us. The civil individual must hide her self away and be wary of its appearance in herself and in others.

In groups and throughout civil society, we find individuals who are defended, immature, split, and in some important sense lacking, obsessed not with being themselves and "doing" what "arises out of being," as Winnicott would put it (1986, 39), but with their own security, with the acquisition of property, with avoiding experiences of domination, with striving to win the unwinnable game of *amour propre* (love or approval contingent upon the opinion of others), with hiding their own 'bad' selves away from a cruel world.

This attitude encourages the dividing of the self, or, in extreme cases, the suppression of the very core of the self, in exchange for the minimal protections afforded by physical safety, property ownership, and group belonging. This exchange expresses itself in the schizoid solutions offered by contract theorists, as well as in the more common "schizoid compromise" of civil privatism and contemporary liberalism (Guntrip 1992), wherein the self offers adaptation and compromise to the world outside while retaining, often simply by hiding, itself from a world that is feared to be unappreciative or unaccommodating to it. Indeed, the real "tragedy of human life in groups," writes Alford, is that individuals undermine groups and groups undermine selves when each needs the other to thrive, that "individuals destroy the one entity that could, if properly organized, help them realize [their individuality]" (1994, 8). As discussed in Chapter 6, a less schizoid account of the relationship between self, society, and state would suggest that secure selves may give something of themselves to groups and institutions, just as institutions and groups need not be designed to protect the society from dangerous selves, but may take as their charge to emancipate and facilitate the self.

Guilt, the real, and the failure to imagine

These reflections permit us to conclude by pursuing a curious, and rarely asked, question regarding the state of nature, one raised briefly in the beginning of this chapter and one alluded to in the opening chapter of this book: Are we, in fact, able to imagine the state of nature, as it has been described in the texts of Hobbes, Locke, Rousseau, and others? Can we, contemporary persons immersed in all of the civilizing influences and encumbered with all of its intellectual and moral baggage, imagine ourselves "strip[ped]" of all faculties obtained by learning, reason, tradition, and civilization (Rousseau 1987, 40)? Or, when we strive to do so, do we find that we encounter, instead, a failure of thought?

Rousseau, himself, suggests that we may *not* be able to do so. Throughout his second *Discourse*, he emphasizes how "unrecognizable" the civilized individual is to the natural one, and how each step of social and scientific progress further removes us from the ability to comprehend "the most important knowledge of all," which is the knowledge of our [imaginary] human origins. Indeed, suggests Rousseau, by "studying man ... we have rendered ourselves incapable of knowing him" (1987, 33). Rousseau's choice of words here is fortuitous, as it is precisely the 'unknown' quality of the being of the state that permits our fantasy and ideology surrounding him to function.

The human being in a state of nature is naïve to the extent that she cannot imagine an alternative condition or an alternative mode of experience. She fails to think, fails to imagine, lives in the moment. Rousseau's racist and degrading account of the Caribbean savage is precisely that of a creature without reason or foresight: "In the morning he sells his bed of cotton and in the evening he returns in tears to buy it back, for want of having foreseen that he would need it that night" (1987, 46).

Is it possible for us as contemporary persons to imagine ourselves in such a state? Must we mock it to imagine it? Is our mockery, then, not also a way of distancing ourselves from and *not* imagining it? Surely, nothing in our experience would seem to prepare us to imagine life in a state of nature. Even the time of life in which we most closely approximate the creature in a state of nature, our very first months of life, is lost from memory. If we cannot imagine a state of nature, then it seems that, in hypothesizing such a state and in locating it at the center of much moral and political thought, we have engaged in an effort to establish something unknowable and unthinkable at the very center of our moral and political lives.

One way to understand this is that in attempts to imaginatively insert ourselves into the state of nature, we encounter, first, the alluring fantasy of de-subjectification discussed above, and permit ourselves to retreat from or negate the capacities of selfhood in ourselves and in others. But if we ultimately fail to imagine ourselves in a state of nature, then might not this very failure to think, this failure to understand what is supposed to be our natural condition, lead us back to a facsimile of the experience we seek? That is, in *failing* to imagine the state of nature, we identify at an unthought level with the inhabitants of the state of nature, who had no power of imagination.

In this way, through our failure of thought, something of the psychic force and putative reality of the state of nature may be *transmitted*, just as Cathy Caruth would claim that in the unthinkable yet "necessary" transmission of trauma, we make an "appointment with the real," with a "site of trauma" that always, inevitably, escapes us but that we find again by "missing" it (1996, 108–110). Or, as Georges Bataille would write in "Experience, Sole Authority, Sole Value":

> Experience attains in the end the fusion of object and subject, being as subject non-knowledge, as object the unknown. It can let the agitation of intelligence break up on that account: repeated failures don't serve it any less than the final docility which one can expect.
>
> *(1988, 9)*

Earlier, we discussed the magical thinking associated with primary narcissism and how we may be tempted to re-describe ourselves as 'born free,' such that our self-destructive actions and schizoid compromises became less narcissistically injurious. The other side of this coin is the failure to imagine ourselves in the state of nature, where this failure transmits an experience of confusion that binds us not only to the state of nature's infantile fantasies but to the terms of social contracts derived from them, much as Freud's vision of totem sacrifice, mourning, and festival bound the group and its members to their gods, to their ancestors, and to each other in a kind of social contract of collective guilt (1938).

If failing to imagine being born free is central to a shared experience of self-lessness, then we may make sense of Martin Jay's otherwise enigmatic claim that "experience is paradoxically not only a proactive 'tearing' of the subject from himself, but also a reactive, post facto reconstruction of that deed" (2005, 398). Here, experience means self-loss, even self-destruction, presumably in the face of an object of experience that demands as much. It is not only the immediate act of "tearing" the self from itself, but the ritualistic, repetitive, and shared remembering of that deed that serves as a means to expiate the guilt of our 'original sin,' which is our awareness of our own destructive, aggressive, and sadistic impulses, an awareness which, if made tolerable, grounds the potential development of a self.

Might we not say, then, that the experience of failing to imagine ourselves in a state of nature, like totem ritual, expresses the need to tear our selves from ourselves, in an attempt to re-establish connection with a lost, unthinkable, yet idealized natural condition in which we are free from this 'sin' of selfhood? Might we not say that when we seek experience, we seek connection with the moment in which we dared to imagine a self, suffered for it, and secretly hoped to 'get back behind' this guilt and this suffering, to a fantasized state of self-less freedom, power, and innocence? If so, then experience, experiences of nature, experiences of trauma, experiences of deprivation, and experiences of failure may be understood, as I have suggested, as efforts to make real an apocalyptic self-imagination, in which we rediscover our seemingly 'natural' capacity for self-destruction, to which we tragically pay homage throughout our private and civil lives.

Notes

1 In response to Hobbes' famous analogy in *De Cive* that we may "consider men as if but even now sprung out of the earth, and suddenly, like mushrooms, come to full maturity, without all kind of engagement with each other" (1972, 205), Astell writes sarcastically, "How I lament my Stars that it was not my good Fortune to live in those Happy Days when Men spring up like so many Mushrooms or *Terrae Filii*, without Mother or Father or any sort of dependency" (quoted in Achinstein 2007, 22).

2 These "savage" people do have "the government of small Families," Hobbes confesses, even though "the concord whereof dependeth on natural lust" and not a common power that could arrange for peace (1985, 187).

3 The general will alone makes the bargain of civility for naturalness a good one, for only living in accordance with the general will is superior to living in accordance with nature. Everything else, all forms of political community in between, are perversions or degenerations of these conditions.

4 Similarly, Rousseau's Émile may misunderstand himself to be free (1979), to encounter only natural hardships and not the wills of superiors, but it would seem odd to suggest, in light of the extensive control and training Émile receives, that he is "born free," or even that he develops freely.

5 I have changed the name and identifying characteristics of this respondent to an interview protocol conducted from 2008–2012 (see Bowker 2014).

6 In David P. Levine's chapter, "The Isolation of the True Self and the Problem of Impingment." In Bowker and Buzby (forthcoming, 2016), this logical yet frequently overlooked consequence of Winnicott's thought regarding the early infant–parent relationship is illuminated with great clarity.

7 It is hard to miss the influence of the state-of-nature doctrine in modern declarations of independence, constitutions, and other charters of freedom. "Men are born and remain free and equal in rights," reads the *Déclaration des droits de l'homme et du citoyen* of 1789. The American Declaration of Independence (1776) likewise holds certain "truths to be self-evident," namely "that all men are created equal ... endowed by their Creator with

certain unalienable Rights, that among these are Life, Liberty and the pursuit of Happiness."

References

Achinstein, S. 2007. "Mary Astell, Religion, and Feminism: Texts in Motion." In *Mary Astell: Reason, Gender, and Faith*, edited by W. Kolbrenner and M. Michelson, 17–30. Burlington, VT: Ashgate.

Alford, C.F. 1991. *The Self in Social Theory: A Psychoanalytic Account of Its Construction in Plato, Hobbes, Locke, Rawls, and Rousseau*. New Haven, CT: Yale University Press.

Alford, C.F. 1994. *Group Psychology and Political Theory*. New Haven, CT: Yale University Press.

Astell, M. 1704. *Moderation, Truly Stated: Or a Review of a Late Pamphlet Entituled Moderation, a Vertue*. London.

Baier, A. 1994. *Moral Prejudices: Essays on Ethics*. Cambridge, MA: Harvard University Press.

Bataille, G. 1988. *Inner Experience*. Translated by L.A. Boldt. Albany, NY: State University of New York Press.

Benhabib, S. 1987. "The Generalized and the Concrete Other: The Kohlberg–Gilligan Controversy and Feminist Theory." In *Feminism as Critique: Essays on the Politics of Gender in Late Capitalist Societies*, edited by S. Benhabib and D. Cornell, 77–95. Minneapolis, MN: University Minnesota Press.

Bowker, M.H. 2014. *Rethinking the Politics of Absurdity: Albert Camus, Postmodernity, and the Survival of Innocence*. Series: Routledge Innovations in Political Theory. New York: Routledge.

Bowker, M.H., and A.L. Buzby, eds. Forthcoming, 2016. *D.W. Winnicott and Political Theory: Self and Society in Transition*. New York: Palgrave Macmillan.

Bowlby, J. 1988. *A Secure Base: Parent–Child Attachment and Healthy Human Development*. New York: Basic Books.

Caruth, C. 1996. *Unclaimed Experience: Trauma, Narrative, and History*. Baltimore, MD: Johns Hopkins University Press.

Curtis, C. 2010. *Postapocalyptic Fiction and the Social Contract: "We'll not Go Home Again."* Lanham, MD: Rowman and Littlefield.

DiStefano, C. 1983. "Masculinity as Ideology in Political Theory: Hobbesian Man Considered." *Women's Studies International Forum* 6(6): 633–644.

DiStefano, C. 1991. *Configurations of Masculinity: A Feminist Perspective on Modern Political Theory*. Ithaca, NY: Cornell University Press.

Foucault, M. 1991. "How an 'Experience-Book' is Born." In *Remarks on Marx: Conversations with Duccio Trombadori*, 25–42. Translated by R. Goldstein and J. Cascaito. New York: Semiotext(e).

Freud, S. 1914. "On Narcissism." In *The Standard Edition of the Complete Psychological Works of Sigmund Freud, Volume XIV*, edited and translated by J. Strachey, 67–102. London: Hogarth.

Freud, S. 1938. "Totem and Taboo: Resemblances between the Mental Lives of Savages and Neurotics." In *The Basic Writings of Sigmund Freud*, edited and translated by A. Brill, 807–930. New York: Random House.

Fromm-Reichmann, F. 1959. "Loneliness." *Psychiatry* 22: 1–15.

Gamble, C. 1999. *The Palaeolithic Societies of Europe*. Cambridge: Cambridge University Press.

Gerson, G. 2004. "Object Relations Psychoanalysis as Political Theory." *Political Psychology* 25(5): 769–794.

Greenberg, J., and S. Mitchell 1983. *Object Relations in Psychoanalytic Theory*. Cambridge, MA: Harvard University Press.

Grenier, J. 1967. *Conversations on the Good Uses of Freedom*. Translated by A. Coleman. Cambridge, MA: Identity.

Guntrip, H. 1992. *Schizoid Phenomena, Object Relations, and the Self*. Madison, CT: International Universities Press.

Held, V. 1993. *Feminist Morality: Transforming Culture, Society, and Politics*. Chicago, IL: University of Chicago Press.

Hobbes, T. 1972. *Thomas Hobbes' De Homine and De Cive*, edited by B. Gert. New York: Anchor Books.

Hobbes, T. 1985. *Leviathan, or The Matter, Forme, and Power of a Common-Wealth Ecclesiasticall and Civill*, edited by C.B. Macpherson. Penguin Classics Edition. London: Penguin.

Holm, B. 2010. *The Music of Failure*. First University of Minnesota Press Edition. Fesler-Lampert Minnesota Heritage Series. Minneapolis and London: University of Minnesota Press.

Jay, M. 1993. *Force Fields: Between Intellectual History and Cultural Critique*. New York: Routledge.

Jay, M. 2005. *Songs of Experience: Modern American and European Variations on a Universal Theme*. Berkeley, CA: University of California Press.

Klein, M. 1975. *The Writings of Melanie Klein, Volume I: Love, Guilt, Reparation and Other Works, 1921–1945*. New York: Free Press.

Leakey, R., and R. Lewin 1978. *People of the Lake: Mankind and its Beginnings*. New York: Avon Books.

Lifton, R.J. 1991. *Death in Life: Survivors of Hiroshima*. Chapel Hill, NC and London: University of North Carolina Press.

Locke, J. 1980. *Second Treatise of Government*, edited by C.B. Macpherson. Indianapolis, IN: Hackett.

Macpherson, C.B. 1971. "The Social Bearing of Locke's Political Theory." In *Life, Liberty and Property: Essays on Locke's Political Ideas*, edited by G. Schochet, 60–85. Belmont, CA: Wadsworth Publishing.

Mills, C. 1997. *The Racial Contract*. Ithaca, NY and London: Cornell University Press.

Montaigne, M. de. 1993. *Essays*, edited and translated by J. Cohen. London: Penguin.

Nussbaum, M. 2000. *Women and Human Development: The Capabilities Approach*. Cambridge: Cambridge University Press.

Pateman, C. 1988. *The Sexual Contract*. Stanford, CA: Stanford University Press.

Rawls, J. 1971. *A Theory of Justice*. Cambridge, MA: Harvard University Press.

Rorty, R. 1989. *Contingency, Irony, and Solidarity*. Cambridge: Cambridge University Press.

Rousseau, J.-J. 1979. *Émile, or on Education*. Translated by A. Bloom. New York: Basic Books.

Rousseau, J.-J. 1987. *The Basic Political Writings*, edited and translated by D. Cress. Indianapolis, IN: Hackett.

Shaffer, P. 2007. *Equus*. Modern Classics International Edition. London: Penguin.

Tolle, E. 2004. *The Power of Now: A Guide to Spiritual Enlightenment*. Novato, CA: New World Library.

Winnicott, D.W. 1965. *The Maturational Processes and the Facilitating Environment: Studies in the Theory of Emotional Development*, edited by M. Khan. London: Hogarth and the Institute of Psycho-Analysis.

Winnicott, D.W. 1971. *Playing and Reality*. London: Routledge.

Winnicott, D.W. 1984. *Deprivation and Delinquency*, edited by C. Winnicott, R. Shepherd, and M. Davis. London and New York: Routledge.

Winnicott, D.W. 1986. *Home Is Where We Start from: Essays by a Psychoanalyst*, edited by C. Winnicott, R. Shepard, and M. Davis. New York: W.W. Norton.

Winnicott, D.W. 1988. *Human Nature*. Philadelphia, PA: Brunner/Mazel.

Winnicott, D.W. 1989. *Psychoanalytic Explorations*, edited by C. Winnicott, R. Shepard, and M. Davis. Cambridge, MA: Harvard University Press.

Winnicott, D.W. 1992. *Through Paediatrics to Psycho-analysis: Collected Papers*, edited by M. Khan. New York: Brunner-Routledge.

Wollstonecraft, M. [1792] 2004. *A Vindication of the Rights of Woman*, edited by M. Brody. New York: Penguin.

INDEX